The Great Doctrines of
the Bible

The Great Doctrines of the Bible

by

WILLIAM EVANS

with eighty additional entries

by

S. MAXWELL CODER

MOODY PRESS
CHICAGO

DEDICATED TO MY WIFE

Contents

Reviser's Preface

William Evans' work on the great doctrines of the Bible has become a classic during the three quarters of a century which have passed since he first gave his classroom lectures in printed form to the people of God.

To read this book is to enjoy the clear, beautifully organized teaching of a man who became justly famous in his generation as one of the most highly gifted men in evangelical circles.

The genius of his remarkable volume has been preserved in the present revision. Except for the recasting of outdated references and antiquated expressions, and the enlarging of some of the material, the language of the original work is unchanged.

A second section has been added, providing summaries of eighty Bible doctrines not developed by Dr. Evans. This material has been prepared in view of the needs of those who may be called upon to teach the Word.

As Dean of Education Emeritus of the Moody Bible Institute, I am delighted to have had a part in making available to believers everywhere a revised and enlarged volume containing something of what has been offered in the classrooms of the Institute ever since 1886 when the school was founded.

S. MAXWELL CODER

EDITOR'S NOTE: Throughout this book, AV (Authorized Version) refers to the King James Version; and RV refers to the American Standard Edition of the Revised Bible (1901).

Foreword

The demand for this book has come from the students in the classroom who have listened to these lectures on the great doctrines of the Bible, and have desired and requested that they be put into permanent form for the purpose of further study and reference. This volume is prepared, therefore, primarily, but not exclusively, for the student, and with his needs in mind.

The doctrines herein treated are dealt with from the standpoint of Biblical rather than dogmatic theology. This is evident from the plan which is followed in the work, namely, to gather together all the Scripture passages dealing with the subject under consideration, and from them choose a required number that may be called representative; then seek to understand the meaning of these references by the study of the text itself as well as its context and parallel passages; and finally, from the selected proof-texts, formulate the doctrinal teaching, and place such results under appropriate headings.

The doctrines of God, Jesus Christ, and the Holy Spirit are more fully dealt with than the doctrines which follow. This is especially true of the doctrine of God. The reason for this is to set forth the method pursued in these studies, and to give a pattern for the study of the doctrines to follow.

It is intended that the doctrines of this book should be studied side by side with the open Bible. It is for this reason that many of the Scripture references are indicated by chapter and verse only. There must be constant reference to the Scriptures themselves.

This volume is in such form as to be of great service in the instruction given in Bible classes. There is probably no greater need in the Christian Church today than that its membership should be made acquainted with the fundamental facts and doctrines of the Christian faith. The Christian layman, therefore, who desires a deeper knowledge of the doctrines of the Christian faith may find all the help he needs in this book. It is hoped that while it is prepared for the student, it is nevertheless not too deep for the average layman.

The special indebtedness of the writer is hereby expressed to the following works: "What the Bible Teaches," by R. A. Torrey, D. D. To this work the writer owes much with regard to the method and plan of this book. "Systematic Theology," by A. H. Strong, D. D., has provided some rich expositions of the sacred text. "Christian Doctrine," by Dr. F. L. Patton, has been found very helpful, especially in connection with the subject of the "Proofs for the Existence of God." Further recognition of indebtedness is also due to the following: "The Problem of the Old Testament," and "The Christian View of God and the World," by Dr. James Orr; "Studies in Christian Doctrine," by George Knapp; "Jesus and the Gospel" and "The Death of Christ," by Prof. James Denny; "The Person and Work of Jesus," by Nathan E. Wood, D. D.

There are doubtless others to whom credit is due of whom the author is not at this time conscious, for, after all, we are "part of all that we have seen, and met, and read." To those unknown authors, therefore, our indebtedness is hereby acknowledged.

WILLIAM EVANS

Los Angeles, California

PART ONE

GREAT DOCTRINES OF THE BIBLE

by

WILLIAM EVANS

THE DOCTRINE OF GOD

THE DOCTRINE OF GOD

I. THE EXISTENCE OF GOD (Vs. Atheism)

1. ASSUMED BY THE SCRIPTURES

2. PROOFS OF THE EXISTENCE OF GOD
a) Universal Belief in the Existence of God
b) Cosmological—Argument from Cause
c) Teleological—Argument from Design
d) Ontological—Argument from Being
e) Anthropological—Moral Argument
f) Argument from Congruity
g) Argument from Scripture

II. THE NATURE OF GOD (Vs. Agnosticism)

1. THE SPIRITUALITY OF GOD (Vs. Materialism)

2. THE PERSONALITY OF GOD (Vs. Pantheism)

3. THE UNITY OF GOD (Vs. Polytheism)

4. THE TRINITY (Vs. Unitarianism)

III. THE ATTRIBUTES OF GOD

1. THE NATURAL ATTRIBUTES
a) Omniscience
b) Omnipotence
c) Omnipresence
d) Eternity and Immutability

2. THE MORAL ATTRIBUTES
a) Holiness
b) Righteousness and Justice
c) Mercy and Loving-kindness
d) Love

THE DOCTRINE OF GOD

I. HIS EXISTENCE

1. Taken for Granted by the Scripture Writers

It does not seem to have occurred to any of the writers of either the Old or the New Testaments to attempt to prove or to argue for the existence of God. Everywhere and at all times it is a fact taken for granted. "A God capable of proof would be no God at all" (Jacobi). He is the self-existent One (Exod. 3:14) and the Source of all life (John 5:26).

The sublime opening of the Scriptures announces the fact of God and His existence: "In the beginning God" (Gen. 1:1). Nor is the rise or dawn of the idea of God in the mind of man depicted. Psa. 14:1: "The fool hath said in his heart, There is no God," indicates not a disbelief in the existence, but rather in the active interest of God in the affairs of men—He seemed to hide Himself from the affairs of men (see Job 22:12-14).

The Scriptures further recognize that men not only know of the existence of God, but have also a certain circle of ideas as to who and what He is (Rom. 1:18, 19).

No one but a "fool" will deny the fact of God. "What! no God? A watch, and no key for it? A watch with a main-spring broken, and no jeweler to fix it? A watch, and no repair shop? A timecard and a train, and nobody to run it? A lamp lit, and nobody to pour oil in to keep the wick burning? A garden, and no gardener? Flowers, and no florist? Conditions, and no conditioner?" He that sitteth in the heavens shall laugh at such absurd atheism.

2. The Arguments for the Existence of God*

These arguments may not prove conclusively that God is, but they do show that in order to argue for the existence of any knowledge, thought, reason, conscience in man, we must assume that God is (Strong). It is said of the beautiful, "It may be shown, but not

---

*A fuller and complete presentation of these arguments for the existence of God may be found in the works of Dr. Augustus H. Strong and Dr. Francis L. Patton, to whom the author is here indebted.

proved." So we say of the existence of God. These arguments are probable, not demonstrative. For this reason they supplement each other, and constitute a series of evidences which is cumulative in its nature. Though taken singly, none of them can be considered absolutely decisive, they together furnish a corroboration of our primitive conviction of God's existence, which is of great practical value, and is in itself sufficient to bind the moral actions of men. A bundle of rods may not be broken even though each one separately may; the strength of the bundle is the strength of the whole. If in practical affairs we were to hesitate to act until we have absolute and demonstrable certainty, we should never begin to move at all.

Instead of doubting everything that can be doubted, let us rather doubt nothing until we are compelled to doubt.

The late Dr. Orr said: "What we mean by the proof of God's existence is simply that there are necessary acts of thought by which we rise from the finite to the infinite, from the caused to the uncaused, from the contingent to the necessary, from the reason involved in the structure of the universe to a universal and eternal reason, which is the ground of all, from morality in conscience to a moral Lawgiver and Judge. In this connection the theoretical proofs constitute an inseparable unity—'constitute together,' as Dr. Stirling declares, 'but the undulations of a single wave, which wave is but a natural rise and ascent to God, on the part of man's own thought, with man's own experience and consciousness as the object before him.' "

Religion was not produced by proofs of God's existence, and will not be destroyed by its insufficiency to some minds. Religion existed before argument; in fact, it is the preciousness of religion that leads to the seeking for all possible confirmations of the reality of God.

a) UNIVERSALITY OF BELIEF IN THE EXISTENCE OF GOD

(1) THE FACT STATED AND PROVEN:

Man everywhere believes in the existence of a supreme Being or beings to whom he is morally responsible and to whom propitiation needs to be made.

Such belief may be crudely, even grotesquely stated and manifested, but the reality of the fact is no more invalidated by such crudeness than the existence of a father is invalidated by the crude attempts of a child to draw a picture of its father.

It has been claimed by some that there are or were tribes in inland Africa that possessed no idea or conception of God. Moffat, Livingstone's father-in-law, made such a claim, but Livingstone, after a thorough study of the customs and languages of such tribes, conclusively showed that Moffat was wrong.

Nor should the existence of such few tribes, even if granted, violate the fact we are here considering, any more than the existence of some few men who are blind, lame, deaf, and dumb would make untrue the statement and fact that man is a seeing, hearing, speaking, and walking creature. The fact that some nations do not have the multiplication table does no violence to arithmetic.

Concerning so-called atheists in Christian lands: it may be questioned if there are really any such beings. Hume, known as a famous skeptic, is reported to have said to Ferguson, as together they looked up into the starry sky: "Adam, there is a God." Voltaire, the atheist, prayed to God in a thunderstorm. Ingersoll, when charged with being an atheist, indignantly refuted the charge, saying: "I am not an atheist; I do not say that there is no God; I am an agnostic; I do not know that there is a God." "I thank God that I am an atheist," were the opening words of an argument to disprove the existence of God. A new convert to atheism was once heard to say to a coterie of unbelievers: "I have gotten rid of the idea of a supreme Being, and I thank God for it."

(2) WHENCE COMES THIS UNIVERSAL BELIEF IN THE EXISTENCE OF GOD?

aa)   *Not from outside sources,* such as reason, tradition, or even the Scriptures

Not from reason or argument, for many who believe in God have not given any time to reasoning and arguing the question; some, indeed, intellectually, could not. Others who have great powers of intellect, and who have reasoned and argued on the subject are professed disbelievers in God. Belief in God is not the result of logical arguments, else the Bible would have given us proofs.

Nor did this universal belief come from tradition, for "Tradition," says Dr. Patton, "can perpetuate only what has been originated."

Nor can it be said that this belief came from the Scriptures even, for, as has been well said, unless a man had a knowledge of the God from whom the Scriptures came, the revelation itself could have no authority for him. The very idea of Scripture as a revelation presupposes belief in a God who can make it.—*Newman Smith*. Revelation must assume the existence of God.

bb)   This universal belief comes from within man.

All the evidence points to the conclusive fact that this universal faith in the existence of God is innate in man, and comes from rational intuition.

(3) THE WEIGHT AND FORCE OF THIS ARGUMENT

The fact that all men everywhere believe in the existence of a supreme Being or beings to whom they are morally responsible, is a strong argument in favor of its truth. So universal an effect must have a cause as universal, otherwise we have an effect without any assignable cause. Certain is it that this argument makes the burden of proof to rest upon those who deny the existence of God.

b) THE ARGUMENT FROM CAUSE: COSMOLOGICAL

When we see a thing we naturally ask for the cause of that thing. We see this world in which we live, and ask how it came to be. Is it self-originating, or is the cause of its being outside of itself? Is its cause finite or infinite?

That it could not come into being of itself seems obvious; no more than nails, brick, mortar, wood, paints, colors, form into a house or building of themselves; no more than the type composing a book came into order of itself. When Liebig was asked if he believed that the grass and flowers which he saw around him grew by mere chemical forces, he replied: "No; no more than I could believe that the books on botany describing them could grow by mere chemical forces." No theory of an "eternal series" can account for this created universe. No matter how long a chain you may have, you must have a staple somewhere from which it depends. An endless perpendicular chain is an impossibility. "Every house is builded by some man," says the Bible; so this world in which we live was built by a designing mind of infinite power and wisdom.

So is it when we consider man. Man exists; but he owes his existence to some cause. Is this cause within or without himself, finite or infinite? Trace our origin back, if you will, to our first parent, Adam; then you must ask, How did he come into being? The doctrine of the eternity of man cannot be supported. Man is an effect; he has not always existed. Geology proves this. That the first Cause must have been an intelligent Being is proven by the fact that we are intelligent beings ourselves.

c) THE ARGUMENT FROM DESIGN: TELEOLOGICAL

A watch proves not only a maker, an artificer, but also a designer; a watch is made for a purpose. This is evident in its structure. A thoughtful, designing mind was back of the watch. So is it with the world in which we live. These "ends" in nature are not to be attributed to "natural results," or "natural selection," results which are produced without intelligence, nor are they "the survival of the fittest," instances in which "accident and fortuity have done the work of mind." No, they are the results of a superintending and originating intelligence and will.

d) THE ARGUMENT FROM BEING: ONTOLOGICAL

Man has an idea of an infinite and perfect Being. From whence this idea? From finite and imperfect beings like ourselves? Certainly not. Therefore this idea argues for the existence of an infinite and perfect Being: such a Being must exist, as a person, and not a mere thought.

e) THE MORAL ARGUMENT: ANTHROPOLOGICAL

Man has an intellectual and a moral nature, hence his Creator must be an intellectual and moral Being, a Judge, and Lawgiver. Man has an emotional nature; only a Being of goodness, power, love, wisdom and holiness could satisfy such a nature, and these things denote the existence of a personal God.

Conscience in man says: "Thou shalt," and "Thou shalt not," "I ought," and "I ought not." These mandates are not self-imposed. They imply the existence of a Moral Governor to whom we are responsible. Conscience—there it is in the breast of man, an ideal Moses thundering from an invisible Sinai the Law of a holy Judge. Said Cardinal Newman: "Were it not for the voice speaking so clearly in my conscience and my heart, I should be an atheist, or a pantheist, when I looked into the world." Some things are wrong, others right: love is right, hatred is wrong. Nor is a thing right because it pleases, or wrong because it displeases. Where did we get this standard of right and wrong? Morality is obligatory, not optional. Who made it obligatory? Who has a right to command my life? We must believe that there is a God, or believe that the very root of our nature is a lie.

f) THE ARGUMENT FROM CONGRUITY

If we have a key which fits all the wards of the lock, we know that it is the right key. If we have a theory which fits all the facts in the case, we know then that we have the right theory. "Belief in a self-existent, personal God is in harmony with all the facts of our mental and moral nature, as well as with all the phenomena of the natural world. If God exists, a universal belief in his existence is natural enough; the irresistible impulse to ask for a first cause is accounted for; our religious nature has an object; the uniformity of natural law finds an adequate explanation, and human history is vindicated from the charge of being a vast imposture. Atheism leaves all these matters without an explanation, and makes, not history alone, but our moral and intellectual nature itself, an imposture and a lie."—*Patton.*

g) THE ARGUMENT FROM SCRIPTURE

A great deal of our knowledge rests upon the testimony of others. Now the Bible is competent testimony. If the testimony of travelers is enough to satisfy us as to the habits, customs, and manners of the peoples of the countries they visit, and which we have never seen, why is not the Bible, if it is authentic history, enough to satisfy us with its evidence as to the existence of God?

Some facts need more evidence than others, we know. This is true of the fact of the existence of God. But the Bible history is sufficient to satisfy every reasonable demand. The history of the Jews, prophecy, is not explainable minus God. If we cannot believe in the existence of God on the testimony of the Bible we might as well burn our books of history. A man cannot deny the truth of the testimony of the Bible unless he says plainly: "No amount of testimony will convince me of the supernatural."

Scripture does not attempt to prove the existence of God; it asserts, assumes, and declares that the knowledge of God is universal, Rom. 1:19-21, 28, 32; 2:15. It asserts that God has wrought this great truth in the very warp and woof of every man's being, so that nowhere is He without this witness. The preacher may, therefore, safely follow the example of the Scripture in assuming that there is a God. Indeed he must unhesitatingly and explicitly assert it as the Scripture does, believing that "His eternal power and divinity" are things that are clearly seen and perceived through the evidences of His handiwork which abound on every hand.

II. THE NATURE OF GOD (Vs. Agnosticism)

1. The Spirituality of God (Vs. Materialism)
"God Is Spirit."

a) STATEMENT OF THE FACT, JOHN 4:24: "GOD IS SPIRIT."

Meaning: The Samaritan woman's question, "Where is God to be found?" etc. On Mt. Zion or Gerizim? Christ's answer: God is not to be confined to any one place (cf. Acts 7:48; 17:25; 1 Kings 8:27). God must be worshipped *in spirit* as distinguished from place, form, or other sensual limitations (John 4:21); and *in truth* as distinguished from false conceptions resulting from imperfect knowledge (4:22).

b) LIGHT ON "GOD IS SPIRIT," FROM OTHER SCRIPTURES

Luke 24:39: "A spirit hath not flesh and bones," i. e., has not body, or parts like human beings; incorporeal; not subject to human limitations.

Col. 1:15: "The image of the invisible God."

1 Tim. 1:17 (R. V.): "Now unto the King incorruptible, invisible."

These passages teach that God has nothing of a material or bodily nature. Sight sees only objects of the material world, but God is not of the nature of the material world, hence He cannot be seen with the material eye—at least not now.

c) LIGHT DERIVED FROM CAUTIONS AGAINST REPRESENTING GOD BY GRAVEN IMAGES

Deut. 4:15-23; Isa. 40:25; Exod. 20:4. Study these passages carefully and note that the reason why images were forbidden was because no one had ever seen God, and consequently could not picture how He looked, and, further, there was nothing on the earth that could resemble Him.

d) DEFINITION OF "GOD IS SPIRIT" IN THE LIGHT OF ALL THIS

God is invisible, incorporeal, without parts, without body, without passions, and therefore free from all limitations; He is apprehended not by the senses, but by the soul; hence God is above sensuous perceptions. 1 Cor. 2:6-16 intimates that without the teaching of God's Spirit we cannot know God. He is not a material Being. "LaPlace swept the heavens with his telescope, but could not find anywhere a God. He might just as well have swept a kitchen with his broom." Since God is not a material Being, He cannot be apprehended by physical means.

e) QUESTIONS AND PROBLEMS WITH REFERENCE TO THE STATEMENT THAT "GOD IS SPIRIT."

(1) What Is Meant By Statement That Man Was Made "In The Image Of God"?

Col. 3:10; Eph. 4:24 declare that this "image" consists in "righteousness, knowledge, and holiness of truth." By that is meant that the image of God in man consisted in intellectual and moral likeness rather than physical resemblance. Some think that 1 Thess. 5:23 indicates that the "trinity of man"—body, soul, and spirit—constitutes that image and likeness.

(2) What Is Meant By The Anthropomorphic Expressions Used Of God?

For example: God is said to have hands, feet, arms, eyes, ears; He sees, feels, hears, walks, etc. Such expressions are to be understood only in the sense of being human expressions used in order to bring the infinite within the comprehension of the finite. How otherwise could we understand God saving by means of human expressions, in figures that we all can understand!

(3) How Are Such Passages As Exod. 24:10 And 33:18-23, In Which It Is Distinctly Stated That Men Saw The God Of Israel, To Be Reconciled With Such Passages As John 1:18: "No Man Hath Seen God At Any Time," And Exod. 33:20: "There Shall No Man See Me And Live"? Answer:

aa) Spirit can be manifested in visible form:

John 1:32: "I saw the Spirit descending from heaven like a dove [or in the form of a dove]." So throughout the ages the invisible God has manifested Himself in visible form. (See Judges 6:34: The Spirit of the Lord clothed Himself with Gideon.)

bb) On this truth is based the doctrine of "The Angel of the Lord"

in the Old Testament: Gen. 16:7, 10, 13. Note here how the Angel of the Lord is identified with Jehovah Himself, cf. vv. 10, 13. Also Gen. 22:12—"The angel of the Lord . . . not withheld from me." In 18:1-16, one of the three angels clearly and definitely identifies himself with Jehovah. Compare chapter 19, where it is seen that only two of the angels have come to Sodom; the other has remained behind. Who was this one, this remaining angel? Gen. 18:17, 20 answers the question; v. 22 reads: "And Abraham stood yet before the LORD." In Exod. 13:21 it is *Jehovah,* while in 14:19 it is the Angel that went before Israel. Thus was the way prepared for the incarnation, for the Angel of the Lord in the Old Testament is undoubtedly the second person of the Trinity. This seems evident from Judges 13:18 compared with Isa. 9:6, in both of which passages, clearly referring to Christ, the name "Wonderful" occurs. Also the omission of the definite article "the" from before the expression "Angel of the Lord," and the substitution of "an" points to the same truth. This change is made in the Revised Version.

cc) *What was it then that the elders of Israel saw when it is said they "saw the God of Israel"?*

Certainly it was not God in His real essence, God as He is in Himself, for no man can have that vision and live. John 1:18 is clear on that point: "No man hath seen God at any time." The emphasis in this verse is on the word "God," and may read, "GOD no one has seen at any time." In 5:37 Jesus says: "Ye have neither heard his voice at any time, nor seen his shape." From this it seems clear that the "seeing" here, the which has been the privilege of no man, refers to the essence rather than to the person of God, if such a distinction can really be made. This is apparent also from the omission of the definite article before God, as well as from the position of God in the sentence. None but the Son has really seen God as God, as He really is. What, then, did these men see?

Evidently an *appearance* of God in some form to their outward senses; perhaps the form of a man, seeing mention is made of his "feet." The vision may have been too bright for human eyes to gaze upon fully, but it was *a* vision of God. Yet it was only a manifestation of God, for, although Moses was conversing with God, he yet said: "If I have found grace in thy sight, show me thy face." Moses had been granted exceeding great and precious privileges in that he had been admitted into close communion with God, more so than any other member of the human race. But still unsatisfied he longed for more; so in v. 18 he asks to see the unveiled glory of God, that very thing which no man in the flesh can ever see and live; but, no, this cannot be. By referring to Exod. 33:18-23 we find God's answer: "Thou canst not see my face . . . thou shalt see my back parts, but my face shall not be seen." (Num. 12:8 throws light upon the subject, if compared with Exod. 33:11.)

"The secret remained unseen; the longing unsatisfied; and the nearest approach to the beatific vision reached by him with whom God spake face to face, as friend with friend, was to be hidden in the cleft of the rock, to be made aware of an awful shadow, and to hear the voice of the unseen."

2. The Personality of God (Vs. Pantheism)

Pantheism maintains that this universe in its ever changing conditions is but the manifestation of the one ever changing universal substance which is God; thus all, everything is God, and God is everything; God is all, all is God. Thus God is identified with nature and not held to be independent of and separate from it. God is, therefore, a necessary but an unconscious force working in the world.

The Bearing of the Personality of God on the Idea of Religion.

True religion may be defined as the communion between two persons: God and man. Religion is a personal relationship between God in heaven, and man on the earth. If God were not a person there could be no communion; if both God and man were one there could be no communion, and, consequently, no religion. An independent personal relationship on both sides is absolutely necessary to communion. Man can have no communion with an influence, a force, an impersonal something; nor can an influence have any moving or affection towards man. It is absolutely necessary to the true definition of religion that both God and man be persons. God is person, not force or influence.

a) DEFINITION OF PERSONALITY

Personality exists where there is intelligence, mind, will, reason, individuality, self-consciousness, and self-determination. There must be not mere consciousness—for the beast has that—but *self*-consciousness. Nor is personality determination—for the beast has this, too, even though this determination be the result of influences from without—but *self*-determination, the power by which man from an act of his own free will determines his acts from within.

Neither corporeity nor substance, as we understand these words, are necessarily, if at all, involved in personality. There may be true personality without either or both of these.

b) SCRIPTURE TEACHING ON THE PERSONALITY OF GOD

(In this connection it will be well to refer to the Ontological Argument for the Existence of God, for which see p. 17.)

(1) Exod. 3:14:—"I Am That I Am."

This name is wonderfully significant. Its central idea is that of existence and personality. The words signify "I AM, I WAS, I SHALL BE," so suggestively corresponding with the New Testament statement concerning God: "Who wast, and art, and art to come."

All the names given to God in the Scripture denote personality. Here are some of them:

Jehovah-Jireh: The Lord will provide (Gen. 22:13, 14).
Jehovah-Rapha: The Lord that healeth (Exod. 15:26).
Jehovah-Nissi: The Lord our Banner (Exod. 17:8-15).
Jehovah-Shalom: The Lord our Peace (Judges 6:24).
Jehovah-Ra-ah: The Lord my Shepherd (Psa. 23:1).
Jehovah-Tsidkenu: The Lord our Righteousness (Jer. 23:6).
Jehovah-Shammah: The Lord is present (Ezek. 48:35).

Moreover, the personal pronouns ascribed to God prove personality: John 17:3, et al. "To know thee"—we cannot know an influence in the sense in which the word "know" is here used.

Statement: All through the Scriptures names and personal pronouns are ascribed to God which undeniably prove that God is a Person.

(2) A Sharp Distinction Is Drawn In The Scriptures Between The Gods Of The Heathen And The Lord God Of Israel (see Jer. 10:10-16).

Note the context: vv. 3-9: Idols are things, not persons; they cannot walk, speak, do good or evil. God is wiser than the men who made these idols; if the idol-makers are persons, much more is God.

See the sharp contrast drawn between dead idols and the living, personal, true and only God: Acts 14:15; 1 Thess. 1:9; Psa. 94:9, 10.

Statement: God is to be clearly distinguished from things which have no life; he is a living Person.

(3) Attributes Of Personality Are Ascribed To God In The Scriptures.

God repents (Gen. 6:6); grieves (Gen. 6:6); is angry (1 Kings 11:9); is jealous (Deut. 6:15); loves (Rev. 3:19); hates (Prov. 6:16).

Statement: God possesses the attributes of personality, and therefore is a Person.

(4) THE RELATION WHICH GOD BEARS TO THE UNIVERSE AND TO MEN, AS SET FORTH IN THE SCRIPTURES, CAN BE EXPLAINED ONLY ON THE BASIS THAT GOD IS A PERSON.

Deism maintains that God, while the Creator of the world, yet sustains no further relations to it. He made it just as the clockmaker makes a self-winding clock: makes it and then leaves it to run itself without any interference on his part. Such teaching as this finds no sanction in the Bible. What are God's relations to the universe and to men?

aa)   He is the Creator of the Universe and Man.

Gen. 1:1, 26; John 1:1-3. These verses contain vital truths. The universe did not exist from eternity, nor was it made from existing matter. It did not proceed as an emanation from the infinite, but was summoned into being by the decree of God. Science, by disclosing to us the marvellous power and accuracy of natural law, compels us to believe in a superintending intelligence who is infinite. Tyndall said: "I have noticed that it is not during the hours of my clearness and vigor that the doctrine of material atheism commends itself to my mind."

(In this connection the Arguments from Cause and Design, pp. 16 and 17, may be properly considered.)

Statement: The creation of the universe and man proves the personality of the Creator—God.

bb)   God sustains certain relations to the Universe and Man which He has made.

Heb. 1:3—"Upholds all things." Col. 1:15-17—"By him all things hold together." Psa. 104:27-30—All creatures wait upon Him for "their meat in due season." Psa. 75:6, 7—"Promotion" among men, the putting down of one man and the setting up of another, is from the hand of God.

What do we learn from these scriptures regarding the relation of God to this universe, to man, and to all God's creatures?

First. That all things are held together by Him; if not, this old world would go to pieces quickly. The uniformity and accuracy of natural law compels us to believe in a personal God who intelligently guides and governs the universe. Disbelief in this fact would mean utter confusion. Not blind chance, but a personal God is at the helm.

Second. That the physical supplies for all God's creatures are in His hand: He feeds them all. What God gives we gather. If He withholds provision we die.

Third. That God has His hand in history, guiding and shaping the affairs of nations. Victor Hugo said: "Waterloo was God."

Fourth. Consider with what detail God's care is described: The sparrows, the lilies, the hairs of the head, the tears of His children, etc. See how these facts are clearly portrayed in the following scriptures: Matt. 6:28-30; 10:29, 30; Gen. 39:21, with 50:20; Dan. 1:9; Job 1:12.

Statement: The personality of God is shown by His active interest and participation in all things, even the smallest things, in the universe, the experience of man, and in the life of all His creatures.

3. The Unity of God (Vs. Polytheism)

There are three monotheistic religions in the world: Judaism, Christianity, and Muhammadanism. The second is a development of the first; the third is an outgrowth of both.

The doctrine of the unity of God is held in contradistinction to *Polytheism,* which is belief in a multiplicity of gods; to *Tritheism,* which teaches that there are three Gods—that is, that the Father, the Son, and the Holy Ghost are, specifically, three distinct Gods; and to *Dualism,* which teaches that there are two independent divine beings or eternal principles, the one good, and the other evil, as set forth especially in Gnostic systems, such as Parseeism.

a) THE SCRIPTURES ASSERT THE UNITY OF GOD.

Deut. 6:4—"Hear, O Israel; the Lord our God is one Lord"; or, "The Lord our God, the Lord is one." Isa. 44:6-8—"First . . . last . . . beside me there is no God." Isa. 45:5—"There is none else, there is no God beside me." 1 Tim. 2:5—"There is one God." 1 Cor. 8:4—"There is none other God but one."

That God is one, that there is no other, that He has no equal is the forceful testimony of above fifty passages in the Scriptures. The fundamental duty of life, namely, the devotion of the entire

being to the Lord, is based upon the unity of God: "The Lord
. . . . is one . . . . therefore thou shalt love the Lord thy God
with *all* thy heart," etc.

No other truth of the Scripture, particularly of the Old Testament, receives more prominence than that of the unity of God.
This truth is clearly pronounced also in the material universe; it
is the introduction and conclusion of all scientific researches. Any
other representation contradicts both creation and revelation. Its
denial is a proper object for the ridicule of every thinking man,
and of the disbelief of every orthodox Christian. Let this, then,
be our first and necessary conclusion—that Deity, whether creating, inspiring, or otherwise manifesting itself, is one God; one,
and no more.—*Cerdo*.

A multiplication of gods is a contradiction; there can be but
one God. There can be but one absolutely perfect, supreme, and
almighty Being. Such a Being cannot be multiplied, nor pluralized.
There can be but one ultimate, but one all-inclusive, but one God.

Monotheism, then, not Tri-theism, is the doctrine set forth in
the Scriptures. "If the thought that wishes to be orthodox had
less tendency to become tri-theistic, the thought that claims to be
free would be less Unitarian."—*Moberly*.

b) THE NATURE OF THE DIVINE UNITY

The doctrine of the unity of God does not exclude the idea of a
plurality of persons in the Godhead. Not that there are three persons in each person of the Godhead, if we use in both cases the
term *person* in one and the same sense. We believe, therefore,
that there are three persons in the Godhead, but one God. Antitrinitarians represent the evangelical church as believing in three
Gods, but this is not true; it believes in one God, but three persons
in the Godhead.

(1) THE SCRIPTURAL USE OF THE WORD "ONE"

Gen. 2:24—"And they two [husband and wife] shall be one
flesh." Gen. 11:6—"The people is one." 1 Cor. 3:6-8—"He
that planteth and he that watereth are one." 12:13—"All baptized into one body." John 17:22, 23—"That they may be one,
even as we are one . . . that they may be made perfect in one."

The word "one" in these scriptures is used in a collective sense;
the unity here spoken of is a compound one, like unto that used in
such expressions as "a cluster of grapes," or "all the people rose as
one man." The unity of the Godhead is not simple but compound.

The Hebrew word for "one" (yacheed) in the absolute sense, and which is used in such expressions as "the only one," is *never* used to express the unity of the Godhead. On the contrary, the Hebrew word "echad," meaning "one" in the sense of a compound unity, as seen in the above quoted scriptures, is the one used always to describe the divine unity.

(2) THE DIVINE NAME "GOD" IS A PLURAL WORD; PLURAL PRONOUNS ARE USED OF GOD.

The Hebrew word for God (Elohim) is used most frequently in the plural form. God often uses plural pronouns in speaking of Himself, e. g., Gen. 1:26—"Let *us* make man." Isa. 6:8—"Who will go for *us?*" Gen. 3:22—"Behold, man is become as one of *us*."

Some would say that the "us" in Gen. 1:26—"Let us make man," refers to God's consultation with the angels with whom He takes counsel before He does anything of importance; but Isa. 40:14—"But of whom took he counsel," shows that such is not the case; and Gen. 1:27 contradicts this idea, for it repeats the statement "in the image of God," not in the image of angels; also that "GOD created man in HIS OWN image, in the image of God [not angels] created he him." The "us" of Gen. 1:26, therefore, is properly understood of plural majesty, as indicating the dignity and majesty of the speaker. The proper translation of this verse should be not "let us make," but "we will make," indicating the language of resolve rather than that of consultation.

4. The Doctrine of the Trinity (Vs. Unitarianism)

The doctrine of the Trinity is, in its last analysis, a deep mystery that cannot be fathomed by the finite mind. That it is taught in the Scripture, however, there can be no reasonable doubt. It is a doctrine to be believed even though it cannot be thoroughly understood.

a) THE DOCTRINE OF THE TRINITY IN THE OLD TESTAMENT

This doctrine is not so much declared as intimated in the Old Testament. The burden of the Old Testament message seems to be the unity of God. Yet the doctrine of the Trinity is clearly intimated in a four-fold way:

First: In the plural names of the Deity; e. g., Elohim

Second: Personal pronouns used of the Deity. Gen. 1:26; 11:7; Isa. 6:8

Third: The Theophanies, especially the "Angel of the Lord."
Gen. 16 and 18

Fourth: The work of the Holy Spirit. Gen. 1:2; Judges 6:34

b) THE DOCTRINE OF THE TRINITY IN THE NEW TESTAMENT

The doctrine of the Trinity is clearly taught in the New Testament; it is not merely intimated, as in the Old Testament, but explicitly declared. This is evident from the following:

First: The baptism of Christ: Matt. 3:16, 17. Here the Father speaks from heaven; the Son is being baptized in the Jordan; and the Spirit descends in the form of a dove.

Second: In the Baptismal Formula: Matt. 28:19—"Baptizing them in the name [sing.] of the Father, and of the Son, and of the Holy Ghost."

Third: The Apostolic Benediction: 2 Cor. 13:14—"The grace of our Lord Jesus Christ . . . love of God . . . communion of the Holy Ghost."

Fourth: Christ Himself teaches it in John 14:16—"I will pray the *Father* . . . He will give you another *Comforter*."

Fifth: The New Testament sets forth:

A Father who is God, Rom. 1:7.

A Son who is God, Heb. 1:8.

A Holy Spirit who is God, Acts 5:3, 4.

The whole is summed up in the words of Boardman: "The Father is all the fulness of the Godhead invisible, John 1:18; the Son is all the fulness of the Godhead manifested, John 1:14-18; the Spirit is all the fulness of the Godhead acting immediately upon the creature, 1 Cor. 2:9, 10."

III. THE ATTRIBUTES OF GOD

It is difficult to clearly distinguish between the attributes and the nature of God. It is maintained by some that such a division ought not to be made; that these qualities of God which we call attributes are in reality part of His nature and essence. Whether this be exactly so or not, our purpose in speaking of the attributes of God is for convenience in the study of the doctrine of God.

It has been customary to divide the attributes of God into two classes: the natural, and the moral. The natural attributes are omniscience, omnipotence, omnipresence, eternity; the moral attributes: holiness, righteousness, faithfulness, mercy and loving-kindness, and love.

1. The Natural Attributes

a) THE OMNISCIENCE OF GOD

God is a Spirit, and as such has knowledge. He is a perfect Spirit, and as such has perfect knowledge. By omniscience is meant that God knows all things and is absolutely perfect in knowledge.

(1) SCRIPTURES SETTING FORTH THE FACT OF GOD'S OMNISCIENCE

In general: Job 11:7, 8—"Canst thou by searching find out God? Canst thou find out the Almighty unto perfection?" Job's friends professed to have discovered the reason for his affliction, for, forsooth, had they not found out the secrets of the divine wisdom unto perfection? No, such is beyond their human, finite ken. Isa. 40:28—"There is no searching of his understanding." Israel's captive condition might lead to loss of trust and faith in God. But Israel has not seen all God's plans—no man has. Job 37:16—"The wondrous works of him which is perfect in knowledge." Could Job explain the wonders of the natural phenomena around him? Much less the purposes and judgments of God. Psa. 147:5—"His understanding is infinite." Of His understanding there is no number, no computation. Israel is not lost sight of. He who can number and name and call the stars is able also to call each of the Jews by name even out of captivity. His knowledge is not to be measured by ours. 1 John 3:20—"God knoweth all things." Our hearts may pass over certain things, and fail to see some things that should be confessed. God, however, sees all things. Rom. 11:33—"How unsearchable are his judgments, and his ways past finding out." The mysterious purposes and decrees of God touching man and his salvation are beyond all human comprehension.

In detail, and by way of illustration:

aa)   His knowledge is absolutely comprehensive.

Prov. 15:3—"The eyes of the Lord are in every place, keeping watch upon the evil and the good." How could He reward and punish otherwise? Not one single thing occurring in any place escapes His knowledge. 5:21—"For the ways of man are before the eyes of the Lord, and he pondereth all his goings." We may have habits hidden from our fellow creatures, but not from God.

bb)   God has a perfect knowledge of all that is in nature.

Psa. 147:4—"He telleth the number of the stars; he calleth

them all by their names." Man cannot (Gen. 15:5). How, then, can Israel say, "My way is hid from the Lord"? Cf. Isa. 40:26, 27. Matt. 10:29—"One . . . . sparrow shall not fall to the ground without your Father." Much less would one of His children who perchance might be killed for His name's sake fall without His knowledge.

cc) *God has a perfect knowledge of all that transpires in human experience.*

Prov. 5:21—"For the ways of man are before the eyes of the Lord, and he pondereth all his goings." All a man's doings are weighed by God. How this should affect his conduct! Psa. 139:2, 3—"Thou knowest my downsitting and mine uprising, thou understandest my thought afar off. Thou compassest my path and my lying down, and art acquainted with all my ways." Before our thoughts are fully developed, our unspoken sentences, the rising feeling in our hearts, our activity, our resting, all that we do from day to day is known and sifted by God. v. 4—"There is not a word in my tongue, but lo, O Lord, thou knowest it altogether." Not only thoughts and purposes, but words spoken, idle, good, or bad. Exod. 3:7—"I have seen the affliction . . . heard the cry: know the sorrows of my people which are in Egypt." The tears and grief which they dared not show to their taskmasters, God saw and noted. Did God know of their trouble in Egypt? It seemed to them as though He did not. But He did. Matt. 10:29, 30—"But the very hairs of your head are all numbered." What minute knowledge is this! Exod. 3:19—"And I am sure that the king of Egypt will not let you go, no, not by a mighty hand." Here is intimate knowledge as to what a single individual will do. Isa. 48:18— "O that thou hadst harkened to my commandments! then had thy peace have been as a river," etc. God knows what our lives would have been if only we had acted and decided differently.

dd) *God has a perfect knowledge of all that transpires in human history.*

With what precision are national changes and destinies foretold and depicted in Dan. 2 and 8! Acts 15:18—"Known unto God are all his works from the beginning of the world [ages]." In the context surrounding this verse are clearly set forth the religious changes that were to characterize the generations to come, the which have been so far literally, though not fully, fulfilled.

ee)   *God knows from all eternity to all eternity what will take place.*

The omniscience of God is adduced as the proof that He alone is God, especially as contrasted with the gods (idols) of the heathen: Isa. 48:5-8—"I have even from the beginning declared it unto thee; before it came to pass I showed it thee. . . . . I have showed thee new things from this time, even hidden things," etc. 46:9, 10—"I am God . . . declaring the end from the beginning, and from ancient times the things that are not yet done, saying, My counsel shall stand, and I will do all my pleasure." Here God is announcing to His prophets things that are to occur in the future which it is impossible for the human understanding to know or reach. There is no past, present, future with God. Everything is one great living present. We are like a man standing by a river in a low place, and who, consequently, can see that part of the river only that passes by him; but he who is aloof in the air may see the whole course of the river, how it rises, and how it runs. Thus is it with God.

(2) CERTAIN PROBLEMS IN CONNECTION WITH THE DOCTRINE OF THE OMNISCIENCE OF GOD

How the divine intelligence can comprehend so vast and multitudinous and exhaustless a number of things must forever surpass our comprehension. "O the depth of the riches both of the wisdom and knowledge of God! How unsearchable are his judgments, and his ways past finding out!" (Rom. 11:33). "There is no searching of his understanding; it is beyond human computation." We must expect, therefore, to stand amazed in the presence of such matchless wisdom, and find problems in connection therewith which must for the time, at least, remain unsolved.

Again, we must not confound the foreknowledge of God with His foreordination. The two things are, in a sense, distinct. The fact that God foreknows a thing makes that thing certain but not necessary. His foreordination is based upon His foreknowledge. Pharaoh was responsible for the hardening of his heart even though that hardening process was foreknown and foretold by God. The actions of men are considered certain but not necessary by reason of the divine foreknowledge.

b) THE OMNIPOTENCE OF GOD

The omnipotence of God is that attribute by which He can bring to pass everything which He wills. God's power admits of no bounds or limitations. God's declaration of His intention is the pledge of the thing intended being carried out. "Hath he said, and shall he not do it?"

(1) SCRIPTURAL DECLARATION OF THE FACT; IN GENERAL:

Job 42:2 (R. V.)—"I know that thou canst do everything [all things], and that no purpose of thine can be restrained." The mighty review of all God's works as it passes before Job (context) brings forth this confession: "There is no resisting thy might, and there is no purpose thou canst not carry out." Gen. 18:14—"Is anything too hard for the Lord?" What had ceased to be possible by natural means comes to pass by supernatural means.

(2) SCRIPTURAL DECLARATION OF THE FACT; IN DETAIL:

aa)   *In the world of nature*

Gen. 1:1-3—"God created the heaven and the earth. And God said, Let there be light, and there was light." Thus "he spake and it was done. He commanded and it stood fast." He does not need even to give His hand to the work; His word is sufficient. Psa. 107:25-29—"He raiseth the stormy wind . . . he maketh the storm calm." "Even the winds and the sea obey him." God's slightest word, once uttered, is a standing law to which all nature must absolutely conform. Nahum 1:5, 6—"The mountains quake at him . . . . the hills melt . . . . the earth is burned at his presence . . . . the rocks are thrown down by him." If such is His power how shall Assyria withstand it? This is God's comforting message to Israel. Everything in the sky, in sea, on earth is absolutely subject to His control.

bb)   *In the experience of mankind*

How wonderfully this is illustrated in the experience of Nebuchadnezzar, Dan. 4; and in the conversion of Saul, Acts 9; as well as in the case of Pharaoh, Exod. 4:11. James 4:12-15—" . . . . For that ye ought to say, If the Lord will, we shall live and do this or that." All human actions, whether present or future, are dependent upon the will and power of God. These things are in God's, not in man's, power. See also the parable of the rich fool, Luke 12:16-21.

cc)   *The heavenly inhabitants are subject to His will and word.*

Dan. 4:35 (R. V.)—"He doeth according to his will in the army of heaven." Heb. 1:14—"Are they [angels] not all ministering spirits, sent forth to minister for them who shall be heirs of salvation?"

dd) Even Satan is under the control of God.

Satan has no power over any of God's children saving as God permits him to have. This fact is clearly established in the case of Job (1:12 and 2:6), and Peter (Luke 22:31, 32), in which we are told that Satan had petitioned God that he might sift the self-righteous patriarch and the impulsive apostle. Finally Satan is to be forever bound with a great chain (Rev. 20:2). God can set a bar to the malignity of Satan just as he can set a bar to the waves of the sea.

c) THE OMNIPRESENCE OF GOD

By the omnipresence of God is meant that God is everywhere present. This attribute is closely connected with the omniscience and omnipotence of God, for if God is everywhere present He is everywhere active and possesses full knowledge of all that transpires in every place.

This does not mean that God is everywhere present in a bodily sense, nor even in the same sense; for there is a sense in which He may be in heaven, His dwelling place, in which He cannot be said to be elsewhere. We must guard against the pantheistic idea which claims that God *is* everything, while maintaining the Scriptural doctrine that He is everywhere present in all things. Pantheism emphasizes the omnipresent activity of God, but denies His personality. Those holding the doctrine of pantheism make loud claims to philosophic ability and high intellectual training, but is it not remarkable that it is in connection with this very phase of the doctrine of God that the Apostle Paul says "they became fools"? (Rom. 1.) God is everywhere and in every place; His center is everywhere; His circumference nowhere. But this presence is a spiritual and not a material presence; yet it is a real presence.

(1) SCRIPTURAL STATEMENT OF THE FACT

Jer. 23:23, 24—"Am I a God at hand, saith the Lord, and not a God afar off? Can any hide himself in secret places that I shall not see him? saith the Lord. Do not I fill heaven and earth? saith the Lord." Did the false prophets think that they could hide their secret crimes from God? Or that He could not pursue them into foreign countries? Or that He knew what was transpiring in heaven only and not upon the earth, and even in its most distant corners? It was false for them to thus delude themselves—their sins would be detected and punished (Psa. 10:1-14).

Psa. 139:7-12—"Whither shall I go from thy Spirit, or whither shall I flee from thy presence," etc. How wondrously the attributes of God are grouped in this psalm. In vv. 1-6 the psalmist speaks of the omniscience of God: God knows him through and through. In vv. 13-19 it is the omnipotence of God which overwhelms the psalmist. The omnipresence of God is set forth in vv. 7-12. The psalmist realizes that he is never out of the sight of God any more than he is outside of the range of His knowledge and power. God is in heaven; "Hell is naked before Him"; souls in the intermediate state are fully known to Him (cf. Job 26:2; Jonah 2:2); the darkness is as the light to Him. Job 22:12-14—"Is not God in the height of heaven? . . . . Can he judge through the dark cloud? Thick clouds are a covering to him that he seeth not," etc. All agreed that God displayed His presence in the heaven, but Job had inferred from this that God could not know and did not take notice of such actions of men as were hidden behind the intervening clouds. Not that Job was atheistic; no, but probably denied to God the attribute of omnipresence and omniscience. Acts 17:24-28—"For in him we live, and move, and have our being." Without His upholding hand we must perish; God is our nearest environment. From these and many other scriptures we are clearly taught that God is everywhere present and acting; there is no place where God is not.

This does not mean that God is everywhere present in the same sense. For we are told that He is in heaven, His dwelling place (1 Kings 8:30); that Christ is at His right hand in heaven (Eph. 1:20); that God's throne is in heaven (Rev. 21:2; Isa. 66:1).

We may summarize the doctrine of the Trinity thus: God the Father is specially manifested in heaven; God the Son has been specially manifested on the earth; God the Spirit is manifested everywhere.

Just as the soul is present in every part of the body so God is present in every part of the world.

(2) SOME PRACTICAL INFERENCES FROM THIS DOCTRINE

First, of Comfort: The nearness of God to the believer. "Speak to Him then for He listens. And spirit with spirit can meet; Closer is He than breathing, And nearer than hands or feet." "God is never so far off, As even to be near; He is within. Our spirit is the home He holds most dear. To think of Him as by our side is almost as untrue, As to remove His shrine beyond those skies of starry blue."—*Faber*. The omnipresence is not only a detective truth—it is protective also. After dwelling on this great and awful attribute in Psalm 139, the psalmist, in vv. 17, 18, exclaims: "How precious are thy thoughts to me. . . . . when I awake, I am still with thee." By this is meant that God stands by our side to help, and as One who loves and understands us (Matt. 28:20).

Second, *of Warning*: "As in the Roman empire the whole world was one great prison to a malefactor, and in his flight to the most distant lands the emperor could track him, so under the government of God no sinner can escape the eye of the judge." Thus the omnipresence of God is detective as well as protective. "Thou God seest me," should serve as warning to keep us from sin.

d) THE ETERNITY AND IMMUTABILITY OF GOD

The word "eternal" is used in two senses in the Bible: figuratively, as denoting existence which may have a beginning, but will have no end, e. g., angels, the human soul; literally, denoting an existence which has neither beginning nor ending, like that of God. Time has past, present, future; eternity has not. Eternity is infinite duration without any beginning, end, or limit—an ever abiding present. We can conceive of it only as duration indefinitely extended from the present moment in two directions—as to the past and as to the future. "One of the deaf and dumb pupils in the institution of Paris, being desired to express his idea of the eternity of the Deity, replied: 'It is duration, without beginning or end; existence, without bounds or dimension; present, without past or future. His eternity is youth, without infancy or old age; life, without birth or death; today, without yesterday or tomorrow.' "

By the immutability of God is meant that God's nature is absolutely unchangeable. It is not possible that He should possess one attribute at one time that He does not possess at another. Nor can there be any change in the Deity for better or for worse. God remains forever the same. He is without beginning and without end; the self-existent "I am"; He remains forever the same, and unchangeable.

(1) SCRIPTURAL STATEMENT OF THE FACT: THE ETERNITY
    OF GOD

Hab. 1:12—"Art thou not from everlasting, O Lord my God,
mine Holy One?" Chaldea had threatened to annihilate Israel.
The prophet cannot believe it possible, for has not God *eternal*
purposes for Israel? Is He not holy? How, then, can evil triumph?
Psa. 90:2—"Before the mountains were brought forth, or ever
thou hadst formed the earth and the world, even from everlasting
to everlasting, thou art God." Short and transitory is the life of
man; with God it is otherwise. The perishable nature of man is
here compared with the imperishable nature of God. Psa. 102:24-
27—"I said, O my God, take me not away in the midst of my
days: thy years are throughout all generations. Of old thou hast
laid the foundations of the earth: and the heavens are the work
of thy hands. They shall perish, but thou shalt endure; yea, all of
them shall wax old like a garment; as a vesture shalt thou
change them, and they shall be changed. But thou art the same,
and thy years shall have no end." With the perishable nature of
the whole material creation the psalmist contrasts the imperishable
nature of God. Exod. 3:14—"And God said unto Moses, I AM
THAT I AM." The past, present and future lie in these words for
the name of Jehovah. Rev. 1:8—"I am Alpha and Omega, the
beginning and the ending, saith the Lord, which is, and which
was, and which is to come, the Almighty."

(2) SCRIPTURAL STATEMENT OF THE IMMUTABILITY OF
    GOD:

Mal. 3:6—"I am the Lord, I change not." Man's hope lies in that
fact, as the context here shows. Man had changed in his life and
purpose toward God, and if God, like man, had changed, man
would have been destroyed. James 1:17—"The Father of lights,
with whom is no variableness, neither shadow of turning." There
is no change—in the sense of the degree or intensity of light such
as is manifested in the heavenly bodies. Such lights are constantly
varying and changing; not so with God. There is no inherent, indwelling, possible change in God. 1 Sam. 15:29—"And also the
Strength of Israel will not lie nor repent: for he is not a man, that
he should repent." From these scriptures we assert that God, in
His nature and character, is absolutely without change.

Does God Repent?

What, then, shall we say with regard to such scriptures as Jonah

3:10 and Gen. 6:6—"And God repented of the evil, that he said
he would do unto them." "And it repented the Lord that he had
made man on the earth, and it grieved him at his heart." In reply
we may say that God does not change, but threatens that men
may change "The repentant attitude in God does not involve any
real change in the character and purposes of God. He ever hates
the sin and ever pities and loves the sinner; that is so both before
and after the sinner's repentance. Divine repentance is therefore
the same principle acting differently in altered circumstances. If
the prospect of punishment answers the same purpose as that intended by the punishment itself, then there is no inconsistency in
its remission, for punishment is not an end, it is only a means to
goodness, to the reign of the law of righteousness." When God
appears to be displeased with anything, or orders it differently
from what we expected, we say, after the manner of men, that He
repents. God's attitude towards the Ninevites had not changed, but
they had changed; and because they had changed from sin unto
righteousness, God's attitude towards them and His intended dealings with them as sinners must of necessity change, while, of course,
God's character had in no wise changed with respect to these
people, although His dealings with them had. So that we may say
that God's *character* never changes, but His *dealings* with men
change as they change from ungodliness to godliness and from disobedience unto obedience. "God's immutability is not that of the
stone, that has no internal experience, but rather that of the
column of mercury that rises and falls with every change in the
temperature of the surrounding atmosphere. When a man bicy-
cling against the wind turns about and goes with the wind instead
of going against it, the wind seems to change, although it is blow-
ing just as it was before."—*Strong.*

2. The Moral Attributes

a) THE HOLINESS OF GOD

If there is any difference in importance in the attributes of God,
that of His holiness seems to occupy the first place. It is, to say the
least, the one attribute which God would have His people remember Him by more than any other. In the visions of Himself
which God granted men in the Scriptures the thing that stood out
most prominent was the divine holiness. This is clearly seen by
referring to the visions of Moses, Job, and Isaiah. Some thirty times
does the Prophet Isaiah speak of Jehovah as "the Holy One," thus

indicating what feature of those beatific visions had most impressed him.

The holiness of God is the message of the entire Old Testament. To the prophets God was the absolutely Holy One; the One with eyes too pure to behold evil; the One swift to punish iniquity. In taking a photograph, the part of the body which we desire most to see is not the hands or feet, but the face. So is it with our vision of God. He desires us to see not His hand and finger, denoting His power and skill, nor even His throne as indicating His majesty. It is His holiness by which He desires to be remembered as that is the attribute which most glorifies Him. Let us bear this fact in mind as we study this attribute of the divine nature. It is just this vision of God that we need today when the tendency to deny the reality or the awfulness of sin is so prevalent. Our view of the necessity of the atonement will depend very largely upon our view of the holiness of God. Light views of God and His holiness will produce light views of sin and the atonement.

(1) SCRIPTURAL STATEMENTS SETTING FORTH THE FACT OF GOD'S HOLINESS

Isa. 57:15—"Thus saith the high and lofty One that inhabiteth eternity, whose name is Holy; I dwell in the high and holy place." Psa. 99:9—"Exalt the Lord our God, and worship at his holy hill: for the Lord our God is holy." Hab. 1:13—"Thou art of purer eyes than to behold evil, and canst not look on iniquity." 1 Pet. 1:15, 16—"But as he which hath called you is holy, so be ye holy in all manner of conversation. Because it is written, Be ye holy: for I am holy." God's personal name is holy. John 17:11—"Holy Father, keep through thine own name those whom thou hast given me." Christ here contemplates the Father as the Holy One, as the source and agent of that which He desires for His disciples, namely, holiness of heart and life, being kept from the evil of this world.

Is it not remarkable that this attribute of holiness is ascribed to each of the three persons of the Trinity? God the Father is the Holy One of Israel (Isa. 41:14); God the Son is the Holy One (Acts 3:14); God the Spirit is called the Holy Spirit (Eph. 4:30).

(2) THE SCRIPTURAL MEANING OF HOLINESS AS APPLIED TO GOD

Job 34:10—"Be it far from God, that he should do wickedness;

and from the Almighty that he should commit iniquity." An evil God, one that could commit evil would be a contradiction in terms, an impossible, inconceivable idea. Job seemed to doubt that the principle on which the universe was conducted was one of absolute equity. He must know that God is free from all evil-doing. However hidden the meaning of His dealings, He is always just. God never did, never will do wrong to any of His creatures; He will never punish wrongly. Men may, yea, often do; God never does. Lev. 11:43-45—"Ye shall not make yourselves abominable with any creeping thing that creepeth, neither shall ye make yourselves unclean with them, that ye should be defiled thereby. For I am the Lord your God; ye shall therefore sanctify yourselves, and ye shall be holy; for I am holy: neither shall ye defile yourselves with any manner of creeping thing that creepeth upon the earth . . . . Ye shall therefore be holy, for I am holy." This means that God is absolutely clean and pure and free from all defilement.

The construction of the Tabernacle, with its holy and most holy place into which the high priest alone entered once a year; the Ten Commandments, with their moral categories; the laws of clean and unclean animals and things—all these speak to us in unmistakable terms as to what is meant by holiness as applied to God.

Two things, by way of definition, may be inferred from these Scriptures: first, negatively, that God is entirely apart from all that is evil and from all that defiles both in Himself and in relation to all His creatures; second, and positively, by the holiness of God is meant the consummate holiness, perfection, purity, and absolute sanctity of His nature. There is absolutely nothing unholy in Him. So the Apostle John declares: "God is light, and in him is no darkness at all."

(3) THE MANIFESTATION OF GOD'S HOLINESS

Prov. 15:9, 26—"The way of the wicked is an abomination unto the Lord. The thoughts of the wicked are an abomination unto the Lord." God hates sin, and is its uncompromising foe. Sin is a vile and detestable thing to God. Isa. 59:1, 2—"Behold, the Lord's hand is not shortened, that it cannot save; neither his ear heavy, that it cannot hear. But your iniquities have separated between you and your God, and your sins have hid his face from you, that he will not hear." Israel's sin had raised a partition wall. The infinite distance between the sinner and God is because of sin. The sinner and God are at opposite poles of the moral universe. This in answer to Israel's charge of God's inability. From these two scriptures it is clear that God's holiness manifests itself in the hatred of sin and the separation of the sinner from Himself.

Herein lies the need of the atonement, whereby this awful distance is bridged over. This is the lesson taught by the construction of the Tabernacle as to the division into the holy place and the most holy place.

Prov. 15:9—"But he loveth him that followeth after righteousness." John 3:16—"For God so loved the world, that he gave his only begotten Son," etc. Here God's holiness is seen in that He loves righteousness in the life of His children to such a degree that He gave His only begotten Son to secure it. The Cross shows how much God loves holiness. The Cross stands for God's holiness before even His love. For Christ died not merely for our sins, but in order that He might provide us with that righteousness of life which God loves. "He died that we might be forgiven; he died to make us good." Do we love holiness to the extent of sacrificing for it?

For other manifestations see under Righteousness and Justice of God.

(4) PRACTICAL DEDUCTIONS FROM THE DOCTRINE OF GOD'S HOLINESS

First, we should approach God with "reverence and godly fear" (Heb. 12:28). In the story of Moses' approach to the burning bush, the smiting of the men at Bethshemesh, the boundary set about Mt. Sinai, we are taught to feel our own unworthiness. There is too much hilarity in our approach unto God. Eccl. 5:1-3 inculcates great care in our address to God.

Second, we shall have right views of sin when we get right views of God's holiness. Isaiah, the holiest man in all Israel, was cast down at the sight of his own sin after he had seen the vision of God's holiness. The same thing is true of Job (40:3-5; 42:4-5). We confess sin in such easy and familiar terms that it has almost lost its terror for us.

Third, that approach to a holy God must be through the merits of Christ, and on the ground of a righteousness which is Christ's and which naturally we do not possess. Herein lies the need of the atonement.

b) THE RIGHTEOUSNESS AND JUSTICE OF GOD

In a certain sense these attributes are but the manifestation of God's holiness. It is holiness as manifested in dealing with the sons of men. Holiness has to do more particularly with the character of God in itself, while in righteousness and justice that character is expressed in the dealings of God with men. Three things may be said in the consideration of the righteousness and justice of God: first, there is the imposing of righteousness, laws and demands, which may be called legislative holiness, and may be known as the righteousness of God; second, there is the executing of the penalties attached to those laws, which may be called judicial holiness; third, there is the sense in which the attributes of the righteousness and justice of God may be regarded as the actual carrying out of the holy nature of God in the government of the world. So that in the righteousness of God we have His love of holiness, and in the justice of God, His hatred of sin.

Again righteousness, as here used, has reference to the very nature of God as He is in Himself—that attribute which leads God always to do right. Justice, as an attribute of God, is devoid of all passion or caprice; it is vindicative, not vindictive. And so the righteousness and justice of the God of Israel were made to stand out prominently as contrasted with the caprice of the heathen gods.

(1) SCRIPTURAL STATEMENT OF THE FACT

Psa. 116:5—"Gracious is the Lord, and righteous; yea, our God is merciful." The context here shows that it is because of this fact that God listens to men, and because, having promised to hear, He is bound to keep His promises. Ezra 9:15—"O Lord God of Israel, thou art righteous." Here the righteousness of Jehovah is acknowledged in the punishment of Israel's sins. Thou art just, and thou hast brought us into the state in which we are today. Psa. 145:17—"The Lord is righteous in all his ways, and holy in all his works." This is evident in the rewards He gives to the upright, in lifting up the lowly, and in abundantly blessing the good, pure, and true. Jer. 12:1—"Righteous art thou, O Lord, when I plead with thee." That is to say, "If I were to bring a charge against Thee I should not be able to convict Thee of injustice, even though I be painfully exercised over the mysteries of Thy providence."

These scriptures clearly set forth not only the fact that God is righteous and just, but also define these attributes. Here we are told that God, in His government of the world, does always that which is suitable, straight, and right.

(2) How The Righteousness And Justice Of God Are Revealed

In two ways: first, in punishing the wicked: retributive justice; second, in rewarding the righteous: remunerative justice.

aa) *In the punishment of the wicked*

Psa. 11:4-7—"The Lord is in his holy temple, the Lord's throne is in heaven: his eyes behold, his eyelids try, the children of men. The Lord trieth the righteous; but the wicked and him that loveth violence his soul hateth. Upon the wicked he shall rain snares, fire and brimstone and an horrible tempest. This shall be the portion of their cup." This is David's reply to his timid advisers. Saul may reign upon the earth and do wickedly, but God reigns from heaven and will do right. He sees who does right and who does wrong. And there is that in His nature which recoils from the evil that He sees, and will lead Him ultimately to punish it. There is such a thing as the wrath of God. It is here described. Whatever awful thing the description in this verse may mean for the wicked, God grant that we may never know. In Exod. 9:23-27 we have the account of the plague of hail, following which are these words: "And Pharaoh sent . . . . for Moses and Aaron, and said unto them, I have sinned this time: the Lord is righteous, and I and my people are wicked." Pharaoh here acknowledges the perfect justice of God in punishing him for his sin and rebellion. He knew that he had deserved it all, even though cavillers today say there was injustice with God in His treatment of Pharaoh. Pharaoh himself certainly did not think so. Dan. 9:12-14 and Rev. 16:5, 6 bring out the same thought. How careful sinners ought to be not to fall into the hands of the righteous Judge! No sinner at last will be able to say, "I did not deserve this punishment."

bb) *In forgiving the sins of the penitent*

1 John 1:9 (R. V.)—"If we confess our sins, he is faithful and righteous to forgive us our sins, and to cleanse us from all unrighteousness." Ordinarily, the forgiveness of sin is associated with the mercy, love, and compassion of God, and not with His righteousness and justice. This verse assures us that if we confess our sins, the righteousness and justice of God are our guarantee for forgiveness—God cannot but forgive and cleanse us from all sin.

cc) *In keeping His word and promise to His children*

Neh. 9:7, 8—"Thou art the Lord the God, who didst choose

Abram . . . . and madest a covenant with him to give the land of the Canaanites . . . . to his seed, and hast performed thy words; for thou art righteous." We need to recall the tremendous obstacles which stood in the way of the fulfillment of this promise, and yet we should remember the eleventh chapter of Hebrews. When God gives His word, and makes a promise, naught in heaven, on earth, or in hell can make that promise void. His righteousness is the guarantee of its fulfillment.

dd) *In showing Himself to be the vindicator of His people from all their enemies*

Psa. 129:1-4—"Many a time have they afflicted me . . . yet they have not prevailed against me. The Lord is righteous: he hath cut asunder the cords of the wicked." Sooner or later, God's people will triumph gloriously as David triumphed over Saul. Even in this life God will give us rest from our enemies; and there shall assuredly come a day when we shall be "where the wicked cease from troubling, and the weary are at rest."

ee) *In the rewarding of the righteous*

Heb. 6:10—"For God is not unrighteous to forget your work and labor of love, which ye have showed towards his name, in that ye have ministered unto the saints, and do minister." Those who had shown their faith by their works would not now be allowed to lose that faith. The very idea of divine justice implies that the use of this grace, thus evidenced, will be rewarded, not only by continuance in grace, but their final perseverance and reward. 2 Tim. 4:8—"Henceforth there is laid up for me a crown of righteousness, which the Lord, the righteous judge, will give me at that day: and not to me only, but unto all them that love his appearing." The righteous Judge will not allow the faithful believer to go unrewarded. He is not like the unrighteous judges of Rome and the Athenian games. Here we are not always rewarded, but some time we shall receive full reward for all the good that we have done. The righteousness of God is the guarantee of all this.

c) THE MERCY AND LOVING-KINDNESS OF GOD

By these attributes is meant, in general, the kindness, goodness, and compassion of God, the love of God in its relation to both the obedient and the disobedient sons of men. The dew drops on the thistle as well as on the rose.

More specifically: Mercy is usually exercised in connection with

guilt; it is that attribute of God which leads Him to seek the welfare, both temporal and spiritual, of sinners, even though at the
cost of great sacrifice on His part. "But God, who is rich in mercy,
for his great love wherewith he loved us. . . . . God commendeth his love towards us, in that, while we were yet sinners, Christ
died for us." (Eph. 2:4; Rom. 5:8.)

Loving-kindness is that attribute of God which leads Him to
bestow upon His obedient children His constant and choice blessing. "He that spared not his own Son, but freely delivered him up
for us all, how shall he not with him freely give us all things?"
(Rom. 8:32.)

(1) Scriptural Statement Of The Fact

Psa. 103:8—"The Lord is merciful and gracious, slow to anger,
and plenteous in mercy." For, instead of inflicting pain, poverty,
death—which are the wages of sin—God has spared our lives,
given us health, increased our blessings and comforts, and given us
the life of the ages. Deut. 4:31—"(For the Lord thy God is a
merciful God); he will not forsake thee, neither destroy thee, nor
forget the covenant of thy fathers." God is ready to accept the
penitence of Israel, even now, if only it be sincere. Israel will return and find God only because He is merciful and does not let go
of her. It is His mercy that forbids His permanently forsaking His
people. Psa. 86:15—"But thou, O Lord, art a God full of compassion, and gracious, long-suffering, and plenteous in mercy and
truth." It was because God had so declared Himself to be of this
nature that David felt justified in feeling that God would not utterly
forsake him in his time of great stress and need. The most striking
illustration of the mercy and loving-kindness of God is set forth
in the parable of the prodigal son (Luke 15:11-32). Here we have
not only the welcome awaiting the wanderer, but also the longing
for his return on the part of the anxious and loving father.

(2) How The Mercy And Loving-kindness Of God Are Manifested

In general: We must not forget that God is absolutely sovereign
in the bestowal of His blessings—"Therefore hath he mercy on
whom he will have mercy" (Rom. 9:18). We should also remember that God wills to have mercy on all His creatures—"For thou,
Lord, art good, and ready to forgive, and plenteous in mercy to all
them that call upon thee" (Psa. 86:5).

aa) Mercy—towards sinners in particular

Luke 6:36—"Be ye therefore merciful, as your Father also is merciful." Matt. 5:45—"That ye may be the children of your Father which is in heaven: for he maketh his sun to rise on the evil and the good, and sendeth rain on the just and the unjust." Here even the impenitent and hard-hearted are the recipients of God's mercy; all sinners, even the impenitent are included in the sweep of His mercy.

Isa. 55:7—"Let the wicked forsake his way, and the unrighteous man his thoughts, and let him return unto the Lord: and he will have mercy upon him; and to our God, for he will abundantly pardon." God's mercy is a holy mercy; it will by no means protect sin, but anxiously awaits to pardon it. God's mercy is a city of refuge for the penitent, but by no means a sanctuary for the presumptuous. See Prov. 28:13, and Psa. 51:1. God's mercy is here seen in pardoning the sin of those who do truly repent. We speak about "trusting in the mercy of the Lord." Let us forsake sin and then trust in the mercy of the Lord and we shall find pardon.

2 Pet. 3:9—"The Lord . . . . is longsuffering to us-ward, not willing that any should perish, but that all should come to repentance." Neh. 9:31—"Nevertheless for thy great mercies' sake thou didst not utterly consume them; for thou art a gracious and merciful God." Here is mercy manifested in forbearance with sinners. If God should have dealt with them in justice they would have been cut off long before. Think of the evil, the impurity, the sin that God must see. How it must disgust Him. Then remember that He could crush it all in a moment. Yet He does not. He pleads; He sacrifices to show His love for sinners. Surely it is because of the Lord's mercies that we are not consumed, and because His compassions fail not. Yet, beware lest we abuse this goodness, for our God is also a consuming fire. "Behold, the goodness and the severity of God." The mercy of God is here shown in His loving forbearance with sinners.

bb) *Loving-kindness towards the saints, in particular*

Psa. 32:10—"But he that trusteth in the Lord, mercy shall compass him about." The very act of trust on the part of the believer moves the heart of God to protect him just as in the case of a parent and his child. The moment I throw myself on God I am enveloped in His mercy—mercy is my environment, like a fiery wall it surrounds me, without a break through which an evil can creep. Resistance surrounds us with "sorrow"; but trust surrounds us with "mercy." In the center of that circle of mercy sits and rests the trusting soul.

Phil. 2:27—"For indeed he was sick nigh unto death; but God had mercy on him; and not on him only, but on me also, lest I should have sorrow upon sorrow." Here God's loving-kindness is seen in healing up His sick children. Yet remember that "He hath mercy on whom He will have mercy." Not every sick child of God is raised. Psa. 6:2, 4—"Have mercy upon me, O Lord, for I am weak: O Lord, heal me. . . . . Deliver my soul for thy mercies' sake." The psalmist asks God to illustrate His mercy in restoring to him his spiritual health. From these scriptures we see that the mercy of God is revealed in healing His children of bodily and spiritual sickness.

Psa. 21:7—"For the king trusteth in the Lord, and through the mercy of the most High he shall not be moved." David feels that, because he trusts in the mercy of the Lord, his throne, whatever may dash against it, is perfectly secure. Is not this true also of the believer's eternal security? More to the mercy of God than to the perseverance of the saints is to be attributed the eternal security of the believer. "He will hold me fast."

d) THE LOVE OF GOD

Christianity is really the only religion that sets forth the Supreme Being as love. The gods of the heathen are angry, hateful beings, and are in constant need of appeasing.

(1) SCRIPTURAL STATEMENTS OF THE FACT

1 John 4:8-16—"God is love." "God is light"; "God is Spirit"; "God is love." Spirit and light are expressions of God's essential nature. Love is the expression of His personality corresponding to His nature. It is the nature of God to love. He dwells always in the atmosphere of love. Just how to define or describe the love of God may be difficult if not impossible. It appears from certain scriptures (1 John 3:16; John 3:16) that the love of God is of such a nature that it betokens a constant interest in the physical and spiritual welfare of His creatures as to lead Him to make sacrifices beyond human conception to reveal that love.

(2) THE OBJECTS OF GOD'S LOVE

aa)   Jesus Christ, God's only-begotten Son, is the special object of His love.

Matt. 3:17—"This is my beloved Son, in whom I am well

pleased." Also Matt. 17:5; Luke 20:13. Jesus Christ shares the love of the Father in a unique sense, just as He is His Son in a unique sense. He is especially "My chosen." "The One in whom my soul delighteth," "My beloved Son"—literally: the Son of mine, the beloved. And we can readily understand how that He who did the will of God perfectly should thus become the special object of the Father's love. Of course, if the love of God is eternal, as is the nature of God, which must be the case, then, that love must have had an eternal object to love. So Christ, in addressing the Father, says: "Thou lovedst me before the foundation of the world."

bb) *Believers in His Son, Jesus Christ, are special objects of God's love.*

John 16:27—"For the Father himself loveth you, because ye have loved me, and have believed that I came out from God." 14:21-23—"He that loveth me shall be loved of my Father. . . . . If a man love me . . . . my Father will love him." 17:23 —"And hast loved them, as thou hast loved me." Do we really believe these words? We are not on the outskirts of God's love, but in its very midst. There stands Christ right in the very midst of that circle of the Father's love; then He draws us to that spot, and, as it were, disappears, leaving us standing there bathed in the same loving-kindness of the Father in which He Himself had basked.

cc) *God loves the world of sinners and ungodly men.*

John 3:16—"For God so loved the world" was a startling truth to Nicodemus in his narrow exclusivism. God loved not the Jew only, but also the Gentile; not a part of the world of men, but every man in it, irrespective of his moral character. For "God commendeth his love towards us, in that, while we were yet sinners, Christ died for us" (Rom. 5:8). This is wonderful when we begin to realize what a world in sin is. The love of God is broader than the measure of man's mind. God desires the salvation of all men (1 Tim. 2:4).

(3) How The Love Of God Reveals Itself

aa) *In making infinite sacrifice for the salvation of men*

1 John 4:9, 10—"In this was manifested the love of God towards us, because that God sent his only-begotten Son into the world, that we might live through him. Herein is love, not that we loved God,

but that God loved us, and sent his Son to be the propitiation for our sins." Love is more than compassion; it hides not itself as compassion may do, but displays itself actively in behalf of its object. The Cross of Calvary is the highest expression of the love of God for sinful man. He gave not only a Son, but His only Son, His well-beloved.

bb)   *In bestowing full and complete pardon on the penitent*

Isa. 38:17—"Thou hast in love to my soul delivered it from the pit of corruption: for thou hast cast all my sins behind thy back." Literally, "Thou hast loved my soul back from the pit of destruction." God had taken the bitterness out of his life and given him the gracious forgiveness of his sins, by putting them far away from Him. Eph. 2:4, 5—"But God, who is rich in mercy, for his great love wherewith he loved us, even when we were dead in sins, hath quickened us together with Christ," etc. Verses 1-3 of this chapter show the race rushing headlong to inevitable ruin. "But" reverses the picture; when all help for man fails, then God steps in, and by His mercy, which springs from "His great love," redeems fallen man, and gives him not only pardon, but a position in His heavenly kingdom by the side of Jesus Christ. All this was "for," or, perhaps better, "in order to satisfy His great love." Love led Him to do it.

cc)   *In remembering His children in all the varying circumstances of life*

Isa. 63:9—"In all their affliction he was afflicted, and the angel of his presence saved them: in his love and in his pity he redeemed them; and he bare them, and carried them all the days of old." Here is retrospection on the part of the prophet. He thinks of all the oppressions of Israel, and recalls how God's interests have been bound up with theirs. He was not their adversary; He was their sympathetic, loving friend. He suffered with them. Isa. 49:15, 16—"Can a woman forget her sucking child? Yea, they may forget, yet will I not forget thee. Behold, I have graven thee on the palms of my hands; thy walls are continually before me." It was the custom those days to trace upon the palms of the hands the outlines of any object of affection; hence a man engraved the name of his god. So God could not act without being reminded of Israel. God is always mindful of His own. Saul of Tarsus learned this truth on the way to Damascus.

THE DOCTRINE OF JESUS CHRIST

THE DOCTRINE OF JESUS CHRIST

A. THE PERSON OF CHRIST

I. THE HUMANITY OF JESUS CHRIST

1. HE HAD A HUMAN PARENTAGE.
2. HE GREW AS OTHER HUMAN BEINGS DO.
3. HE HAD THE APPEARANCE OF A MAN.
4. HE WAS POSSESSED OF A BODY, SOUL, AND SPIRIT.
5. HE WAS SUBJECT TO THE SINLESS INFIRMITIES OF HUMANITY.
6. HUMAN NAMES ARE GIVEN TO HIM.

II. THE DEITY OF JESUS CHRIST

1. DIVINE NAMES ARE GIVEN TO HIM.
2. DIVINE WORSHIP IS ASCRIBED TO HIM.
3. DIVINE QUALITIES AND PROPERTIES ARE POSSESSED BY HIM.
4. DIVINE OFFICES ARE ASCRIBED TO HIM.
5. DIVINE ATTRIBUTES ARE POSSESSED BY HIM.
6. CHRIST'S NAME IS COUPLED WITH THAT OF THE FATHER.
7. THE SELF-CONSCIOUSNESS OF JESUS CHRIST AS MANIFESTED:
   a) In His Visit to the Temple
   b) In His Baptism
   c) In His Temptation
   d) In the Calling of the Twelve and the Seventy
   e) In the Sermon on the Mount

B. THE WORK OF CHRIST

I. THE DEATH OF JESUS CHRIST

1. ITS IMPORTANCE
2. THE SCRIPTURAL DEFINITION OF CHRIST'S DEATH
3. UNSCRIPTURAL VIEWS OF CHRIST'S DEATH
4. THE NECESSITY OF CHRIST'S DEATH
5. THE EXTENT OF CHRIST'S DEATH
6. THE EFFECTS OF CHRIST'S DEATH

II. THE RESURRECTION OF JESUS CHRIST

1. ITS IMPORTANCE
2. THE NATURE OF THE RESURRECTION OF JESUS CHRIST
3. THE CREDIBILITY OF THE RESURRECTION OF JESUS CHRIST
4. THE RESULTS OF THE RESURRECTION OF JESUS CHRIST

III. THE ASCENSION AND EXALTATION OF JESUS CHRIST

1. THE MEANING OF THESE TERMS
2. THE SCRIPTURAL DATA FOR THE DOCTRINE
3. THE NECESSITY OF THE ASCENSION AND EXALTATION OF JESUS CHRIST
4. THE NATURE OF THE ASCENSION AND EXALTATION OF JESUS CHRIST
5. THE PURPOSE OF THE ASCENSION AND EXALTATION OF JESUS CHRIST
6. THE RESULTS OF THE ASCENSION AND EXALTATION OF JESUS CHRIST

THE DOCTRINE OF JESUS CHRIST

A. THE PERSON OF CHRIST

The close kinship of Christ with Christianity is one of the distinctive features of the Christian religion. If you take away the name of Buddha from Buddhism and remove the personal revealer entirely from his system; if you take away the personality of Muhammad from Muhammadanism, or the personality of Zoroaster from the religion of the Parsees, the entire doctrine of these religions would still be left intact. Their practical value, such as it is, would not be imperilled or lessened. But take away from Christianity the name and person of Jesus Christ and what have you left? Nothing! The whole substance and strength of the Christian faith centres in Jesus Christ. Without Him there is absolutely nothing.—*Sinclair Patterson.*

From beginning to end, in all its various phases and aspects and elements, the Christian faith and life is determined by the person and the work of Jesus Christ. It owes its life and character at every point to Him. Its convictions are convictions about Him. Its hopes are hopes which He has inspired and which it is for Him to fulfill. Its ideals are born of His teaching and His life. Its strength is the strength of His spirit.—*James Denney.*

I. THE HUMANITY OF JESUS CHRIST

1. *The Scriptures Distinctly Teach that He had a Human Parentage: That He Was Born of a Woman—The Virgin Mary.*

Matt. 1:18—"Mary . . . . was found with child of the Holy Ghost." 2:11—"The young child with Mary his mother." 12:47 —"Behold, thy mother and thy brethren." 13:55—"Is not his mother called Mary?" John 1:14—"The Word was made flesh, and dwelt among us." 2:1—"The mother of Jesus was there." Acts 13:23—"Of this man's seed hath God . . . . raised . . . . Jesus." Rom. 1:3—"Of the seed of David according to the flesh." Gal. 4:4—"Made of a woman."

53

In thus being born of a woman Jesus Christ submitted to the conditions of a human life and a human body; became humanity's son by a human birth. Of the "seed of the woman," of the "seed of Abraham," and of line and lineage of David, Jesus Christ is undeniably human.

We must not lose sight of the fact that there was something supernatural surrounding the birth of the Christ. Matt. 1:18—"On this wise," and Luke 1:35—"The Holy Ghost shall come upon thee, and the power of the Highest shall overshadow thee; therefore also that holy thing which shall be born of thee shall be called the Son of God." "On this wise" indicates that this birth was different from those recorded before it. Luke 1:35 is explicit about the matter. To assail the virgin birth is to assail the Virgin's life. He was of "the seed of the woman," not of the man. (See Luke 1:34—"How shall this be, seeing I know not a man?") No laws of heredity are sufficient to account for His generation. By a creative act God broke through the chain of human generation and brought into the world a supernatural being.

The narrative of the virgin birth need not stagger us. The abundance of historical evidence in its favor should lead to its acceptance. All the manuscripts in all the ancient versions contain the record of it. All the traditions of the early church recognize it. Mention of it is made in the earliest of all the creeds: the Apostles' Creed. If the doctrine of the virgin birth is rejected it must be on purely subjective grounds. If one denies the possibility of the supernatural in the experience of human life, it is, of course, easy for him to deny this doctrine. To one who believes that Jesus was human only it would seem comparatively easy to deny the supernatural birth on purely subjective grounds. The preconceptions of thinkers to a great degree determine their views. It would seem that such a wonderful life as that lived by Christ, having as it did such a wonderful finish in the resurrection and ascension, might, indeed should, have a wonderful and extraordinary entrance into the world. The fact that the virgin birth is attested by the Scriptures, by tradition, by creeds, and that it is in perfect harmony with all the other facts of that wonderful life should be sufficient attestation of its truth.*

---

*The Virgin Birth, by James Orr, D.D., deals fully and most ably with this subject.

It has been thought strange that if, as is claimed, the virgin birth is so essential to the right understanding of the Christian religion, that Mark, John, and Paul should say nothing about it. But does such silence really exist? John says "the Word became flesh"; while Paul speaks of "God manifest in the flesh." Says L. F. Anderson: "This argument from silence is sufficiently met by the considerations that Mark passes over thirty years of our Lord's life in silence; that John presupposes the narratives of Matthew and Luke; that Paul does not deal with the story of Jesus' life. The facts were known at first only to Mary and Joseph; their very nature involved reticence until Jesus was demonstrated to be the Son of God with power by the resurrection from the dead; meantime the natural development of Jesus and His refusal to set up an earthly kingdom have made the miraculous events of thirty years ago seem to Mary like a wonderful dream; so only gradually the marvelous tale of the mother of the Lord found its way into the Gospel tradition and the creeds of the church, and into the innermost hearts of the Christians of all countries."

2. He Grew in Wisdom and Stature as Other Human Beings Do. He Was Subject to the Ordinary Laws of Human Development in Body and Soul.

Luke 2:40, 52, 46—"And the child grew, and waxed strong in spirit, filled with wisdom: and the grace of God was upon him. And Jesus increased in wisdom and stature, and in favor with God and man. And . . . . they found him in the temple, sitting in the midst of the doctors, both hearing them, and asking them questions."

Just to what extent His sinless nature influenced His growth we may not be able to say. It seems clear, however, from the Scriptures, that we are to attribute Jesus' growth and advancement to the training He received in a godly home; to the instruction given at the synagogue and the temple; from His own personal study of the Scriptures, and from His fellowship and communion with His Father. Both the human and divine element entered into His training and development, which were as real in the experience of Jesus as in that of any other human being. We are told that "Jesus grew, and increased in widom and stature." He "increased," i. e., He kept advancing; He "grew," and the reflective form of the verb would seem to indicate that His growth was due to His own efforts. From all this it seems clear that Jesus received His training along the lines of ordinary human progress—instruction, study, thought.

Nor should the fact that Christ possessed divine attributes, such as omniscience and omnipotence, militate against a perfectly human development. Could He not have possessed them and yet not have used them? Self-emptying is not self-extinction. Is it incredible to think that, although possessing these divine attributes, He should have held them in subjection in order that the Holy Spirit might have His part to play in that truly human, and yet divine, life?

3. He Had the Appearance of a Man.

John 4:9—"How is it that thou, being a Jew." Luke 24:13— The two disciples on the way to Emmaus took Him to be an ordinary man. John 20:15—"She, supposing him to be the gardener." 21:4, 5—"Jesus stood on the shore; but the disciples knew not that it was Jesus."

The woman of Samaria evidently recognized Jesus as a Jew by His features or speech. To her He was just an ordinary Jew, at least to begin with. There is no Biblical warrant for surrounding the head of Christ with a halo, as the artists do. His pure life no doubt gave Him a distinguished look, just as good character similarly distinguishes men today. Of course we know nothing definite as to the appearance of Jesus, for no picture or photograph of Him do we possess. The apostles draw attention only to the tone of His voice (Mark 7:34; 15:34). After the resurrection and ascension Jesus seems still to have retained the form of a man (Acts 7:56; 1 Tim. 2:5).

4. He Was Possessed of a Human Physical Nature: Body, Soul and Spirit.

John 1:14—"And the Word was made flesh." Heb. 2:14— "Forasmuch then as the children are partakers of flesh and blood, he also himself likewise took part of the same." Matt. 26:12— "She hath poured this ointment on my body." v. 38—"My soul is exceeding sorrowful." Luke 23:46—"Father, into thy hands I commend my spirit." 24:39—"Behold my hands and my feet, that it is I myself: handle me, and see; for a spirit hath not flesh and bones, as ye see me have."

By his incarnation Christ came into possession of a real human nature; He came not only unto His own, but came unto them in the likeness of their own flesh. Of course we must distinguish between a human nature and a carnal nature. A carnal nature is really not an integral part of man as God made him in the beginning. Christ's human nature was truly human, yet sinless: "Yet without sin" (Heb. 4:15).

5. He Was Subject to the Sinless Infirmities of Human Nature.

Matt. 4:2—"He was afterward an hungred." John 19:28— "Jesus . . . . saith, I thirst." 4:6—"Jesus . . . . being wearied with his journey." Matt. 8:24—"But he was asleep." John 19:30 —"He bowed his head, and gave up the ghost." He mourns over Jerusalem (Matt. 23:37); weeps over His dead friend Lazarus (John 11:35); craves for human sympathy in the garden (Matt. 26:36, 40); tempted in all points like as we are (Heb. 4:15). There is not a note in the great organ of our humanity which, when touched, does not find a sympathetic vibration in the mighty range and scope of our Lord's being, saving, of course, the jarring discord of sin. But sin was not an integral part of *un*fallen human nature. We speak of natural depravity, but, in reality, sin is *un*natural. God made Adam perfect and without sin. Since Adam's fall, however, men are "born in sin" (Ps. 51:5).

6. Human Names Are Given to Him By Himself and Others.

Luke 19:10—"Son of Man." Matt. 1:21—"Thou shalt call his name Jesus." Acts 2:22—"Jesus of Nazareth." 1 Tim. 2:5—"The man Christ Jesus."

No less than eighty times in the Gospels does Jesus call Himself the Son of Man. Even when acquiescing in the title Son of God as addressed to Himself He sometimes immediately after substitutes the title Son of Man (John 1:49-51; Matt. 26:63, 64).

While we recognize the fact that there is something official in the title Son of Man, something connected with His relation to the Kingdom of God, it is nevertheless true that in using this title He as-

suredly identifies Himself with the sons of men. While He is rightly called THE Son of Man, because, by His sinless nature and
life He is unique among the sons of men, He is nevertheless A Son
of Man in that He is bone of our bone and flesh of our flesh.

II. THE DEITY OF JESUS CHRIST

1. Divine Names Are Given to Him.

a) HE IS CALLED GOD.

John 1:1—"The Word was God." Heb. 1:8—"But unto the Son
he saith, Thy throne, O God, is for ever." John 1:18—"The only
begotten Son [or better "only begotten God"]." Absolute deity is
here ascribed to Christ. 20:28—"My Lord and my God." Not an
expression of amazement, but a confession of faith. This confession
accepted by Christ, hence equivalent to the acceptance of deity,
and an assertion of it on Christ's part. Rom. 9:5—"God blessed
forever." Tit. 2:13—"The great God and our Saviour Jesus Christ."
1 John 5:20—"His Son Jesus Christ. This is the true God." In all
these passages Christ is called God.

It may be argued that while Christ is here called God, yet that
does not argue for nor prove His deity, for human judges are
also called "gods" in John 10:35—"If he called them gods unto
whom the word of God came." True, but it is then used in a
secondary and relative sense, and not in the absolute sense as
when used of the Son.

b) HE IS CALLED THE SON OF GOD.

The references containing this title are numerous. Among others
see Matt. 8:29; 14:33; 16:16, 17; Mark 1:1; 14:61; Luke 1:35;
4:41. While it may be true that in the synoptic Gospels Jesus may
not be said to have claimed this title for Himself, yet He unhesitatingly accepted it when used of Him and addressed to Him by
others. Further, it seems clear from the charges made against Him
that He did claim such an honor for Himself. Matt. 27:40, 43—
"For he said, I am the Son of God." Mark 14:61, 62—"Art thou
the Christ, the Son of the Blessed? and Jesus said, I am." Luke
22:70—"Art thou then the Son of God? And he said unto them,
Ye say that I am." In John's Gospel however, Jesus plainly calls
Himself "the Son of God" (5:25; 10:36; 11:4). Indeed, John's

Gospel begins with Christ as God: "The Word was God," and ends with the same thought: "My Lord and my God" (20:28). (Chapter 21 is an epilogue.)

Dr. James Orr says, in speaking of the title Son of God as ascribed to Christ: "This title is one to which there can be no finite comparison or analogy. The oneness with God which it designates is not such reflex influence of the divine thought and character such as man and angels may attain, but identity of essence constituting him not God-like alone, but God. Others may be children of God in a moral sense; but by this right of elemental nature, none but He; He is herein, the *only* Son; so little separate, so close to the inner divine life which He expresses, that He is in the bosom of the Father. This language denotes two natures homogeneous, entirely one, and both so essential to the Godhead that neither can be omitted from any truth you speak of it."

If when He called Himself "the Son of God" He did not mean more than that He was *a* son of God, why then did the high priest accuse Him of blasphemy when He claimed this title (Matt. 26: 61-63)? Does not Mark 12:6—"Having yet therefore one son, his well-beloved, he sent him also last unto them, saying, They will reverence my son," indicate a special sonship? The sonship of Christ is human and historical, it is true; but it is more: it is transcendent, unique, solitary. That something unique and solitary lay in this title seems clear from John 5:18—"The Jews sought the more to kill Him . . . . because he . . . . said . . . . also that God was His [own] Father, making Himself equal with God."

The use of the word "only begotten" also indicates the uniqueness of this sonship. For use of the word see Luke 7:12—"The only son of his mother." 9:38—"For he is mine only child." This word is used of Christ by John in 1:14, 18; 3:16, 18; 1 John 4:9, and distinguishes between Christ as the only Son, and the "many . . . . children of God" (John 1:12, 13). In one sense Christ has no brethren: He stands absolutely alone. This contrast is clearly emphasized in John 1:14, 18—"only begotten Son," and 1:12 (R. V.)—"many . . . . children." He is the Son from eternity: they "become" sons in time. He is one; they are many. He is Son by nature; they are sons by adoption and grace. He is Son of the same essence with the Father; they are of different substance from the Father.

c) HE IS CALLED THE LORD.

Acts 4:33; 16:31; Luke 2:11; Acts 9:17; Matt. 22:43-45. It is true that this term is used of men, e. g., Acts 16:30—"Sirs [Lords], what must I do to be saved?" John 12:21—"Sir [Lord], we would see Jesus." It is not used, however, in this unique sense, as the cqnnection will clearly show. In our Lord's day, the title "Lord" as used of Christ was applicable only to the Deity, to God. "The ptolemies and the Roman Emperors would allow the name to be applied to them only when they permitted themselves to be deified. The archaeological discoveries at Oxyrhyncus put this fact beyond a doubt. So when the New Testament writers speak of Jesus as Lord, there can be no question as to what they mean." —*Wood.*

d) OTHER DIVINE NAMES ARE ASCRIBED TO HIM:

"The first and the last" (Rev. 1:17). This title used of Jehovah in Isa. 41:4; 44:6; 48:12. "The Alpha and Omega" (Rev. 22:13, 16); cf. 1:8 where it is used of God.

2. Divine Worship Is Ascribed to Jesus Christ.

The Scriptures recognize worship as being due to God, to Deity alone: Matt. 4:10—"Worship the Lord thy God, and him only." Rev. 22:8, 9—"I fell down to worship before the feet of the angel . . . . Then saith he unto me, See thou do it not: . . . . worship God." John was not allowed even to worship God at the feet of the angel. Acts 14:14, 15; 10:25, 26—Cornelius fell down at the feet of Peter, and worshipped him. "But Peter took him up, saying, Stand up; I myself also am a man." See what an awful fate was meted out to Herod because he dared to accept worship that belonged to God only (Acts 12:20-25). Yet Jesus Christ unhesitatingly accepted such worship, indeed, called for it (John 4:10). See John 20:28; Matt. 14:33; Luke 24:52; 5:8.

The homage given to Christ in these scriptures would be nothing short of sacrilegious idolatry if Christ were not God. There seemed to be not the slightest reluctance on the part of Christ in the acceptance of such worship. Therefore either Christ was God or He was an imposter. But His whole life refutes the idea of imposture. It was He who said, "Worship God only"; and He had no right to take the place of God if He were not God.

God himself commands all men to render worship to the Son,

even as they do to Him. John 5:23, 24—"That all men should honor the Son, even as they honor the Father." Even the angels are commanded to render worship to the Son. Heb. 1:6—"And let all the angels of God worship him." Phil. 2:10—"That at the name of Jesus every knee should bow."

It was the practice of the apostles and the early church to render worship to Christ: 2 Cor. 12:8-10—"I besought the Lord." Acts 7:59—"And they stoned Stephen, calling upon God, and saying, Lord Jesus, receive my spirit." 1 Cor. 1:2—"Them that . . . call upon the name of Jesus Christ our Lord."

The Christians of all ages have not been satisfied with admiring Christ, they have adored and worshipped Him. They have approached His person in the attitude of self-sacrifice and worship as in the presence of and to God.

Robert Browning quoted, in a letter to a lady in her last illness, the words of Charles Lamb, when in a gay fancy with some friends as to how he and they would feel if the greatest of the dead were to appear suddenly in flesh and blood once more—on the first suggestion, "and if Christ entered this room?" changed his tone at once, and stuttered out as his manner was when moved: "You see—if Shakespeare entered, we should all rise; if Christ appeared, we must kneel."

3. He Possesses the Qualities and Properties of Deity.

a) PRE-EXISTENCE

John 1:1—"In the beginning"; cf. Gen. 1:1. John 8:58—"Before Abraham was, I am." That is to say: "Abraham's existence presupposes mine, not mine his. He was dependent upon me, not I upon him for existence. Abraham came into being at a certain point of time, but I am." Here is simple being without beginning or end. See also John 17:5; Phil. 2:6; Col. 1:16, 17.

b) SELF-EXISTENCE AND LIFE-GIVING POWER

John 5:21, 26—"For as the Father raiseth up the dead and quickeneth them, even so the Son quickeneth whom he will." "For as the Father hath life in himself, so hath he given to the Son to have life in himself." 1:4—"In him was life." See also 14:6; Heb. 7:16; John 17:3-5; 10:17, 18. These scriptures teach that all life—physical, moral, spiritual, eternal—has its source in Christ.

c) IMMUTABILITY

Heb. 13:8—"Jesus Christ the same yesterday, and today, and for ever." See also 1:12. All nature, which like a garment He throws around Him, is subject to change and decay; Jesus Christ is the same always, He never changes. Human teachers, such as are spoken of in the context, may change, but He, the Christ, never.

d) ALL THE FULNESS OF THE GODHEAD DWELT IN HIM

Col. 2:9. Not merely the divine perfections and attributes of Deity, but (*theotes*) the very essence and nature of the Godhead. He was not merely God-like; He was God.

4. Divine Offices Are Ascribed to Him.

a) HE IS THE CREATOR:

John 1:3—"All things were made by Him." In the creation He was the acting power and personal instrument. Creation is the revelation of His mind and might. Heb. 1:10 shows the dignity of the Creator as contrasted with the creature. Col. 1:16 contradicts the Gnostic theory of emanations, and shows Christ to be the creator of all created things and beings. Rev. 3:14—"The beginning of the creation of God," means "beginning" in the active sense, *the origin,* that by which a thing begins to be. Col. 1:15— "first-born," not made; compare with Col. 1:17, where the "for" of v. 16 shows Him to be not included in the "created things," but the origin of and superior to them all. He is the Creator of the universe (v. 16), just as He is the Head of the Church (v. 18).

b) HE IS THE UPHOLDER OF ALL THINGS:

Col. 1:17; Heb. 1:3. The universe is neither self-sustaining nor is it forsaken by God (Deism). Christ's power causes all things to hold together. The pulses of universal life are regulated and controlled by the throbbings of the mighty heart of Christ.

c) HE HAS THE RIGHT TO FORGIVE SINS:

Mark 2:5-10. Luke 7:48—"And he said unto her, Thy sins are forgiven." Certain it is that the Pharisees recognized that Christ was here assuming a divine prerogative. No mere man had any right to forgive sins. God alone could do that. Hence the Pharisees' charge of blasphemy. This is no declaration of forgiveness, based upon the knowledge of the man's penitence. Christ does not merely *declare* sins forgiven. He *actually* forgives them. Further, Jesus, in the parable of the two debtors (Luke 7), declares that sins were committed against Himself (cf. Psa. 51:4—"Against thee, thee only, have I sinned").

d) THE RAISING OF THE BODIES OF MEN IS ASCRIBED TO HIM:

John 6:39, 40, 54; 11:25. Five times it is here declared by Jesus that it is His prerogative to raise the dead. It is true that others raised the dead, but under what different conditions? They worked by a delegated power (Acts 9:34); but Christ, by His own power (John 10:17, 18). Note the agony of Elisha and others, as compared with the calmness of Christ. None of these claimed to raise the dead by his own power, nor to have any such power in the general resurrection of all men. Christ did make such claims.

e) HE IS TO BE THE JUDGE OF ALL MEN:

John 5:22—"For the Father judgeth no man, but hath committed all judgment unto the Son." 2 Tim. 4:1; Acts 17:31; Matt. 25:31-46. The Man of the Cross is to be the Man of the throne. The issues of the judgment are all in His hand.

5. Divine Attributes Are Possessed By Him.

a) OMNIPOTENCE

Matt. 28:18—"All power is given unto me in heaven and in earth." Rev. 1:8; John 17:2; Eph. 1:20-22. Here is power over three realms: First, all power on earth: over disease (Luke 4:38-41); death (John 11); nature, water into wine (John 2); tempest (Matt. 8). Second, all power in hell: over demons (Luke 4:35, 36, 41); evil angels (Eph. 6). Third, all power in heaven (Eph. 1:20-22). Finally, power over all things (Heb. 2:8; 1:3; Matt. 28:18).

b) OMNISCIENCE

John 16:30—"Now are we sure that thou knowest all things." 2:24, 25; Matt. 24; 25; Col. 2:3. Illustrations: John 4:16-19; Mark 2:8; John 1:48. "Our Lord always leaves the impression that He knew all things in detail, both past and future, and that this knowledge comes from His original perception of the events.

He does not learn them by acquisition. He simply knows them by immediate perception. Such utterances as Matt. 24 and Luke 21 carry in them a subtle difference from the utterances of the prophets. The latter spoke as men who were quite remote in point of time from their declaration of unfolding events. Jesus spoke as one who is present in the midst of the events which He depicts. He does not refer to events in the past as if He were quoting from the historic narrative in the Old Testament. The only instance which casts doubt upon this view is Mark 13:32. The parallel passage in Matthew omits, in many ancient versions, the words: 'Neither the Son.' The saying in Mark is capable of an interpretation which does not contradict this view of His omniscience. This is an omniscience nevertheless, which in its manifestation to men is under something of human limitation."—*Wood.*

This limitation of knowledge is no argument against the infallibility of those things which Jesus did teach: for example, the Mosaic authorship of the Pentateuch. That argument, says Liddon, involves a confusion between limitation of knowledge and liability to error; whereas, plainly enough, a limitation of knowledge is one thing, and fallibility is another. St. Paul says, "We know in part," and "We see through a glass darkly." Yet Paul is so certain of the truth of that which he teaches, as to exclaim, "But though we, or an angel from heaven, preach any other gospel unto you than that which we have preached unto you, let him be accursed." Paul clearly believed in his own infallibility as a teacher of religious truth, and the Church of Christ has ever since regarded his epistles as part of an infallible literature. But it is equally clear that Paul believed his knowledge of truth to be limited. Infallibility does not imply omniscience, any more than limited knowledge implies error. If a human teacher were to decline to speak upon a given subject, by saying that he did not know enough about it, this would not be a reason for disbelieving him when he proceeded to speak confidently upon a totally different subject, thereby at least implying that he did not know enough to warrant his speaking. On the contrary, his silence in the one case would be a reason for trusting his statements in the other. The argument which is under consideration in the text would have been really sound, if our Saviour had fixed the date of the day of judgment and the event had shown Him to be mistaken.

Why stumble over the limitation of this attribute and not over the others? Did He not hunger and thirst, for example? As God He is omnipresent, yet as man He is present only in one place. As God He is omnipotent; yet, on one occasion at least, He could do no mighty works because of the unbelief of men.

c) OMNIPRESENCE

Matt. 18:20—"For where two or three are gathered together in my name, there am I in the midst of them." He is with every missionary (Matt. 28:20). He is prayed to by Christians in every place (1 Cor. 1:2). Prayer would be a mockery if we were not assured that Christ is everywhere present to hear. He fills all things, every place (Eph. 1:23). But such an all pervading presence is true only of Deity.

6. His Name Is Coupled With That of God the Father

The manner in which the name of Jesus Christ is coupled with that of God the Father clearly implies equality of the Son with the Father. Compare the following:

a) THE APOSTOLIC BENEDICTION

2 Cor. 13:14. Here the Son equally with the Father is the bestower of grace.

b) THE BAPTISMAL FORMULA

Matt. 28:19; Acts 2:38. "In the name," not the names (plural). How would it sound to say, "In the name of the Father" *and of Moses?* Would it not seem sacrilegious? Can we imagine the effect of such words on the apostles?

c) OTHER PASSAGES

John 14:23—"We will come": the Father and I. 17:3—"And this is life eternal, that they might know thee the only true God, *and Jesus Christ.*" The content of saving faith includes belief in Jesus Christ equally with the Father. 10:30—"I and my Father are one." "One" is neuter, not masculine, meaning that Jesus and the Father constitute one power by which the salvation of man is secured. 2 Thess. 2:16, 17—"Now our Lord Jesus Christ himself, and God, even our Father . . . comfort your hearts." These two names, with a verb in the singular, intimate the oneness of the Father with the Son.

7. *The Self-Consciousness of Jesus Regarding His Own Person and Work*

It will be interesting to search the Gospel records to ascertain what was in the mind of Jesus concerning Himself—His relation to the Father in particular. What bearing has the testimony of Jesus upon the question of His Deity? Is the present Christian consciousness borne out by the Gospel narratives? Is Jesus Christ a man of a much higher type of faith than ours, yet one with whom we believe in God? Or is He, equally with God, the object of our faith? Do we believe *with* Him, or *on* Him? Is there any indication in the words ascribed to Jesus, as recorded in the Gospels, of a consciousness on His part of His unique relation to God the Father? Is it Jesus Himself who is responsible for the Christian's consciousness concerning His deity, or is the Church reading into the Gospel accounts something that is not really there? Let us see.

a) AS SET FORTH IN THE NARRATIVE OF HIS VISIT TO THE TEMPLE

Luke 2:41-52. This is a single flower out of the wonderfully enclosed garden of the first thirty years of our Lord's life. The emphatic words, for our purpose, are "thy father," and "my Father." These are the first recorded words of Jesus. Is there not here an indication of the consciousness on the part of Jesus of a unique relationship with His heavenly Father? Mary, not Joseph, asked the question, so contrary to Jewish custom. She said: "Thy father"; Jesus replied in substance: "Did you say *my* Father has been seeking me?" It is remarkable to note that Christ omits the word "father" when referring to His parents, cf. Matt. 12:48; Mark 3:33, 34. *"My* Father!" No other human lips had ever uttered these words. Men said, and He taught them to say, *"Our* Father." It is not too much to say that in this incident Christ sees, rising before Him, the great truth that God, and not Joseph, is His Father, and that it is in His true Father's house that He now stands.

b) AS REVEALED AT HIS BAPTISM

Matt. 3:13-17; Mark 1:9-11; Luke 3:21. Here are some things to remember in connection with Christ's baptism: First, Jesus was well acquainted with the relation of John and his ministry to the Old Testament prophecy, as well as of John's own announcement that he was the Messiah's forerunner, and that he

(John) was not worthy to untie the latchet of Christ's shoes. Second, to come then to John, and to submit to baptism at his hands, would indicate that Jesus conceded the truth of all that John had said. This is emphasized when we remember Jesus' eulogy of John (Matt. 11). Thirdly, there is the descent of the Spirit, and the voice; what meaning did these things have to Jesus? If Christ's sermon in the synagogue at Nazareth is of any help here, we must believe that at His baptism, so much more than at the age of twelve, He was conscious that in thus being anointed He was associating Himself in some peculiar way with the prophecy of Isaiah, chapters 42 and 61: "Behold my Servant . . . I have put my Spirit upon Him." All, therefore, that must have been wrapped up in the thought of the "Servant of the Lord" in the Old Testament would assuredly be quickened in His consciousness that day when the Spirit descended upon Him. See also Luke 4:16-17; Acts 10:38; Matt. 12:28.

But what did the heavenly voice signify to Christ? "This is my beloved Son" takes us back to the second Psalm where this person is addressed as the ideal King of Israel. The last clause—"in whom I am well pleased"—refers to Isaiah 42, and portrays the servant who is anointed and empowered by the endowment of God's Spirit. We must admit that the mind of Jesus was steeped in the prophecies of the Old Testament, and that He knew to whom these passages referred. The ordinary Jew knew that much. Is it too much to say that on that baptismal day Jesus was keenly conscious that these Old Testament predictions were fulfilled in Him? We think not.

c) AS SET FORTH IN THE RECORD OF THE TEMPTATION

Matt. 4:1-11; Mark 1:12, 13; Luke 4:1-13. That Jesus entered into the temptation in the wilderness with the consciousness of the revelation He received, and of which He was conscious at the baptism, seems clear from the narratives. Certain it is that Satan based his temptations upon Christ's consciousness of His unique relation to God as His Son. Throughout the whole of the temptation Satan regards Christ as being in a unique sense the Son of God, the ideal King, through whom the kingdom of God is to be established upon the earth. Indeed, so clearly is the kingship of Jesus recognized in the temptation narrative that the whole question agitated there is as to how that kingdom may be established in the world. It must be admitted that a careful reading of the narratives forces us to the conclusion that throughout all the temptation Christ was conscious of His position with reference to the founding of God's kingdom in the world.

d) AS SET FORTH IN THE CALLING OF THE TWELVE AND THE SEVENTY

The record of this event is found in Matt. 10; Mark 3:13-19; 6:7-13; Luke 9:1-6; 10:1-14. This important event in the life of our Lord had an important bearing upon His self-consciousness as to His person and work. Let us note some of the details:

First, as to the number, twelve. Is there no suggestion here with reference to the New Jerusalem when the Messiah shall sit upon the throne surrounded by the twelve apostles seated on their thrones? Is not Jesus here conscious of Himself as being the centre of the scene thus described in the Apocalypse?

Second, He gave them power. Is not Jesus here repeating what had been done for Him at His baptism: conveying super-human power? Who can give this power that is strong enough to make even demons obey? No one less than God surely.

Third, note that the message which He committed to the twelve concerned matters of life and death. Not to receive that message would be equivalent to the rejection of the Father.

Fourth, all this is to be done in *His* name, and for *His* name's sake. Fidelity to Jesus is that on which the final destiny of men depends. Everything rises or falls in its relation to Him. Could such words be uttered and there be no consciousness on the part of the speaker of a unique relationship to the Father and the things of eternity? Know you of anything bolder than this?

Fifth, He calls upon men to sacrifice their tenderest affections for Him. He is to be chosen before even father and mother (Matt. 10:34-39).

e) AS REVEALED IN THE SERMON ON THE MOUNT

Matt. 5-7; Luke 6:20-49. Two references will be sufficient here. Who is this that dares to set Himself up as superior to Moses and the law of Moses, by saying, "But *I* say unto you"? Then, again, listen to Christ as He proclaims Himself to be the Judge of all men at the last day (Matt. 7:21). Could Jesus say all this without having any consciousness of His unique relationship to all these things? Assuredly not.

B. THE WORK OF JESUS CHRIST

I. THE DEATH OF JESUS CHRIST

1. *Its Importance*

a) IT HAS A SUPREME PLACE IN THE CHRISTIAN RELIGION

Christianity is a religion of atonement distinctively. The elimination of the doctrine of the death of Christ from the religion that bears His name would mean the surrender of its uniqueness and claim to be the only true religion, the supreme and final revelation from God to the sons of men. It is its redemption feature that distinguishes Christianity from any and all other religions. If you surrender this distinctive Christian doctrine from its creed, then this supreme religion is brought down to the level of many other prevailing religious systems. Christianity is not merely a system of ethics; it is the history of redemption through Jesus Christ, the personal Redeemer.

b) ITS VITAL RELATION TO JESUS CHRIST

The atonement is so closely related to Jesus Christ, so allied to His work, as set forth in the Scriptures, that it is absolutely inseparable from it. Christ was not primarily a religious teacher, a philanthropist, an ethical example; He was all these, yea, and much more—He was first and foremost the world's Saviour and Redeemer. Other great men have been valued for their lives; He, above all, for His death, around which God and man are reconciled. The Cross is the magnet which sends the electric current through the telegraph between earth and heaven, and makes both Testaments thrill, through the ages of the past and future, with living, harmonious, and saving truth. Other men have said: "If I could only live, I would establish and perpetuate an empire." The Christ of Galilee said: "My death shall do it." Let us understand that the power of Christianity lies not in hazy indefiniteness, not in shadowy forms, not so much even in definite truths and doctrines, but in *the* truth, and in *the* doctrine of Christ crucified and risen from the dead. Unless Christianity be more than ethical, it is not, nor can it really be ethical at all. It is redemptive, dynamic through that redemption, and ethical withal.

c) ITS RELATION TO THE INCARNATION

It is not putting the matter too strongly when we say that the incarnation was for the purpose of the atonement. At least this seems to be the testimony of the Scriptures. Jesus Christ partook of flesh and blood in order that He might die (Heb. 2:14). "He was manifested to take away our sins" (1 John 3:5). Christ came into this world to give His life a ransom for many (Matt. 20:28). The very purpose of the entire coming of Christ into the world, in all its varying aspects, was that, by assuming a nature like unto our own, He might offer up His life as a sacrifice for the sins of men. The faith of the atonement presupposes the faith of the incarnation. So close have been the relation of these two fundamental doctrines that their relation is one of the great questions which have divided men in their opinions in the matter: which is primary and which secondary; which is to be regarded as the most necessary to man's salvation, as the primary and the highest fact in the history of God's dealings with man. The atonement naturally arises out of the incarnation so that the Son of God could not appear in our nature without undertaking such a work as the word atonement denotes. The incarnation is a pledge and anticipation of the work of atonement. The incarnation is most certainly the declaration of a purpose on the part of God to save the world. But how was the world to be saved if not through the atonement?

d) ITS PROMINENCE IN THE SCRIPTURES

It was the claim of Jesus, in His conversation with the two disciples on the way to Emmaus, that Moses, and all the prophets, indeed, all the Scriptures, dealt with the subject of His death (Luke 24:27, 44). That the death of Christ was the one great subject into which the Old Testament prophets searched deeply is clear from 1 Pet. 1:11, 12. The atonement is the scarlet cord running through every page in the entire Bible. Cut the Bible anywhere, and it bleeds; it is red with redemption truth. It is said that one out of every forty-four verses in the New Testament deals with this theme, and that the death of Christ is mentioned in all one hundred and seventy-five times. When you add to these figures the typical and symbolical teaching of the Old Testament, some idea is gained as to the important place which this doctrine occupies in the sacred Scriptures.

e) THE FUNDAMENTAL THEME OF THE GOSPEL

Paul says: "I delivered unto you first of all [i. e., first in order; the first plank in the Gospel platform; the truth of primary importance] . . . that Christ died for our sins" (1 Cor. 15:1-3). There can be no Gospel story, message or preaching without the story of the death of Christ as the Redeemer of men.

f. THE ONE GRAND THEME IN HEAVEN

Moses and Elias, the heavenly visitors to this earth, conversed about it (Luke 9:30, 31), even though Peter was ashamed of the same truth (Matt. 16:21-25). The theme of the song of the redeemed in heaven is that of Christ's death (Rev. 5:8-12).

2. The Scriptural Definition of Christ's Death

The Scriptures set forth the death of Jesus Christ in a fourfold way:

a) AS A RANSOM

Matt. 20:28; 1 Pet. 1:18; 1 Tim. 2:6; Gal. 3:13.

The meaning of a ransom is clearly set forth in Lev. 25:47-49: To deliver a thing or person by paying a price; to buy back a person or thing by paying the price for which it is held in captivity. So sin is like a slave market in which sinners are "sold under sin" (Rom. 7:14); souls are under sentence of death (Ezek. 18:4). Christ, by His death, buys sinners out of the market, thereby indicating complete deliverance from the service of sin. He looses the bonds, sets the prisoners free, by paying a price—that price being His own precious blood.

To whom this ransom is paid is a debatable question: whether to Satan for his captives, or to eternal and necessary holiness, to the divine law, to the claims of God who is by His nature the holy Lawgiver. The latter, referring to God and His holiness, is probably preferable.

Christ redeemed us from the curse of a broken law by Himself being made a curse for us. His death was the ransom price paid for our deliverance.

b) A PROPITIATION

Rom. 3:25; 1 John 2:2; Heb. 2:17 (R. V.).

Christ is the propitiation for our sins; He is set forth by God to be a propitiation through His blood.

Propitiation means mercy-seat, or covering. The mercy-seat covering the ark of the covenant was called a propitiation (Exod. 25:22; Heb. 9:5). It is that by which God covers, overlooks, and pardons the penitent and believing sinner because of Christ's death. Propitiation furnishes a ground on the basis of which God could set forth His righteousness, and yet pardon sinful men, Rom. 3:25, 26; Heb. 9:15. Christ Himself is the propitiatory sacrifice, 1 John 2:2. The death of Jesus Christ is set forth as the ground on which a righteous God can pardon a guilty and sinful race without in any way compromising His righteousness.

c) AS A RECONCILIATION

Rom. 5:10; 2 Cor. 5:18, 19; Eph. 2:16; Col. 1:20.

We are reconciled to God by the death of His Son, by His Cross, and by the blood of His Cross—that is the message of these scriptures.

Reconciliation has two sides; active and passive. In the *active* sense we may look upon Christ's death as removing the enmity existing between God and man, and which had hitherto been a barrier to fellowship (see the above quoted texts). This state of existing enmity is set forth in such scriptures as Rom. 8:7—"Because the carnal mind is enmity against God." Also Eph. 2:15; Jas. 4:4. In the *passive* sense of the word it may indicate the change of attitude on the part of man toward God, this change being wrought in the heart of man by a vision of the Cross of Christ; a change from enmity to friendship thus taking place, cf. 2 Cor. 5:20. It is probably better to state the case thus: God is propitiated, and the sinner is reconciled (2 Cor. 5:18-20).

d) AS A SUBSTITUTION

Isa. 53:6; 1 Pet. 2:24; 3:18; 2 Cor. 5:21.

The story of the passover lamb (Exod. 12), with 1 Cor. 5:7, illustrates the meaning of substitution as here used: one life given in the stead of another. "The Lord hath laid on him the iniquity of us all." God made Christ, who knew no sin, to be sin for us. Christ

Himself bore our sins in His own body on the tree—this is substitution. Christ died in our place, bore our sins, paid the penalty due our sins; and all this, not by force, but willingly (John 10:17, 18). The idea of substitution is well illustrated by the nature of the preposition used in connection with this phase of Christ's death: In Matt. 20:28 Christ is said to give His life a ransom *for* all (also 1 Tim. 2:6). That this preposition means *instead of* is clear from its use in Matt. 2:22—"Archelaus did reign in the room [or in the stead] of his father Herod." Also in Luke 11:11 —"Will he *for* a fish give him a serpent?" (See Heb. 12:2, 16.) Substitution, then, as used here means this: That something happened to Christ, and because it happened to Christ, it need not happen to us. Christ died for our sins; we need not die for them if we accept His sacrifice. For further illustrations, see Gen. 22:13; God providing a ram instead of Isaac; also Barabbas freed and Christ bearing his cross and taking his place.

> Upon a life I did not live;
>   Upon a death I did not die;
> Upon another's death, another's life,
>   I risk my soul eternally.

3. Unscriptural Views of Christ's Death

There are certain so-called *modern* views of the atonement which it may be well to examine briefly, if only to show how unscriptural they are. That the modern mind fails to see in the doctrine of the atonement what the orthodox faith has held for centuries to be the truth of God regarding this fundamental Christian doctrine, there is certainly no doubt. To some minds today the death of Jesus Christ was but the death of a martyr, counted in the same category as the death of John Huss or Savonarola. Or perchance Christ's death was an exhibition to a sinful world of God's wondrous love. Or it may be that Christ, in His suffering of death, remains forever the sublime example of adherence to principles of righteousness and truth, even to the point of death. Or, again, Calvary may be an episode in God's government of the world. God, being holy, deemed it necessary to show to the world His hatred of sin, and so His wrath fell on Christ. The modern mind does not consider Christ's death as in any sense vicarious, or substitutionary. Indeed, it fails to see the justice as well as the need or possibility of one man, and He so innocent, suffering for the sins of the whole race—past, present and future. Every man must bear the penalty of his own sin, so we are told; from that there is no escape, unless, and it is fervently hoped and confidently expected, that God, whose wondrous love surpasses all human conception, should, as He doubtless will, overlook the eternal consequences of man's sin because of the great love wherewith He loves the race. The love of God is the hope of the race's redemption.

What shall the Christian Church say to these things, and what shall be her reply? To the Word of God must the Church resort for her weapons in this warfare. If the so-called modern mind and its doctrinal views agree with the Scriptures, then the Christian Church may allow herself to be influenced by the spirit of the age. But if the modern mind and the Scriptures do not agree in their results, then the Church of Christ must part company with the modern mind. Here are some of the modern theories of the atonement:

a) THE ACCIDENT THEORY

Briefly stated, this is the theory: The Cross was something unforeseen in the life of Christ. Calvary was not in the plan of God for His Son. Christ's death was an accident, as unforeseen and unexpected as the death of any other martyr was unforeseen and unexpected.

To this we reply: Jesus was conscious all the time of His forthcoming death. He foretold it again and again. He was always conscious of the plots against His life. This truth is corroborated by the following scriptures: Matt. 16:21; Mark 9:30-32; Matt. 20:17-19; Luke 18:31-34; Matt. 20:28; 26:2, 6, 24, 39-42; Luke 22:19, 20. Further, in John 10:17, 18 we have words which distinctly contradict this false theory: "Therefore doth my Father love me, because I lay down my life, that I might take it again. No man taketh it from me, but I lay it down of myself. I have power to lay it down, and I have power to take it again. This commandment have I received of my Father."

In addition to this we may make mention of the many, many references and prophecies of the Old Testament to the fact of Christ's death. Then there is Christ's own testimony to the fact of His death being predicted and foretold by the prophets (Luke 24:26, 27, 44). See also Isa. 53; Psa. 22; 69.

b) THE MARTYR THEORY

It is as follows: Christ's death was similar in kind to that of

John Huss, or Polycarp, or any other noble man who has given up his life as a sacrifice for a principle and for truth.

To this we reply: Then Christ should have so declared Himself. Paul should have said so. That word was used for other Christian deaths, why not for Christ's? Then there is no mystery about the atonement, and the wonder is that Paul should have said anything about the mystery. Further, if Christ died as a martyr He might, at least, have had the same comforting presence of God afforded other martyrs in the hour of their death. Why should He be God-forsaken in that crucial hour? Is it right that God should make the holiest man in all the ages the greatest sufferer, if that man were but a martyr? When you recall the shrinking of Gethsemane, could you really—and we say it reverently—call Jesus as brave a man facing death as many another martyr has been? Why should Christ's soul be filled with anguish (Luke 22:39-46), while Paul the Apostle was exultant with joy (Phil. 1:23)? Stephen died a martyr's death, but Paul never preached forgiveness through the death of Stephen. Such a view of Christ's death may beget martyrs, but it can never save sinners.

c) THE MORAL EXAMPLE THEORY

Christ's death has an influence upon mankind for moral improvement. The example of His suffering ought to soften human hearts, and help a man to reform, repent, and better his condition. So God grants pardon and forgiveness on simple repentance and reformation. In the same way a drunkard might call a man his saviour by whose influence he was induced to become sober and industrious. But did the sight of His suffering move the Jews to repentance? Does it move men today? Such a view of Christ's death does not deal with the question with which it is always connected, viz., the question of sin.

d) THE GOVERNMENTAL THEORY

This means that the benevolence of God requires that He should make an example of suffering in Christ in order to exhibit to man that sin is displeasing in His sight. God's government of the world necessitates that He show His wrath against sin.

True, but we reply: Why do we need an incarnation for the manifestation of that purpose? Why not make a guilty, and not an absolutely innocent and guileless man such an example of God's displeasure upon sin? Were there not men enough in existence? Why create a new being for such a purpose?

e) THE LOVE OF GOD THEORY

He died to show men how much God loved them. Men ever after would know the feeling of the heart of God toward them.

True, the death of Christ did show the great love of God for fallen man. But men did not need such a sacrifice to know that God loved them. They knew that before Christ came. The Old Testament is full of the love of God. Read Psalm 103. The Scriptures which speak of God's love as being manifested in the gift of His Son, tell us also of another reason why He gave His Son: "That whosoever believeth in him should not perish, but have everlasting life"(John 3:16); "Herein is love, not that we loved God, but that he loved us, and sent his Son to be the propitiation for our sins" (1 John 4:10).

We believe that Christ's Cross reveals the love of God, and that throughout all these ages men have been bowed in penitence as they have caught a vision of the One who hung thereon. But if you were to question the multitudes that have believed in God because of the Cross, you would find that what moved them to repentance was not merely, if at all, certainly not primarily, that the Cross revealed the love of God in a supreme way, but the fact that there at that Cross God had dealt with the great and awful fact of sin, that the Cross had forever removed it.

"I examine all these views, beautiful as some of them are, appealing to the pride of man, but which leave out all thought of vicarious atonement, and say, 'But what shall be done with my sin? Who shall put it away? Where is its sacrifice? If without shedding of blood there is no remission of sin, where is the shed blood?' These views are neat, measurable, occasionally pathetic, and frequently beautiful, but they do not include the agony of the whole occasion and situation. They are aspect theories, partial conceptions. They do not take in the whole temple from its foundation to its roof. No man must set up his judgment against that of another man in a dogmatic way, but he may, yea, he must, allow his heart to speak through his judgment; and in view of this liberty, I venture to say that all these theories of the atonement are as nothing, most certainly shallow and incomplete to me . . . As I speak now, at this very moment, I feel that the Christ on the Cross is doing something for me, that His death is my life, His atonement my pardon, His crucifixion the satisfaction for my sin, that from Calvary, that place of a skull, my flowers of peace and joy blossom forth, and that in the Cross of Christ I glory."—*Joseph Parker.*

4. The Necessity of Christ's Death

The necessity of the atonement lay in a two-fold fact: The holiness of God, and the sinfulness of man. The doctrine of the atonement is a related subject, and it cannot be properly understood unless it is viewed as such. It is related to certain conditions existing between God and man—a condition and relation which has been affected by sin. It is necessary, therefore, to know this relation and how it has been affected by sin. This relation between God and man is a personal one. No other construction can legitimately be put upon the passages setting forth this relationship. *"Thou* hast searched *me,* and known *me."* *"I* am continually with *Thee."* It is, moreover, an ethical relationship, and that which is ethical is at the same time personal and universal, that is to say, that God's dealings with mankind are expressed in a moral constitution of universal and eternal validity. These relationships are disordered by sin. No matter how sin came to be here we are morally conscious, by the testimony of a bad conscience, that we are guilty, and that our sin is not merely a matter of personal guilt but a violation of a universal moral law.

a) THE HOLINESS OF GOD

We should carefully note the emphasis laid upon the doctrine of God's holiness in the Old Testament (see under Attributes of God, p. 37). The Levitical law, the laws of clean and unclean, the Tabernacle and the Temple with its outer court, its holy and most holy place, the priestly order and the high priest, the bounds set around Mt. Sinai, things and persons that might not be touched without causing defilement, sacred times and seasons, these, and much more, speak in unmistakable terms of the holiness of God. We are thus taught that if sinful man is to approach unto God, it must be through the blood of atonement. The holiness of God demands that before the sinner can approach unto and have communion with Him, some means of propitiation must be provided. This means of approach is set forth in the shed blood.

b) THE SIN OF MAN

Light and erroneous views of the atonement come from light and erroneous views of sin. If sin is regarded as merely an offence against man, a weakness of human nature, a mere disease, rather than as rebellion, transgression, and enmity against God, and therefore something condemning and punishable, we shall not, of course, see any necessity for the atonement. We must see sin as the Bible depicts it, as something which brings wrath, condemnation, and eternal ruin in its train. We must see it as guilt that needs expiation. We must see sin as God sees it before we can denounce it as God denounces it. We confess sin today in such light and easy terms that it has almost lost its terror.

In view of these two thoughts, the holiness of God and the sinfulness of man, the question naturally arises: How is the mercy of God to be manifested so that His holiness will not be compromised by His assuming a merciful attitude towards sinful men in the granting of forgiveness, pardon, justification? The answer is: The only way in which this can be done is by means of the atonement.

c) THE FULFILLMENT OF THE SCRIPTURES

We may add this third thought to the two already mentioned. There is a sense in which the atonement was necessary in order to the fulfillment of the predictions of the Old Testament—predictions inseparable from the person and work of the Messiah. If Jesus Christ were the true Messiah, then these predictions regarding His sufferings and death must be fulfilled in Him (Luke 24:25-27, 44; Isa. 53; Psa. 22; 69).

5. The Extent of Christ's Death

Was the death of Jesus Christ for all mankind—for every human being in the world, or for man actually and ultimately regenerate only—the chosen Church? Was it for all mankind, irrespective of their relation to Jesus Christ, or must we limit the actual benefits of the atonement to those who are spiritually united to Christ by faith? That the death of Christ is intended to benefit all mankind seems clear from the following scriptures: Isa. 53:6; 1 Tim. 2:6; 1 John 2:2, cf. 2 Cor. 5:19; Rom. 14:15; 1 Cor. 8:11. The scriptures which to some seem to limit the effects of the atonement are John 10:15, cf. vv. 26, 29; Eph. 5:25-27.

Certain it is that the doctrine of the atonement is presented in the Scriptures as competent to procure and secure salvation for all. Indeed, not only competent but efficacious to do this very thing. It might seem that there is an apparent contradiction in the above-named scriptures. The atonement, in its actual issue, should realize and actualize the eternal purpose of God, the which is set forth as a desire that all men should be saved and come to a saving knowledge of the truth as it is in Jesus Christ. This is testified to be the general and universal invitation of the Scriptures to partake of the blessings of Christ's death. Thus the offer of the Gospel to all is not a pretence but a reality on the part of God. The divine willingness that all men should share the benefits of the atonement is all-inclusive, and really means what is offered. Yet on the other hand, we can not overlook the fact that, from another point of view the effects of the atonement—shall we say the *purpose* of the atonement?—seems to be limited to the sphere of the true Church, so that only those who are really united to Christ by faith actually share in the merits of the atonement. Let us put it this way: "The atonement is *sufficient* for all; it is *efficient* for those who believe in Christ. The atonement itself, so far as it lays the basis for the redemptive dealing of God with all men, is *unlimited*; the *application* of the atonement is limited to those who actually believe in Christ. He is the Saviour of all men *potentially* (1 Tim. 1:15); of believers alone *effectually* (1 Tim. 4:10). The atonement is limited only by men's unbelief.

a) FOR THE WHOLE WORLD

The Scriptures set forth this fact in the following statements: "And he is the propitiation for our sins: and not for ours only, but also for the sins of the whole world" (1 John 2:2). Christ's death was the ground on which God, who is absolutely holy, could deal with the whole race of men in mercy, and pardon their sins.

John 1:29—"Behold the Lamb of God, which taketh away the sin of the world." Not the sin of a few individuals, or of an elect race, like Israel, but the sin of the whole world. This was a striking truth to reveal to a Jew.

1 Tim. 2:6—"Who gave himself a ransom for all, to be testified in due time." It is for this reason, as the context of this passage shows, that we may pray for all men. If all men were not capable of being saved, how then could we pray to that end?

b) FOR EACH INDIVIDUAL MAN

This is but a detailed statement of the fact that He died for the whole world. Not a single individual man, woman, or child is excluded from the blessings offered in the atonement.

Heb. 2:9—"But we see Jesus, who was made a little lower than the angels for the suffering of death, crowned with glory and honor; that he by the grace of God should taste death for every man." Leo the Great (461) affirmed that "So precious is the shedding of Christ's blood for the unjust, that if the whole universe of captives would believe in the Redeemer, no chain of the devil could hold them." General Booth once said: "Friends, Jesus shed His precious blood to pay the price of salvation, and bought from God enough salvation to go around."

c) FOR THE SINFUL, UNJUST, AND UNGODLY

Sinners of all sorts, degrees, and conditions may have a share in the redemptive work of Christ. Greece invited only the cultured, Rome sought only the strong. Judea bid for the religious only. Jesus Christ bids all those that are weary and heavy-hearted and over-burdened to come to Him (Matt. 11:28).

Rom. 5:6-10—"Christ died for the ungodly. . . . While we were yet sinners, Christ died for us. . . . When we were enemies, we were reconciled to God by the death of his Son." 1 Pet. 3:18— "For Christ also hath once suffered for sins, the just for the unjust." Christ died for *sinners*—those in open opposition to God; for the *unjust*—those who openly violate God's laws; for the *ungodly*— those who violently and brazenly refuse to pay their dues of prayer, worship, and service to God; for *enemies*—those who are constantly fighting God and His cause. For all of these Christ died.

1 Tim. 1:15—"Christ Jesus came into the world to save sinners; of whom I am chief." Paul was a *blasphemer,* a *persecutor, injurious* (v. 13), a *murderer* (Acts 22 and 26), yet God saved him; he was included in the atonement. Note also that it is in this very connection that the apostle declares that the reason God saved him was in order that his salvation might be a pattern, or an encouragement to other great sinners, that God could and would save them, if they desired Him to do so.

d) FOR THE CHURCH

There is a peculiar sense in which it may be said that Christ's death is for the Church, His body, the company of those who believe in Him. There is a sense in which it is perfectly true that Christ's death avails only for those who believe in Him; so in that sense it can be said that He died for the Church more particularly. He is "the Saviour of all men, specially of those that believe" (1 Tim. 4:10). Herein lies the truth that is contained in the theory of a limited atonement.

Eph. 5:25-27—"Christ also loved the church, and gave himself for it." Not for any one particular denomination; not for any one organization within any four walls; but for all those whom He calls to Himself and who follow Him here.

Gal. 2:20—"The Son of God, who loved me, and gave himself for me." Here the individual member of the Church, the body of Christ, is specifically mentioned as being included in the efficacy of the atonement. When Luther first realized this particular phase of the atonement, he was found sobbing beneath a crucifix, and moaning: "Mein Gott, Mein Gott, Für Mich! Für Mich!"

1 Cor. 8:11—"And through thy knowledge shall the weak brother perish, for whom Christ died?" Also Rom. 14:15. Note the connection in which this truth is taught. If Christ was willing to die for the weak brother—whom we, perchance, sneer at for his conscientious scruples—we ought to be willing to deny ourselves of some habit for his sake.

How all-inclusive, all-comprehensive, far-reaching is the death of Christ in its effects! Not a few, but many shall be saved. He gave his life a ransom for *many*. God's purposes in the atonement shall not be frustrated. Christ shall see of the travail of His soul, and shall be satisfied. Many shall come from the north, the south, and east and the west and sit down in the kingdom. In that great day it will be seen (Rev. 7:9-15).

6. The Effects of Christ's Death

a) IN RELATION TO THE PHYSICAL OR MATERIAL UNIVERSE

Just as the material universe was in some mysterious manner affected by the fall of man (Rom. 8:19-23, R. V.), so also is it affected by the death of Jesus Christ, which is intended to neutralize the effect of sin upon the creation. There is a cosmical effect in the atonement. The Christ of Paul is larger than the second Adam—the Head of a new humanity; He is also the center of a universe which revolves around Him, and is in some mysterious way reconciled by His death. Just how this takes place we may not be able definitely to explain.

Col. 1:20—"And, having made peace through the blood of his cross, by him to reconcile all things unto himself; by him, I say, whether they be things in earth, or things in heaven." Some day there shall be a new heaven and a new earth, wherein dwelleth righteousness (2 Pet. 3:13). See also Heb. 9:23, 24; Isa. 11 and 35.

b) IN RELATION TO THE WORLD OF MEN

(1) THE ENMITY EXISTING BETWEEN GOD AND MAN IS REMOVED.

Rom. 5:10; Col. 1:20-22. For explanation, see under Scriptural Definition of Christ's Death (p. 72). The ground of enmity between God and man—whether in the active or passive sense of *reconciliation*—is removed by Christ's death. The world of mankind is, through the atonement, reconciled to God.

(2) A PROPITIATION FOR THE WORLD'S SIN HAS BEEN PROVIDED.

1 John 2:2; 4:10. See under A Propitiation (p. 72). The propitiation reaches as far as does the sin.

(3) SATAN'S POWER OVER THE RACE HAS BEEN NEUTRALIZED.

John 12:31, 32—"Now is the judgment of this world: now shall the prince of this world be cast out. And I, if I be lifted up from the earth, will draw all men unto me." Also John 16:9, 10; Col. 2:10. The lifting up of Christ on the Cross meant the casting down of Satan. Satan no longer holds undisputed sway over the sons of men. The power of darkness has been broken. Man need no longer be the slave of sin and Satan.

(4) THE QUESTION OF THE WORLD'S SIN IS SETTLED.

It need no longer stand as a barrier between God and man. Strictly speaking, it is not now so much of a *sin* question as it is a *Son* question; not, What shall be done with my sin? but, What shall I do with Jesus, which is called Christ? The sins of the Old

Testament saints, which during all the centuries had been held, as it were, in abeyance, were put away at the Cross (Rom. 3:25, 26). Sins present and future were also dealt with at the Cross. By the sacrifice of Himself, Christ forever put away sin (Heb. 9:26).

(5) THE CLAIMS OF A BROKEN LAW HAVE BEEN MET, AND THE CURSE RESTING UPON MAN BECAUSE OF A BROKEN LAW REMOVED.

Col. 2:14—"Blotting out the handwriting of ordinances that was against us, which was contrary to us, and took it out of the way, nailing it to his cross." Thus every claim of the holy law of God, which sinful man had violated, had been met.

Gal. 3:13—"Christ hath redeemed us from the curse of the law, being made a curse for us: for it is written, Cursed is every one that hangeth on a tree." (See v. 10 for the description of the curse.) The wages of sin, and the curse of sin, is death. Christ by His death on the Cross paid that debt and removed that curse.

(6) JUSTIFICATION, ADOPTION, SANCTIFICATION, ACCESS TO GOD, AN INHERITANCE, AND THE REMOVAL OF ALL FEAR OF DEATH—ALL THIS IS INCLUDED IN THE EFFECT OF THE DEATH OF CHRIST IN THE BEHALF OF THE BELIEVER.

Rom. 5:9; Gal. 4:3-5; Heb. 10:10; 10:19, 20; 9:15; 2:14, 15. How comforting, how strengthening, how inspiring are these wonderful aspects of the effects of the death of our Lord and Saviour, Jesus Christ!

c) THE EFFECT OF CHRIST'S DEATH ON SATAN

See under (3) above. The devil must submit to the victory of Christ. The dominion of Satan, so far as the believer in Christ is concerned, is now at an end: his dominion over the disobedient sons of men, too, will soon be at an end. Christ's death was the pronouncement of Satan's doom; it was the loss of his power over men. The power of the devil, while not yet absolutely destroyed, has been neutralized (Heb. 2:14). The evil principalities and powers, and Satan himself, did their worst at the Cross, but there they received their deathblow (Col. 2:14, 15).

II. THE RESURRECTION OF JESUS CHRIST

1. Its Importance

a) IT HOLDS A UNIQUE PLACE IN CHRISTIANITY

Christianity is the only religion that bases its claim to acceptance upon the resurrection of its founder. For any other religion to base its claim on such a doctrine would be to court failure. Test all other religions by this claim and see.

b) IT IS FUNDAMENTAL TO CHRISTIANITY

In that wonderful chapter on the resurrection (1 Cor. 15) Paul makes Christianity answer with its life for the literal truth of the resurrection of Jesus Christ. That the body of the founder of the Christian religion did not lie in the grave after the third day is fundamental to the existence of the religion of Christ: "And if Christ be not risen, then is our preaching vain, and your faith is also vain" (v. 14). "If Christ be not raised . . . ye are yet in your sins" (v. 17). "Then they also which are fallen asleep in Christ are perished" (v. 18). Remove the resurrection from Paul's Gospel, and his message is gone. The resurrection of Jesus Christ is not an appendage to Paul's Gospel; it is a constitutive part of it.

The importance of this doctrine is very evident from the prominent part it played in the preaching of the Apostles: Peter—Acts 2:24, 32; 3:15; 4:10; 5:30; 10:40; 1 Peter 1:21, 23. Paul—Acts 13:30, 34; 17:31; 1 Cor. 15; Phil. 3:21. It was belief in such preaching that led to the establishment of the Christian church. Belief in the resurrection of Christ was the faith of the early church (Acts 4:33). The testimony to this great fact of Christian faith was borne in the midst of the fiercest opposition. Nor was it controverted, although the grave was well known and could have been pointed out. It was in this fact that Christianity acquired a firm basis for its historical development. There was not only an "Easter Message," there was also an "Easter Faith."

Our Lord's honor was, in a sense, staked upon the fact of His resurrection. So important did He regard it that He remained forty days upon the earth after His resurrection, giving many infallible proofs of the great fact. He appealed to it again and again as evidence of the truth of His claims: Matt. 12:39, 40; John 2: 20-22.

Both the friends and the enemies of Christianity admit that the resurrection of Jesus Christ is vital to the religion that bears His name. The Christian confidently appeals to it as an incontrovertible fact; the skeptic denies it altogether as a historical reality. "If the resurrection really took place," says an assailant of it, "then Christianity must be admitted to be what it claims to be— a direct revelation from God." "If Christ be not risen," says the Apostle Paul, "then is our preaching vain, and your faith is also vain." The one tries all he can to do away with the proofs submitted for the accepted fact; the other plainly says that if the resurrection cannot be believed, then Christianity is nothing but a sham. If the resurrection of Christ can be successfully denied, if it can be proven to be absolutely untrue, then the whole fabric of the Gospel falls to pieces, the whole structure of the Christian religion is shaken at its foundation, and the very arch of Christianity crumbles into dust. Then it has wrought only imaginary changes, deluded its most faithful adherents, deceived and disappointed the hopes of its most devoted disciples, and the finest moral achievements that adorn the pages of the history of the Christian church have been based upon a falsehood.

Nor must we ignore the prominent place the resurrection of Jesus Christ occupies in the Scriptures. More than one hundred times is it spoken of in the New Testament alone.

2. *The Nature of the Resurrection of Jesus Christ*

a) JESUS CHRIST ACTUALLY DIED

Some who disbelieve in the resurrection of Christ assert that Jesus merely swooned, and that pitying hands took Him down from the cross, thinking that He had died. The cool air of the tomb in which He was placed revived Him, so that He came forth from the tomb as though He had really risen from the dead. The disciples believed that He had really died and risen again.

This theory is false for the following reasons:

Jesus Christ appeared to the disciples after the third day, not as a weak, suffering, half-dead man, but as a conquering, triumphant victor over death and the grave. He never could have made the impression upon the disciples that He did, if He had presented the picture of a sick, half-dead man.

From John 19:33-37 we learn that when the soldiers pierced the side of Christ, *there came forth blood and water*. Physiologists and physicists agree that such a condition of the vital organs, including the heart itself, precludes the idea of a mere swoon, and proves conclusively that death had taken place.

Joseph of Arimathaea asked permission to bury the body of Jesus because he knew that Jesus had been pronounced dead (Matt. 27:57, 58).

When the news was brought to Pilate that Christ had died, it is said that "Pilate marvelled if he were already dead: and calling unto him the centurion, he asked him whether he had been any while dead. And when he knew it of the centurion, he gave the body to Joseph" (Mark 15:44, 45).

The women brought spices to anoint a dead body, not a half-dead Christ (Mark 16:1).

The soldiers pronounced Him dead: "But when they came to Jesus, and saw that he was dead already, they brake not his legs" (John 19:33).

Jesus Christ Himself, He who is the Truth, testifies to the fact that He had really died: Rev. 1:18—"I am he that liveth, and was dead."

b) THE FACT THAT CHRIST'S BODY WAS ACTUALLY RAISED FROM THE DEAD

The resurrection of Christ is not a spiritual resurrection, nor were his appearances to the disciples spiritual manifestations. He appeared to His disciples in a bodily form. The body that was laid in Joseph's tomb came forth on that first Easter morn twenty centuries ago.

Some maintain that it is not vital to belief in the resurrection of Christ that we insist on a literal resurrection of the body of Jesus; all that we need to insist on is that Christ was ever afterwards known to be the victor over death, and that He had the power of an endless life. So it comes to pass that we have what is called an "Easter Message," as contrasted with an "Easter Faith" which believes in the literal resurrection of Jesus Christ from the dead. "Faith has by no means to do with the knowledge of the form in which Jesus lives, but only with the conviction that He is the living Lord."—*Harnack* in *What is Christianity?* According to this theory, belief in Christ's resurrection means nothing more than belief in the survival of the soul of Jesus—that somehow or other Jesus was alive, and lived with God, while His body yet saw corruption in the grave.

We reply: This cannot be, for all the facts in the Gospel narratives contradict such a theory. Let us examine these narratives.

(1) WE ARE CONFRONTED BY THE FACT OF AN EMPTY TOMB.

Matt. 28:6; Mark 16:6; Luke 24:3, 12; John 20:1, 2. The fact that the tomb was empty is testified to by competent witnesses—both friends and enemies: by the women, the disciples, the angels, and the Roman guards. How shall we account for the absence of the body of Jesus from the tomb? That it had not been stolen by outside parties is evident from the testimony of the soldiers who were bribed to tell that story (Matt. 28:11-15). Such a guard never would have allowed such a thing to take place. Their lives would have been thereby jeopardized. And if they were asleep (v. 13), how could they know what took place? Their testimony under such circumstances would be useless.

The condition in which the linen cloths were found lying by those who entered the tomb precludes the possibility of the body being stolen. Had such been the case the cloths would have been taken with the body, and not left in perfect order, thereby showing that the body had gone out of them. Burglars do not leave things in such perfect order. There is no order in haste.

Then again, we have the testimony of angels to the fact that Jesus had really risen as foretold (Matt. 28:6; Mark 16:6). The testimony of angels is surely trustworthy (Heb. 2:2).

(2) THERE ARE OTHER RESURRECTIONS MENTIONED IN THE GOSPEL RECORDS WHICH WERE UNDOUBTEDLY BODILY RESURRECTIONS.

Matt. 9:18-26; Luke 7:11-18; John 11:1-44. These incidents, although they are doubtless more properly called restorations, do throw light upon the resurrection of Jesus. Why did the officers say that they were afraid "that his disciples should come by night and steal him away" if they did not refer to the *body* of Jesus? They surely could not steal His soul.

(3) THOSE WHO SAW HIM AFTER THE RESURRECTION RECOGNIZED HIM AS HAVING THE SAME BODY AS HE HAD BEFORE, EVEN TO THE WOUND PRINTS.

John 20:27; Luke 24:37-39. It is true that there were occasions on which He was not recognizable by the disciples, but such occasions were the result of the eyes of the disciples being holden in order that they might not know him. There was divine intervention on these occasions. Does Christ still retain the prints of the nails? Is He still the Lamb as though it had been slain? (Rev. 5 and 6).

(4) THERE CAN BE NO DOUBT OF THE FACT THAT THE APOSTLE PAUL BELIEVED IN THE BODILY RESURRECTION OF CHRIST.

The Corinthians, to whom the apostle wrote that wonderful treatise on the resurrection (1 Cor. 15), were not spending their time denying a *spiritual* resurrection; nor was the apostle spending his time trying to produce convincing arguments for a *spiritual* resurrection. (See also Rom. 8:11.)

(5) IT IS CLEAR ALSO FROM CHRIST'S OWN TESTIMONY BEFORE AND AFTER THE RESURRECTION.

Matt. 17:23; Luke 24:39; Rev. 1:18. No other construction can legitimately be put upon these words than that Christ here refers to the resurrection of His body.

(6) THE APOSTOLIC TESTIMONY CORROBORATES THIS FACT.

Acts 2:24-32; 1 Pet. 1:3, 21; 3:21. Peter was at the tomb; he it was who stepped inside and saw the linen cloths lying. His testimony ought to be beyond question as to the fact at issue.

(7) THE RECORD OF THE APPEARANCES OF CHRIST PROVES A LITERAL, PHYSICAL RESURRECTION.

Matt. 28:9, 10; John 20:14-18, cf. Mark 16:9; Luke 24:13-32; John 21, etc. All these appearances bear witness to the fact that it was not an incorporeal spirit or phantom, but a real, bodily Christ that they saw. He could be seen, touched, handled; He was recognizable; He ate and drank in their presence.

(8) LASTLY, MANY PASSAGES IN THE SCRIPTURES WOULD BE UNINTELLIGIBLE EXCEPT ON THE GROUND OF A BODILY RESURRECTION OF JESUS CHRIST FROM THE GRAVE.

Rom. 8:11, 23; Eph. 1:19, 20; Phil. 3:20, 21; 1 Thess. 4:13-17.

c) THE NATURE OF THE RESURRECTION BODY OF CHRIST

(1) IT WAS A REAL BODY: NOT A GHOST, NOR A PHANTOM.

That the resurrection body of Jesus was not a phantom, but a body composed of "flesh and bones" is evident from Luke 24:36-43. It could be "touched" (John 20:20), and bore the marks of His passion (John 20:24-29). The likeness to His earthly body was not wholly parted with. [NOTE: Does this throw any light on the matter of recognition in heaven? Has Jesus Christ still this body in the glory? Shall we know Him by the prints?]

(2) YET THE BODY OF JESUS WAS MORE THAN A MERE NATURAL BODY.

It bore marks and possessed attributes which proclaimed a relation to the celestial or supra-terrestrial sphere. For example: It could pass through barred doors (John 20:19), thus transcending physical limitations. It was not recognizable at times (Luke 24:13-16; John 20:14, 15; 21:4, 12; Mark 16:12). This fact may be accounted for in two ways: First, supernaturally—their eyes were holden; Second, that in that risen life the spiritual controls the material rather than as here, the material the spiritual; so that the spirit could change the outward form of the body at will and at any given time. [Yet, note how Jesus had power to make Himself known by little acts, such as the breaking of the bread, and the tone of His voice. Do we carry these little characteristics into the other life? Shall we know our loved ones by these things?] Then again, Jesus was able to vanish out of sight of His friends (Luke 24:31; John 20:19, 26; Luke 24:51; Acts 1:9). And so He could be in different places at very short intervals of time.

Can we explain these facts? No, not fully. Yet we must not be so material as to totally disbelieve them. "Daily, indeed, are men being forced to recognize that the world holds more mysteries than they formerly imagined it to do. Probably physicists are not so

sure of the impenetrability of matter, or even of the conserva-
tion of energy, as they once were; and newer speculations on the
etheric basis of matter, and on the relation of the seen to the unseen universe (or universes) with forces and laws largely unknown, open up vistas of possibility which may hold in them the
key to phenomena even as extraordinary as those in question."—
James Orr.

(3) CHRIST'S RESURRECTION BODY WAS IMMORTAL.

Not only is it true that Christ's body has not seen death since
His resurrection, but it cannot die again. Rom. 6:9, 10; Rev.
1:18, cf. Luke 20:36. [The lesson for us from this: Christ is the
firstfruits (1 Cor. 15:20).]

3. The Credibility of the Resurrection of Jesus Christ

Credibility refers to the acceptance of a fact in a manner that
deserves belief; it is belief based upon good authority, reliable
facts, and competent witnesses. Credulity is belief in a thing without respect to the strength or weakness, reliability or unreliability
of the authority, facts, or witnesses; it is a believing too readily, and
with no reason for the faith or hope. The resurrection of Christ
is a fact proven by competent evidence, and a deserving of intelligent acceptance and belief. It is a doctrine buttressed by "many
infallible proofs."

The lines of proof for the credibility of Christ's resurrection
which may be followed in harmony with our purpose are as follows:

a) THE ARGUMENT FROM CAUSE AND EFFECT

Certain things, conditions, institutions exist in our midst today;
they are effects of causes, or a cause; what is that cause? Among
these we may mention—

(1) THE EMPTY TOMB

That was an effect; what was its cause? How did that grave become empty? (See p. 87). The fact of an empty tomb must be
accounted for. How do we account for it? Renan, the French
skeptic, wittingly said, and yet how truly: "You Christians live on
the fragrance of an empty tomb."

(2) THE LORD'S DAY

The Lord's Day is not the original Sabbath. Who dared change it? For what reason, and on what ground was it changed? Ponder the tenacity with which the Jews held on to their Sabbath given in Eden and made known amid the thunders of Sinai. Recall how Jews would sooner die than fight on the Sabbath day (cf. Titus' invasion of Jerusalem on the Sabbath). The Jews never celebrated the birthdays of great men; they celebrated events, like the Passover. Yet, in the New Testament times we find Jews changing their time-honored seventh day to the first day of the week, and, contrary to all precedent, calling that day after a man—the Lord's Day. Here is an effect, a tremendous effect; what was its cause? We cannot have an effect without a cause. The resurrection of our Lord was the cause for this great change in the day of worship.

(3) THE CHRISTIAN CHURCH

We know what a grand and noble institution the Christian Church is. What would this world be without it? Its hymns, worship, philanthropy, ministrations of mercy are all known to us. Where did this institution come from? It is an effect, a glorious effect; what is its cause? When the risen Christ appeared unto the discouraged disciples and revived their faith and hope, they went forth, under the all-conquering faith in a risen and ascended Lord, and preached the story of His life, death, resurrection, ascension, and coming again. Men believed these teachings; gathered themselves together to study the Scriptures, to pray, to worship Christ, and to extend His kingdom among men. This is how the Church came into existence. Its cause was the resurrection of Christ.

(4) THE NEW TESTAMENT

If Jesus Christ had remained buried in the grave, the story of His life and death would have remained buried with Him. The New Testament is an effect of Christ's resurrection. It was the resurrection that put heart into the disciples to go forth and tell its story. Skeptics would have us believe that the resurrection of Christ was an afterthought of the disciples to give the story of Christ's life a thrilling climax, a decorative incident which satisfies the dramatic feeling in man, a brilliant picture at the end of an heroic life. We reply: There would have been no beautiful story to put a climax to if there had been no resurrection of the Christ of the story. The resurrection does not grow out of the beautiful story of His life, but the beautiful story of Christ's life grew out of the fact of the resurrection. The New Testament is the book of the resurrection.

b) THE ARGUMENT FROM TESTIMONY

(1) As to the Number of the Witnesses

The resurrection of Christ as a historical fact is verified by a sufficient number of witnesses: over five hundred (1 Cor. 15:3-9). In our courts, one witness is enough to establish murder; two, high treason; three, the execution of a will; seven, an oral will. Seven is the greatest number required under our law. Christ's resurrection had five hundred and fourteen. Is not this a sufficient number?

(2) As to the Character of the Witnesses

The value of the testimony of a witness depends much upon his character; if that is impeached, then the testimony is discounted. Scrutinize carefully the character of the men who bore witness to the fact of Christ's resurrection. Impeach them if you can. They are unassailable on ethical grounds. "No honorable opponent of the Gospel has ever denied this fact. Their moral greatness awakened an Augustine, a Francis of Assisi, and a Luther. They have been the unrivalled pattern of all mature and moral manhood for nearly two thousand years." In law much is made of the question of *motive*. What motive could the apostles have had in perpetrating the story of Christ's resurrection upon people? Every one of them (except one) died a martyr's death for his loyalty to the story of Christ's resurrection. What had they to gain by fraud? Would they have sacrificed their lives for what they themselves believed to be an imposture?

Nor are we to slight the testimony to Christ's resurrection that comes to us from sources other than that of the inspired writers of the New Testament. Ignatius, a Christian, and a contemporary of Christ, a martyr for his faith in Christ, in his *Letter to the Philadelphians,* says: "Christ truly suffered, as He also truly raised up Himself. I *know* that after the resurrection He was in the flesh, and I believe Him to be so still. And when He came to those who were with Peter, He said to them, 'Take, handle me, and see that I am not an incorporeal phantom!'" Tertullian, in his *Apolegeticus,* says: "The fame of our Lord's remarkable resurrection and ascension being now spread abroad, Pontius Pilate, according to an ancient custom of communicating novel occurrences to the emperor, that nothing might escape him, transmitted to Tiberius, Emperor of Rome, an account of the resurrection of our Lord from the dead. . . . Tiberius referred the whole matter to the Senate, who, being unacquainted with the facts, rejected it." The integrity of this passage is unquestioned by even the most skeptical critics.

Alleged Discrepancies.*

The seeming differences in the testimony of the witnesses to the resurrection may be largely, if not altogether, reconciled by a correct knowledge of the manner and order of the *appearances* of Christ after His resurrection.

The following order of appearances may help in the understanding of the testimony to the resurrection:

1. The women at the grave see the vision of angels.
2. The women separate at the grave to make known the news —Mary Magdalene going to tell Peter and John, who doubtless lived close by (for it seems that they reached the grave in a single run). The other women go to tell the other disciples who, probably, were at Bethany.
3. Peter and John, hearing the news, run to the grave, leaving Mary. They then return home.
4. Mary follows; lingers at the grave; gets vision of the Master, and command to go tell the disciples.
5. The other women see Christ on the way.
6. Christ appears to the two on the way to Emmaus.
7. To Simon Peter.
8. To the ten apostles, and other friends.
9. To the apostles at Tiberias.
10. To the apostles and multitude on the mount.
11. To the disciples and friends at the ascension.
12. To James (1 Cor. 15:7).
13. To Paul (1 Cor. 15:8).

---

*The following extract from Dr. Orr's book, *The Resurrection of Jesus*, will throw some light on the matter of differences in testimony, while maintaining the credibility of the fact itself. "An instructive example is furnished in a recent issue of the *Bibliotheca Sacra*. A class in history was studying the French Revolution, and the pupils were asked to look the matter up, and report next day by what vote Louis XVI was condemned. Nearly half the

4. *The Results of the Resurrection of Jesus Christ*

a) AS TO JESUS CHRIST HIMSELF

Rom. 1:4—"And declared to be the Son of God with power, according to the spirit of holiness, by the resurrection from the dead." To "declare" means to mark off, to define, to set apart (Acts 10:42; Heb. 4:7). NOTE: Christ was not *made* the Son of God by the resurrection, but *declared* such. Had Christ remained in the grave as other men had done, there would then have been no reasonable ground to impose faith in Him. The empty tomb testifies to the deity of Christ.

Matt. 12:38-42; John 2:13-22. In these scriptures Jesus Christ bases His authority for His teaching and the truth of all His claims on His resurrection from the dead. (See p. 84.) See also Matt. 28:6—"Risen, as he said."

b) AS TO THE BELIEVER IN JESUS CHRIST

(1) ASSURES HIM OF HIS ACCEPTANCE WITH GOD.

Rom. 4:25—"Who was delivered for our offences, and was raised again for our justification." So long as Christ lay in the grave there was no assurance that His redemptive work had been acceptable to God. The fact that God raised Jesus from the dead was evidence that the Father was satisfied with the sacrifice Christ had made for the sins of men. "Of righteousness, because I go unto my Father" (John 16:10). Believing sinners may now rest satisfied that in Him they are justified. This thought is illustrated by the picture of the Jews waiting outside the temple for the coming out

---

class reported that the vote was unanimous. A considerable number protested that he was condemned by a majority of one. A few gave the majority as 145 in a vote of 721. How utterly irreconcilable these reports seemed! Yet for each the authority of reputable historians could be given. In fact, all were true, and the full truth was a combination of all three. On the first vote as to the king's guilt there was no contrary voice. Some tell only of this. The vote on the penalty was given individually, with reasons, and a majority of 145 declared for the death penalty, at once or after peace was made with Austria, or after confirmation by the people. The votes for immediate death were only 361 as against 360. History abounds with similar illustrations. As an example of another kind, reference may be made to Rev. R. J. Campbell's volume of *Sermons Addressed to Individuals,* where, on pp. 145-6 and pp. 181-2, the same story of a Brighton man is told with affecting details. The story is no doubt true in substance; but for 'discrepancies'—let the reader compare them, and never speak more (or Mr. Campbell either) of the Gospels!"

of the high priest (Luke 1:21), thereby indicating that their sacrifice had been accepted.

(2) ASSURES HIM OF AN INTERCEDING HIGH PRIEST IN THE HEAVENS.

Rom. 8:34—"Who is he that condemneth? It is Christ that died, yea rather, that is risen again, who is even at the right hand of God, who also maketh intercession for us." Also Heb. 7:25. Salvation was not completed at the Cross; there is still need of daily forgiveness, and so of the continual presenting of the shed blood before the mercy-seat. The accusations of Satan still need to be answered (Zec. 3:1-5; Job 1 and 2; Heb. 7:25). We need a Moses, not only to deliver us from bondage, but also to plead for us and intercede for us because of our sins committed in the wilderness journey. Herein is our assurance of forgiveness of sins committed after conversion—that our great High Priest is always heard (John 11:42), and that He prays constantly for us that our faith fail not (Luke 22:32). Our temporary falls shall not condemn us, for our Priest intercedes for us.

(3) ASSURES HIM OF ALL NEEDED POWER FOR LIFE AND SERVICE.

Eph. 1:19-22—"The exceeding greatness of his power . . . which he wrought in Christ, when he raised him from the dead, and set him at his own right hand in the heavenly places, far above all principality, and power, and might, . . . and gave him to be the head over all things to the church." Also Phil. 3:10. There are two standards in the Bible by which God's power is gauged: In the Old Testament, when God would have His people know the extent of His power, it is according to the power by which He brought Israel out of Egypt (Micah 7:15); in the New Testament, the unit of measurement of God's power is "According to the working of his mighty power, which he wrought in Christ . . . when he raised him from the dead." The connection of Phil. 3:10 gives the believer the promise and assurance not only of present power and victory, but also of future glorification. If we desire to know what God is able to do for and through us we are invited to look at the resurrection of Jesus Christ.

(4) THE ASSURANCE OF HIS OWN RESURRECTION AND IMMORTALITY.

1 Thess. 4:14—"For if we believe that Jesus died and rose

again, even so them also which sleep in Jesus will God bring with him." 2 Cor. 4:14—"Knowing that he which raised up the Lord Jesus shall raise up us also by Jesus, and shall present us with you." John 14:19—"Because I live, ye shall live also."

c) AS TO THE WORLD

(1) THE CERTAINTY OF A RESURRECTION.

1 Cor. 15:22—"As in Adam all die; even so in Christ shall all be made alive." Paul is here discussing a *bodily,* and not a *spiritual,* resurrection (see p. 88). As in Adam all men die physically, so in Christ all men are raised physically. The resurrection of Jesus Christ guarantees the resurrection of all men (see under Resurrection, p. 245).

(2) THE CERTAINTY OF A JUDGMENT DAY.

Acts 17:31—"Because he hath appointed a day, in the which he will judge the world in righteousness by that man whom he hath ordained; whereof he hath given assurance unto all men, in that he hath raised him from the dead." The resurrection of Christ is God's unfailing testimony to the fact of a coming day of judgment for the world. The one is as sure as the other.

III. THE ASCENSION AND EXALTATION OF JESUS CHRIST

1. The Meaning of These Terms

When we speak of the *ascension* of Christ we refer to that event in the life of our risen Lord in which He departed visibly from His disciples into heaven. This event is recorded in Acts 1:9-11—"This same Jesus which is taken up from you into heaven," etc.

By the *exaltation* of Jesus Christ we mean that act of God by which the risen and ascended Christ is given the place of power at the right hand of God. Phil. 2:9—"Wherefore God also hath highly exalted him and given him a name which is above every name." Eph. 1:20, 21—"Which he [God] wrought in Christ, when he raised him from the dead, and set him at his own right hand in the heavenly places, far above all principality and power." See also Heb. 1:3.

2. The Scriptural Data for the Doctrine

Foregleams of this truth were granted to the prophets of the Old Testament times, Psa. 110:1; 68:18. They saw Christ in prophetic vision not only as the meek and lowly One, but as the ascended and glorified Lord.

Our Lord Himself, on many occasions, foretold His ascension and exaltation. These events were constantly before His mind's eye: Luke 9:51; John 6:62; 20:17.

The New Testament writers record the event: Mark 16:19; Luke 24:51; John 3:13; Acts 1:9-11; Eph. 4:8-10; Heb. 10:12.

Stephen, in his dying moments, was granted a vision of the exalted Christ. He saw the "Son of Man standing on the right hand of God" (Acts 7:55, 56).

The apostles taught and preached these great truths: Peter, Acts 2:33, 34; 5:31; 1 Peter 3:22; Paul: Eph. 4:8-10; Heb. 4:14; 1 Tim. 3:16.

3. The Necessity of the Ascension and Exaltation of Jesus Christ

The nature of the resurrection body of our Lord necessitated His ascension and exaltation. Such a body could not be subject to ordinary laws; it could not permanently abide here.

Christ's unique personality also required such an exit from the world. Should not the exit of Christ from this world be as unique as His entrance into it? Then, again, consider the sinlessness of His life. If a miraculous exit was granted to men like Elijah and Enoch, who were sinful men, why should we marvel if such was granted to Christ? Indeed it seems perfectly natural, and quite in keeping with His whole life, that just such an event as the ascension and exaltation should form a fitting finish to such a wonderful career.

The ascension and exaltation were necessary to complete the redemptive work of Christ. His work was not finished when He arose from the dead. He had not yet presented the blood of the atonement in the presence of the Father; nor had He yet been given His place at the right hand of the Father as the bestower of all spiritual gifts, and especially the gift of the Holy Spirit.

The apostles were thus able to furnish to an unbelieving and inquisitive world a satisfactory account of the disappearance of the body of Christ which had been placed in the tomb, and which they claimed to have seen after the resurrection. "Where is your Christ?" the scoffing world might ask. "We saw Him ascend up into the heaven, and He is now at the Father's right hand," the apostles could reply.

It was further necessary in order that Christ might become an ideal object of worship for the whole human race. We should not forget that Christ's earthly ministry was a purely local one: He could be but in one place at a time. Those who worshipped at His feet in Jerusalem could not, at the same time, worship Him in any other place. This was the lesson, doubtless, that the Master desired to teach Mary when she would fain hold on to Him, and when He said, "Touch me not." Mary must worship now by faith, not by sight.

4. The Nature of the Ascension and Exaltation of Jesus Christ

a) IT WAS A BODILY AND VISIBLE ASCENSION.

Acts 1:9-11; Luke 24:51. It was the same Christ they had known in life, only glorified, who had tarried with them now for the space of forty days, who had delivered unto them certain commandments, and whose hands were even then outstretched in blessing that they saw slowly vanishing from their view up into the heavens. It was a body of flesh and bones, not flesh and blood. So will be our translation (1 Cor. 15:51, 52).

b) HE PASSED UP THROUGH THE HEAVENS.

Heb. 4:14 (R. V.); Eph. 4:10; Heb. 7:26. Whatever and how many created heavens there may be between the earth and the dwelling place of God, we may not know, but we are here told that Christ passed through them all, and up to the highest heaven, indeed was made higher than the heavens. This means that He overcame all those evil principalities and powers that inhabit these heavenlies (Eph. 6) and who doubtless tried their best to keep Him from passing through the heavens to present His finished work before the Father. Just as the high priest passed through the vail into the holy place, so Christ passed through the heavens into the presence of God.

c) HE TOOK HIS PLACE AT THE RIGHT HAND OF THE FATHER.

He was exalted to the right hand of God. Eph. 1:20—"Set him at his own right hand in the heavenly places, far above all principality and power." Col. 3:1—"Christ sitteth on the right hand of God." This place was not taken by Christ without conflict with these evil principalities and powers. But "He made a show of them openly, triumphing over them in it" (Col. 2:15). See also Acts 5:31.

What is meant by "the right hand of God"? Is it a definite place, or is it simply a figure of speech denoting a place of authority and power? Why can not both things be included? God has His dwelling place in heaven, and it is not incredible to believe that from the throne there Christ exercises His divine prerogatives. Stephen saw Christ standing at the right hand of God in heaven.

The "right hand of God" assuredly indicates the place of the accuser whom Christ casts out (Zec. 3:1; Rev. 12:10); the place of intercession which Christ now occupies (Rom. 8:34); the place of acceptance where the Intercessor now sits (Psa. 110:1); the place of highest power and richest blessing (Gen. 48:13-19); the place of power (Psa. 110:5). All these powers and prerogatives are Christ's by reason of His finished work of redemption.

5. The Purpose of the Ascension and Exaltation of Jesus Christ

a) HE HAS ENTERED HEAVEN AS A FORERUNNER.

Heb. 6:20—"Whither the forerunner is for us entered, even Jesus." The forerunner is one who enters into a place where the rest are to follow; one who is sent before to make observations; a scout, a spy. The Levitical high priest was not a forerunner; no one could follow him. But where Christ goes His people may go also.

b) HE HAS GONE TO PREPARE A PLACE FOR HIS PEOPLE.

Heb. 9:21-24; John 14:2. He is there making all necessary preparations for the coming of His Bride, the Church. In some way it seems that the heavenly sanctuary had been defiled by sin. It was necessary, therefore, that Christ purge it with His blood. What a home that will be if He prepares it!

c) HE IS NOW APPEARING BEFORE GOD IN OUR BEHALF.

Heb. 9:24—"To appear in the presence of God for us." He is there to act as High Priest in our behalf; to present the blood of atonement. "Before the throne my Surety stands." And yet not sò much before the throne as on the throne. He is the Kingly Priest. With authority He asks, and His petitions are granted.

d) HE HAS TAKEN HIS PLACE AT THE FATHER'S RIGHT HAND THAT HE MAY FILL ALL THINGS, AWAITING THE DAY WHEN HE SHALL HAVE UNIVERSAL DOMINION.

Eph. 4:10. He fills all things with His presence, with His work, with Himself. He is not a local Christ any longer (cf. Jer. 23:24).

Heb. 10:12, 13; Acts 3:20, 21—"He shall send Jesus Christ . . . whom the heaven must receive until the times of restitution of all things." Having won His victory, Christ is now waiting for all the spoils to be gathered. He is expecting, not doubting, but assuredly waiting; already His feet are upon the neck of the enemy. The Apocalypse pictures Christ entering upon the actual possession of His kingdom.

6. The Results of the Ascension and Exaltation of Jesus Christ

a) IT ASSURES US OF A FREE AND CONFIDENT ACCESS INTO THE PRESENCE OF GOD.

Heb. 4:14-16 (R. V.)—"Having then a great high priest, who hath passed through the heavens, Jesus the Son of God, let us hold fast our confession. . . . Let us therefore draw near with boldness unto the throne of grace." Our great High Priest is before the throne to present petitions, secure pardons for His people, and to communicate blessings in answer to their faith and prayers. We may have a free and fearless confidence in our approach to God.

b) AN ASSURED HOPE OF IMMORTALITY.

2 Cor. 5:1-8 describes the longing of the Christian to be clothed with a body after he has been called upon to lay aside this earthly tabernacle. He has no desire for a bodiless existence. The

ascension and exaltation of Christ assures the believer that like Christ he also will take his place in heaven with a body like unto Christ's own glorious body.

c) IT GIVES THE BELIEVER CONFIDENCE IN GOD'S PROVIDENCE TO BELIEVE THAT ALL THINGS ARE WORKING TOGETHER FOR HIS GOOD.

Seeing that Christ, the believer's Head, is exalted far above all things in heaven and earth, it is possible for the believer to be master of circumstances, and superior to all his environment (Eph. 1:22; cf. Col. 1:15-18).

d) CHRIST HAS BEEN MADE HEAD OVER ALL THINGS FOR THE CHURCH.

That is to say, everything is subject to Christ, and that for the Church's sake. Eph. 1:22 (R. V.)—"And he put all things in subjection under his feet, and gave him to be head over all things to the church." Christ is the fullness of the Father for the Church (Col. 1:19; 2:9, 10). Christ bestows the Holy Spirit upon the Church (Acts 2:33-36; John 7:37-39). He receives for and bestows upon the Church spiritual gifts (Eph. 4:8-12).

THE DOCTRINE OF THE
HOLY SPIRIT

THE DOCTRINE OF THE HOLY SPIRIT

I. THE PERSONALITY OF THE HOLY SPIRIT

1. WHY THE PERSONALITY OF THE HOLY SPIRIT IS QUESTIONED.

  a) The Spirit Seems Impersonal.

  b) The Names Given to the Holy Spirit.

  c) The Holy Spirit Is Not Usually Associated with the Greetings and Salutations of the New Testament.

  d) The Word "Spirit" Is Neuter.

2. METHOD OF PROVING THE PERSONALITY OF THE HOLY SPIRIT.

  a) Names Implying Personality Are Given to the Spirit.

  b) Personal Pronouns Are Used of the Spirit.

  c) Identified with Father and Son to Indicate Personality.

  d) Personal Characteristics Are Ascribed to the Spirit.

  e) Personal Acts Are Ascribed to the Spirit.

  f) The Spirit Is Susceptible to Personal Treatment.

II. THE DEITY OF THE HOLY SPIRIT

1. DIVINE NAMES ARE GIVEN TO THE SPIRIT.

2. DIVINE ATTRIBUTES

3. DIVINE WORKS

4. NAME OF THE SPIRIT ASSOCIATED WITH NAMES OF THE DEITY

5. COMPARISON OF OLD TESTAMENT PASSAGES WITH SOME IN THE NEW TESTAMENT

III. THE NAMES OF THE HOLY SPIRIT

1. THE HOLY SPIRIT

2. THE SPIRIT OF GRACE

3. THE SPIRIT OF BURNING

4. THE SPIRIT OF TRUTH

5. THE SPIRIT OF LIFE

6. THE SPIRIT OF WISDOM AND KNOWLEDGE

7. THE SPIRIT OF PROMISE

8. THE SPIRIT OF GLORY

9. THE SPIRIT OF GOD AND OF CHRIST

IV. THE WORK OF THE HOLY SPIRIT

1. IN RELATION TO THE WORLD
   a) The Universe
   b) The World of Mankind

2. IN RELATION TO THE BELIEVER

3. IN RELATION TO THE SCRIPTURES

4. IN RELATION TO JESUS CHRIST

V. OFFENCES AGAINST THE HOLY SPIRIT

1. BY THE SINNER
   a) Resisting
   b) Insulting
   c) Blaspheming

2. BY THE BELIEVER
   a) Grieving
   b) Lying to
   c) Quenching

THE DOCTRINE OF THE
HOLY SPIRIT

We are living in the Age of the Spirit. The Old Testament period may be called the Age of the Father; the period covered by the Gospels, the Age of the Son; from Pentecost until the second advent of Christ, the Age of the Spirit.

All matters pertaining to the doctrine of the Holy Spirit should, therefore, be of special interest to us who live in this age of special privilege. Yet how ignorant is the average Christian concerning matters pertaining to the Spirit. The Christian church today needs to heed Paul's exhortation: "Now concerning spiritual gifts [or, perhaps better, "matters pertaining to the Spirit"], I would not have you ignorant." May it not be that the reason why the sin against the Holy Spirit is so grievous is because it is a sin committed in the light and with the knowledge of the clearest and fullest revelation of the Godhead. We cannot, therefore, afford to remain in ignorance of this all-important doctrine.

I. THE PERSONALITY OF THE HOLY SPIRIT

It seems strange that it should be necessary to discuss this phase of the subject at all. Indeed, in the light of the last discourse of the Master (John 14-16), it seems superfluous, if not really insulting. During all the ages of the Christian era, however, it has been necessary to emphasize this phase of the doctrine of the Spirit (cf. Arianism, Socinianism, Unitarianism).

1. *Why the Personality of the Holy Spirit Is Questioned.*

a) BECAUSE, AS CONTRASTED WITH THE OTHER PERSONS OF THE GODHEAD, THE SPIRIT SEEMS IMPERSONAL.

The visible creation makes the personality of God the Father somewhat easy to conceive; the incarnation makes it almost, if not altogether, impossible to disbelieve in the personality of Jesus Christ; but the acts and workings of the Holy Spirit are so secret and mystical, so much is said of His influence, graces, power and gifts, that we are prone to think of Him as an influence, a power, a manifestation or influence of the divine nature, an agent rather than a Person.

b) BECAUSE OF THE NAMES GIVEN TO THE HOLY SPIRIT

He is called *breath, wind, power.* The symbols used in speaking of the Spirit are *oil, fire, water,* etc. See John 3:5-8; Acts 2:1-4; John 20:22; 1 John 2:20. It is not strange that in view of all this some students of the Scriptures may have been led to believe, erroneously of course, that the Holy Spirit is an impersonal influence emanating from God the Father.

c) BECAUSE THE HOLY SPIRIT IS NOT USUALLY ASSOCIATED WITH THE FATHER AND THE SON IN THE GREETINGS AND SALUTATIONS OF THE NEW TESTAMENT.

For illustration, see 1 Thess. 3:11—"Now God himself and our Father, and our Lord Jesus Christ, direct our way unto you." Yet we must remember, in this connection, that the apostolic benediction in 2 Cor. 13:14 does associate the three persons of the Trinity, thereby asserting their personality equally.

d) BECAUSE THE WORD OR NAME "SPIRIT" IS NEUTER.

It is true that the same Greek word is translated *wind* and *Spirit;* also that the Authorized Version uses the neuter pronoun "itself," when speaking of the Holy Spirit (Rom. 8:16, 26). As we shall see later, the Revised Version substitutes "himself" for "itself."

The importance of the personality of the Spirit and of our being assured of this fact is forcibly set forth by Dr. R. A. Torrey: "If the Holy Spirit is a Divine Person and we know it not, we are robbing a Divine Being of the love and adoration which are His due. It is of the highest practical importance whether the Holy Spirit is a power that we, in our ignorance and weakness, are somehow to get hold of and use, or whether the Holy Spirit is a personal Being . . . who is to get hold of us and use us. It is of the highest experimental importance. . . . Many can testify to the blessing that came into their lives when they came to know the Holy Spirit, not merely as a gracious influence . . . but as an ever-present, loving friend and helper."

2. *Method of Proving the Personality of the Holy Spirit*

It is difficult to define *personality* when used of the divine Being. God cannot be measured by human standards. God was not made in the image of man, but man in the image of God. God is not a deified man; man is rather a limited God ("a little . . . less than God." Heb. 2:7, R. V.). Only God has a perfect personality. When, however, one possesses the attributes, properties and qualities of personality, then personality may be unquestionably predicated of such a being. Does the Holy Spirit possess such properties? Let us see.

a) NAMES THAT IMPLY PERSONALITY ARE GIVEN TO THE SPIRIT.

The Comforter: John 14:16; 16:7. "Comforter" means one who is called to your side—as a client calls a lawyer. That this name cannot be used of any abstract, impersonal influence is clear from the fact that in 1 John 2:1 the same word is used of Christ. (See Rom. 8:26.) Again in John 14:16 the Holy Spirit, as the Paraclete, is to take the place of a person—Christ Himself, and to personally guide the disciples just as Jesus had been doing. No one but a person can take the place of a person; certainly no mere influence could take the place of Jesus Christ, the greatest personality that ever lived. Again, Christ, in speaking of the Spirit as the Comforter, uses the masculine definite article, and thus, by His choice of gender, teaches the personality of the Holy Spirit. There can be no parity between a person and an influence.

b) PERSONAL PRONOUNS ARE USED OF THE HOLY SPIRIT.

John 16:7, 8, 13-15: Twelve times in these verses the Greek masculine pronoun *ekeinos* (that one, He) is used of the Spirit. This same word is used of Christ in 1 John 2:6, 3:3, 5, 7, 16. This is especially remarkable because the Greek word for spirit *(pneuma)* is neuter, and so should have a neuter pronoun; yet, contrary to ordinary usage, a masculine pronoun is here used. This is not a pictorial personification, but a plain, definite, clear-cut statement asserting the personality of the Holy Spirit. Note also that where, in the Authorized Version, the neuter pronoun is used, the same is corrected in the Revised Version: not "itself," but "Himself" (Rom. 8:16, 26).

c) THE HOLY SPIRIT IS IDENTIFIED WITH THE FA-
THER AND THE SON—AND, INDEED, WITH CHRIS-
TIANS—IN SUCH A WAY AS TO INDICATE PER-
SONALITY.

The Baptismal Formula. Matt. 28:19. Suppose we should read,
"Baptizing them in the name of the Father, and of the Son, and
of *the wind or breath.*" Would that sound right? If the first two
names are personal, is not the third? Note also: "In the name"
(singular), not names (plural), implying that all three are Persons equally.

The Apostolic Benediction. 2 Cor. 13:14. The same argument
may be used as that in connection with the baptismal formula
just cited.

Identification with Christians. Acts 15:28. "For it seemed good
to the Holy Ghost, and to us." Shall we say, "It seemed good to
the wind and to us"? It would be absurd. 10:38—"How God
anointed Jesus of Nazareth with the Holy Ghost and with
power." Shall we read, "Anointed . . . with *power* and power?"
Rom. 15:13—"That ye may abound in hope, through the power of
the Holy Ghost." Shall we read, "That ye may abound in hope
through the power of the *power"?* See also Luke 4:14. Would not
these passages rebel against such tautological and meaningless
usage? Most assuredly.

d) PERSONAL CHARACTERISTICS ARE ASCRIBED TO
THE HOLY SPIRIT.

The Holy Spirit is represented as searching the deepest and
profoundest truths of God, and possessing knowledge of His counsels sufficiently to understand His purposes (1 Cor. 2:10, 11).
Could a mere influence do this? See also Isa. 11:3; 1 Pet. 1:11.

Spiritual gifts are distributed to believers according to the *will*
of the Spirit (1 Cor. 12). Here is wisdom, prudence and discre-
tion, all of which are distinguishing marks of personality. The
Spirit not only bestows spiritual gifts, but bestows them discreet-
ly according as He thinks best. See John 3:8 also.

The Spirit is said to have a *mind,* and that implies thought, purpose, determination: Rom. 8:27, cf. v. 7. Mind is an attribute of
personality.

e) PERSONAL ACTS ARE ASCRIBED TO THE HOLY
SPIRIT.

The Spirit *speaks*: Rev. 2:7 (cf. Matt. 17:5—"Hear ye him.")

It is the Spirit who speaks through the apostles (10:20). Speech is an attribute of personality.

The Spirit *maketh intercession*: Rom. 8:26 (R. V.), cf. Heb. 7:25; 1 John 2:1, 2, where Christ is said to "make intercession." Acts 13:2; 16:6, 7; 20:28. In these passages the Holy Spirit is seen *calling* missionaries, *overseeing* the church, and *commanding* the life and practice of the apostles and the whole church. Such acts indicate personality.

f) THE HOLY SPIRIT IS SUSCEPTIBLE TO PERSONAL TREATMENT.

He may be *grieved* (Eph. 4:30); *insulted* (Heb. 10:29); *lied to* (Acts 5:3); *blasphemed* and *sinned against* (Matt. 12:31, 32). Indeed, the sin against the Holy Spirit is a much more grievous matter than the sin against the Son of Man. Can such be said of an influence? Can it be said even of any of the sons of men?

II. THE DEITY OF THE HOLY SPIRIT

By the Deity of the Holy Spirit is meant that the Holy Spirit is God. This fact is clearly set forth in the Scriptures, in a fivefold way:

1. Divine Names Are Given to the Holy Spirit.

In Acts 5:4, the Spirit is called *God*. And this in opposition to man, to whom, alone, Ananias thought he was talking. Can any statement allege Deity more clearly? In 2 Cor. 3:18—"We . . . are transformed into the same image from glory to glory, even as from the Lord the Spirit" (R. V.). Here the Spirit is called the *Lord*. For the meaning of "Lord" see under the Deity of Christ, p. 60.

2. The Holy Spirit Possesses Divine Attributes.

He is *eternal* in his nature (Heb. 9:14, R. V.); *omnipresent* (Psa. 139:7-10); *omnipotent* (Luke 1:35); *omniscient* (1 Cor. 2:10, 11). For the meaning of these attributes, see under the Doctrine of God and Jesus Christ, pp. 28 and 63.

3. Divine Works Are Ascribed to the Holy Spirit.

Creation (Gen. 1:2; Psa. 104:30, R. V.); Job 33:4—"The Spirit of God hath made me, and the breath of the Almighty hath given me life." *Regeneration* (John 3:5-8); *resurrection* (Rom. 8:11).

4. The Name of the Holy Spirit Is Associated with that of the Father, and of the Son.

See under Personality of the Spirit, p. 107. The same arguments which there prove the personality of the Spirit may be used here to prove the Deity of the Spirit. It would be just as absurd to say, "Baptizing them in the name of the Father, and of the Son, and of *Moses,*"—thus putting Moses on an equality with the Father and the Son—as it would be to say, "Baptizing them in the name of the Father, and of the Son, and of the *wind*"—thus making the wind as personal as the Father and the Son. The Spirit is on an equality with the Father and the Son in the distribution of spiritual gifts (1 Cor. 12:4-6).

5. Passages Which in the Old Testament Refer to God Are in the New Testament Made to Refer to the Holy Spirit.

Compare Isa. 6:8-10 with Acts 28:25-27; and Exod. 16:7 with Heb. 3:7-9.

III. THE NAMES OF THE HOLY SPIRIT

Just as the Father and the Son have certain names ascribed to them, setting forth their nature and work, so also does the Holy Spirit have names which indicate His character and work.

1. The Holy Spirit

Luke 11:13—"How much more shall your heavenly Father give the Holy Spirit to them that ask him?" Rom. 1:4—"The spirit of holiness." In these passages it is the moral character of the Spirit that is set forth. Note the contrast: "Ye, being evil," and "the Holy Spirit." The Spirit is *holy* in Himself and produces holiness in others.

2. The Spirit of Grace

Heb. 10:29—"And hath done despite unto the Spirit of grace." As the executive of the Godhead, the Spirit confers grace. To resist the Spirit, therefore, is to shut off all hope of salvation. To resist His appeal is to insult the Godhead. That is why the punishment mentioned here is so awful.

3. The Spirit of Burning

Matt. 3:11, 12—"He shall baptize you with the Holy Ghost, and with fire." Isa. 4:4—"When the Lord shall have washed away the filth of the daughters of Zion . . . by the spirit of judgment and the spirit of burning." This cleansing is done by the blast of the Spirit's burning. Here is the searching, illuminating, refining, dross-consuming character of the Spirit. He burns up the dross in our lives when He enters and takes possession.

4. The Spirit of Truth

John 14:17; 15:26; 16:13; 1 John 5:6. As God is Love, so the Spirit is Truth. He possesses, reveals, confers, leads into, testifies to, and defends the truth. Thus He is opposed to the "spirit of error" (1 John 4:6).

5. The Spirit of Life

Rom. 8:2—"For the law of the Spirit of life in Christ Jesus hath made me free from the law of sin and death." That which had been the actuating principle of life, namely, the flesh, is now deposed, and its controlling place taken by the Spirit. The Spirit is thus the dynamic of the believer's experience that leads him into a life of liberty and power.

6. The Spirit of Wisdom and Knowledge

That the references in Isa. 11:2; 61:1, 2 are to be understood as referring to the Spirit that abode upon the Messiah, is clear from Luke 4:18 where "Spirit" is capitalized. Christ's wisdom and knowledge resulted, in one aspect of the case, from His being filled with the Spirit. "Wisdom and understanding" refer to intellectual and moral apprehension; "counsel and might," the power to scheme, originate, and carry out; "knowledge and the fear of the Lord," acquaintance with the true will of God, and the determination to carry it out at all costs. These graces are the result of the Spirit's operations on the heart.

7. The Spirit of Promise

Eph. 1:13—"Ye were sealed with that holy Spirit of promise." The Spirit is the fulfillment of Christ's promise to send the Comforter, and so He is the promised Spirit. The Spirit also confirms and seals the believer, and thus assures him that all the promises made to him shall be completely fulfilled.

8. The Spirit of Glory

1 Pet. 4:14—"The spirit of glory and of God resteth upon you." What is glory? Glory as used in the Scripture means character. The Holy Spirit is the One who produces godlike character in the believer (cf. 2 Cor. 3:18).

9. The Spirit of God, and of Christ

1 Cor. 3:16—"The Spirit of God dwelleth in you." Rom. 8:9— "Now if any man have not the Spirit of Christ, he is none of his." The fact that the Spirit is sent from the Father and the Son, that He represents them, and is their executive, seems to be the thought conveyed here.

10. The Comforter (p. 109)

IV. THE WORK OF THE HOLY SPIRIT

The work of the Spirit may be summed up under the following headings: His work in the universe; in humanity as a whole; in the believer; with reference to the Scriptures; and, finally, with reference to Jesus Christ.

1. In Relation to the World

a) WITH REGARD TO THE UNIVERSE

There is a sense in which the creation of the universe may be ascribed to God's Spirit. Indeed Psa. 33:6—"By the word of the Lord were the heavens made; and all the host of them by the breath [Spirit] of his mouth," attributes the work of creation to the Trinity, the Lord, the Word of the Lord, and the Spirit of the Lord. The creation of man is attributed to the Spirit. Job 33:4—"The Spirit of God hath made me, and the breath of the Almighty hath given me life." It would be proper, doubtless, to say that the Father created all things through the agency of the Word and the Spirit. In the Genesis account of creation (1:3) the Spirit is seen actively engaged in the work of creation.

Not only is it true that the Spirit's agency is seen in the act of creation, but His power is seen also in the preservation of nature.

Isa. 40:7—"The grass withereth, the flower fadeth, because the spirit of the Lord bloweth upon it." A staggering declaration. The Spirit comes in the fierce east wind with its keen, biting blast of death. He comes also in the summer zephyr, which brings life and beauty.

b) WITH REGARD TO HUMANITY AS A WHOLE

John 16:8-11—"And when he is come, he will reprove the world of sin, and of righteousness, and of judgment; of sin, because they believe not on me; of righteousness, because I go unto my Father and ye see me no more; of judgment, because the prince of this world is judged." Here are three great facts of which the Spirit bears witness to the world: the sin of unbelief in Christ; the fact that Christ was righteous and absolutely true in all that He claimed to be; the fact that the power of Satan has been broken. Of sin: the sin in which all other sins are embraced; of righteousness: the righteousness in which all other righteousness is manifested and fulfilled; of judgment: the judgment in which all other judgments are decided and grounded. Of sin, belonging to man; of righteousness, belonging to Christ; of judgment, belonging to Satan.

John 15:26—"The Spirit of truth . . . shall testify of me." Acts 5:32—"And we are his witnesses of these things; and so is also the Holy Ghost." It is the work of the Holy Spirit to constantly bear witness of Christ and His finished work to the world of sinful and sinning men. This He does largely, although hardly exclusively, through the testimony of believers to the saving power and work of Christ: "Ye also shall bear witness" (John 15:27).

2. The Work of the Spirit in Relation to the Believer

a) HE REGENERATES THE BELIEVER.

John 3:3-5—"Born of . . . the Spirit." Tit. 3:5—"The . . . renewing of the Holy Ghost." Sonship and membership in the kingdom of God come only through the regenerating of the Holy Spirit. "It is the Spirit that quickeneth." Just as Jesus was begotten of the Holy Ghost, so must every child of God who is to be an heir to the kingdom.

b) THE SPIRIT INDWELLS THE BELIEVER.

1 Cor. 6:19—"Your body is the temple of the Holy Ghost which is in you." Also 3:16; Rom. 8:9. Every believer, no matter how

weak and imperfect he may be, or how immature his Christian experience, still has the indwelling of the Spirit. Acts 19:2 does not contradict this statement. Evidently some miraculous outpouring of the Spirit is intended there, the which followed the prayer and laying on of the hands of the apostles. "Now if any man have not the Spirit of Christ, he is none of his." "No man can say that Jesus is the Lord, but by the Holy Ghost" (Rom. 8:9; 1 Cor. 12:3).

c) THE SPIRIT SEALS THE BELIEVER.

Eph. 1:13, 14—"In whom also after that ye believed, ye were sealed with that Holy Spirit of promise which is the earnest of our inheritance." Also 4:30—"Sealed unto the day of redemption." This sealing stands for two things: ownership and likeness (2 Tim. 2:19-21). The Holy Spirit is "the Spirit of adoption" which God puts into our hearts, by which we know that we are His children. The Spirit bears witness to this great truth (Gal. 4:6; Rom. 8:14-16). The sealing has to do with the heart and the conscience—satisfying both as to the settlement of the sin and sonship question.

d) THE HOLY SPIRIT INFILLS THE BELIEVER.

Acts 2:4—"And they were all filled with the Holy Ghost." Eph. 5:18—"Be filled with the Spirit." The filling differs somewhat from the indwelling. We may speak of the baptism of the Spirit as that initial act of the Spirit by which, at the moment of our regeneration, we are baptized by the Spirit into the body of Christ; the Spirit then comes and takes up His dwelling within the believer. The filling with the Spirit, however, is not confined to one experience, or to any one point of time exclusively; it may be repeated times without number. There is one baptism, but many infillings with the Spirit. The experience of the apostles in the Acts bears witness to the fact that they were repeatedly filled with the Spirit. Whenever a new emergency arose they sought a fresh infilling with the Spirit (cf. Acts 2:4 with 4:31, showing that the apostles who were filled on the day of Pentecost were again filled a few days after).

There is a difference between possessing the Spirit and being filled with the Spirit. All Christians have the first; not all have the second, although all may have. Eph. 4:30 speaks of believers as being "sealed," whereas 5:18 commands those same believers to "be filled [to be being filled again and again] with the Spirit."

Both the baptism and the infilling may take place at once. There need be no long wilderness experience in the life of the believer. It is the will of God that we should be filled (or, if you prefer the expression, "be baptized") with the Spirit at the moment of conversion, and remain filled all the time. Whenever we are called upon for any special service, or for any new emergency, we should seek a fresh infilling of the Spirit, either for life or service, as the case may be.

The Holy Spirit seeks—so we learn from the story of the Acts —for men who are not merely possessed by but also filled with the Spirit, for service (6:3, 5; 9:17; 11:24). Possession touches assurance; infilling, service.

e) THE HOLY SPIRIT EMPOWERS THE BELIEVER FOR LIFE AND SERVICE.

Rom. 8:2—"For the law of the Spirit of life in Christ Jesus hath made me free from the law of sin and death" (also vv. 9-11). There are two natures in the believer: the flesh and the Spirit (Gal. 5:17). But while the believer is still in the flesh, he does not live after the flesh (Rom. 8:12, 13). The Holy Spirit enables the believer to get constant and continual victory over sin. A single act of sin a believer may commit; to live in a state of sin is impossible for him, for the Spirit which is within him gives him victory, so that sin does not *reign* over him. If sinless perfection is not a Scriptural doctrine, sinful imperfection is certainly less Scriptural. The eighth chapter of Romans exhibits a victorious life for the believer; a life so different from that depicted in the seventh chapter. And the difference lies in the fact that the Holy Spirit is hardly, if at all, mentioned in the seventh chapter, while in the eighth He is mentioned over twelve times. The Spirit in the heart is the secret of victory over sin.

Then note how the Holy Spirit produces the blessed fruit of the Christian life (Gal. 5:22, 23). What a beautiful cluster of graces! How different from the awful catalogue of the works of the flesh (vv. 19-21). Look at this cluster of fruit. There are three groups: the first, in relation to God—love, joy, peace; the second, in relation to our fellowman—longsuffering, gentleness, goodness; the third, for our individual Christian life—faith, meekness, self-control.

f) THE HOLY SPIRIT IS THE GUIDE OF THE BELIEVER'S LIFE.

He guides him as to the details of his daily life, Rom. 8:14; Gal. 5:16, 25—"Walk in the Spirit." There is no detail of the believer's life that may not be under the control and direction of the Spirit. "The steps [and, as one has well said, 'the stops'] of a good man are ordered by the Lord."

The Holy Spirit guides the believer as to the field in which he should labor. How definitely this truth is taught in the Acts: 8:27-29; 16:6, 7; 13:2-4. What a prominent part the Spirit played in selecting the fields of labor for the apostles! Every step in the missionary activity of the early church seemed to be under the direct guidance of the Spirit.

g) THE HOLY SPIRIT ANOINTS THE BELIEVER.

This anointing stands for three things:

First, for *knowledge and teaching.* 1 John 2:27—"But the anointing which ye have received of him abideth in you, and ye need not that any man teach you; but as the same anointing teacheth you of all things, and is truth . . . ye shall abide in him." Also 2:20. It is not enough to learn the truth from human teachers, we must listen to the teaching of the Spirit. 1 Cor. 2:9-14 teaches us that there are some great truths that are spiritually discerned; they cannot be understood saving by the Spirit-filled man, for they are "spiritually discerned." See also John 14:26; 16:13.

Second, for *service.* How dependent Christ was upon the Holy Spirit for power in which to perform the duties of life is clear from such passages as Luke 4:18—"The Spirit of the Lord is upon me, because he hath anointed me to preach," etc. Also Acts 10:38—"How God anointed Jesus of Nazareth with the Holy Ghost and with power: who went about doing good." Ezekiel teaches a lesson by his vivid picture of the activity of God portrayed in the wheels within wheels. The moving power within those wheels was the Spirit of God. So in all our activity for God we must have the Spirit of power.

Third, for *consecration.* Three classes of persons in the Old Testament were anointed: the prophet, the priest, and the king. The result of anointing was consecration—"Thy vows are upon me, O God"; knowledge of God and His will—"Ye know all things"; influence—fragrance from the ointment. Just as the incense at Mecca clings to the pilgrim when he passes through the streets, so it is with him who has the anointing of the Spirit. All his garments smell of myrrh, and aloes, and cassia. He has about him the sweet odor and scent of the Rose of Sharon and the Lily of the Valley.

3. *The Relation of the Holy Spirit to the Scriptures*

a) HE IS THE AUTHOR OF THE SCRIPTURES.

Holy men of God spake as they were moved by the Holy Spirit. 2 Pet. 1:20, 21. The Scriptures came by the inbreathing of God, 2 Tim. 3:16. "Hear what the Spirit saith to the churches," Rev. 2 and 3. It was the Spirit who was to guide the apostles into all the truth, and show them things to come (John 16:13).

b) THE SPIRIT IS ALSO THE INTERPRETER OF THE SCRIPTURES.

1 Cor. 2:9-14. He is "the Spirit of wisdom and revelation," Eph. 1:17. "He shall receive of mine and show it unto you," John 16:14, 15. (See under the Inspiration of the Bible, p. 194.)

4. *The Relation of the Holy Spirit to Jesus Christ*

How dependent Jesus Christ was, in His state of humiliation, on the Holy Spirit! If He needed to depend solely upon the Spirit, can we afford to do less?

a) HE WAS CONCEIVED BY THE HOLY SPIRIT, BORN OF THE SPIRIT, LUKE 1:35.

b) HE WAS LED BY THE SPIRIT, MATT. 4:1.

c) HE WAS ANOINTED BY THE SPIRIT FOR SERVICE, ACTS 10:38.

d) HE WAS CRUCIFIED IN THE POWER OF THE SPIRIT, HEB. 9:14.

e) HE WAS RAISED BY THE POWER OF THE SPIRIT, ROM. 1:4; 8:11.

f) HE GAVE COMMANDMENT TO HIS DISCIPLES AND CHURCH THROUGH THE SPIRIT, ACTS 1:2.

g) HE IS THE BESTOWER OF THE HOLY SPIRIT, ACTS 2:33.

V. OFFENCES AGAINST THE HOLY SPIRIT

Scarcely any phase of the doctrine of the Spirit is more solemn than this. It behooves us all, believer and unbeliever alike, to be careful as to how we treat the Holy Spirit. Sinning against the Spirit is fraught with terrific consequences.

For convenience sake we are classifying the offences against the Spirit under two general divisions, namely, those committed by the unbeliever, and those committed by the believer. Not that there is absolutely no overlapping in either case. For, doubtless, in the very nature of the case there must be. This thought will be kept in mind in the study of the offences against the Spirit.

1. Offences Committed by the Unbeliever

a) RESISTING THE HOLY GHOST

Acts 7:51—"Ye do always resist the Holy Ghost." Here the picture is that of the Holy Spirit attacking the citadel of the soul of man, who violently resists the gracious attempts of the Spirit to win him. In spite of the plainest arguments and the most incontestable facts, this man wilfully rejects the evidence and refuses to accept the Christ so convincingly presented. Thus is the Holy Ghost resisted. (See Acts 6:10.) That this is a true picture of resistance to the Holy Spirit is clearly seen from Stephen's recital of the facts in Acts 7:51-57.

b) INSULTING, OR DOING DESPITE UNTO THE HOLY SPIRIT

Heb. 10:29 (cf. Luke 18:32). It is the work of the Spirit to present the atoning work of Christ to the sinner as the ground of his pardon. When the sinner refuses to believe or accept the testimony of the Spirit, he thereby insults the Spirit by esteeming the whole work of Christ as a deception and a lie, or accounts the death of Christ as the death of an ordinary or common man, and not as God's provision for the sinner.

c) BLASPHEMING THE HOLY SPIRIT

Matt. 12:31, 32. This seems to be the most grievous sin of all, for the Master asserts that there is no forgiveness for this sin. Sins against the Son of Man may be forgiven because it was easily possible, by reason of His humble birth, lowly parentage, etc., to question the claims He put forth to deity. But when, after Pentecost, the Holy Spirit came, and presented to every man's conscience evidence sufficient to prove the truth of these claims, the man who then refused to yield to Christ's claims was guilty of resisting, insulting, and that amounts to blaspheming the testimony of the whole Godhead, of which the Spirit is the executive.

2. Offences Committed by the Believer

a) GRIEVING THE SPIRIT

Eph. 4:30, 31; Isa. 63:10 (R. V.). To grieve means to make sad or sorrowful. It is the word used to describe the experience of Christ in Gethsemane; and so the sorrow of Gethsemane may be endured by the Holy Spirit. The Spirit is the most sensitive person of the Godhead. He is called the "Mother-heart" of God. The context of this passage (v. 31) tells us how the Spirit may be grieved: by "foolish talking and jesting." Whenever the believer allows any of the things mentioned in this verse (and those stated also in Gal. 5:17-19) to find place in his heart and expression in his words and life; when these things abide in his heart and actively manifest themselves, then the Spirit is sad and grieved. Indeed to refuse any part of our moral nature to the full sway of the Spirit is to grieve Him. If we continue to grieve the Spirit, then the grief turns into vexation (Isa. 63:10).

b) LYING TO THE HOLY SPIRIT

Acts 5:3, 4. The sin of lying to the Spirit is very prominent during services for dedication. We stand up and say, "I surrender all" when in our hearts we know that we have not surrendered *all*. Yet, like Ananias, we like to have others believe that we have consecrated our all. We do not wish to be one whit behind others in our profession. Read carefully in this connection the story of Achan (Joshua 7), and that of Gehazi (2 Kings 5:20-27).

c) QUENCHING THE SPIRIT

1 Thess. 5:19—"Quench not the Spirit." The thought of quenching the Spirit seems to be used in connection with fire: "Smoking flax shall he not quench" (Matt. 12:20); "Quench the fiery darts" (Eph. 6:16). It is therefore related more to the thought of service than to that of life. The context of 1 Thess. 5:19 shows this. The manifestation of the Spirit in prophesying was not to be quenched. The Holy Spirit is seen as coming down upon this

gathered assembly for praise, prayer, and testimony. This manifestation of the Spirit must not be quenched. Thus we may quench
the Spirit not only in our hearts, but also in the hearts of others.
How? By disloyalty to the voice and call of the Spirit; by disobedience to His voice whether it be to testify, praise, to do any
bit of service for God, or to refuse to go where He sends us to labor
—the foreign field, for example. Let us be careful also lest in
criticizing the manifestation of the Spirit in the testimony of some
believer, or the sermon of some preacher, we be found guilty of
quenching the Spirit. Let us see to it that the gift of the Holy
Ghost for service be not lost by any unfaithfulness, or by the
cultivation of a critical spirit on our part, so that the fire in our
hearts dies out and nothing but ashes remain—ashes, a sign
that fire was once there, but has been extinguished.

From what has been said the following may be summarily
stated:

Resisting has to do with the regenerating work of the Spirit;

Grieving has to do with the indwelling Holy Spirit;

Quenching has to do with the enduement of the Spirit for service.

THE DOCTRINE OF MAN

THE DOCTRINE OF MAN

I. THE CREATION AND ORIGINAL CONDITION OF MAN

1. IMAGE AND LIKENESS OF GOD

a) The Image of God Does Not Denote Physical Likeness.

b) "Image" and "Likeness" Are Not Exhausted in Creation.

c) Scriptures Teach In What Image and Likeness Consisted.

d) Man Was Endowed with Intellectual Faculties.

e) Man Possessed Moral and Spiritual Faculties.

II. THE FALL OF MAN

1. THE SCRIPTURAL ACCOUNT

2. VARIOUS INTERPRETATIONS

3. THE NATURE OF THE FALL

4. THE RESULTS OF THE FALL

a) On Adam and Eve

b) On the Race
   Various Theories
   Scriptural Declarations

THE DOCTRINE OF MAN

I. THE CREATION AND ORIGINAL CONDITION OF MAN

1. Man Made in the Image and Likeness of God

Gen. 1:26—"And God said, Let us make man in our image, after our likeness." 9:6—"For in the image of God made he man." What is meant by the terms *image* and *likeness? Image* means the shadow or outline of a figure, while *likeness* denotes the resemblance of that shadow to the figure. The two words, however, are practically synonymous. That man was made in the image and likeness of God is fundamental in all God's dealings with man (1 Cor. 11:7; Eph. 4:21-24; Col. 3:10; James 3:9). We may express the language as follows: Let us make man in our image to be our likeness.

a) THE IMAGE OF GOD DOES NOT DENOTE PHYSICAL LIKENESS.

God is Spirit; He does not have parts and passions as a man. (See under Doctrine of God; The Spirituality of God, pp. 18-22). Consequently Mormon and Swedenborgian views of God as a great human are wrong. Deut. 4:15 contradicts such a physical view of God (see p. 19). Some would infer from Psa. 17:15 —"I shall be satisfied, when I awake, with thy likeness," that in some remote way, a physical likeness is suggested. The R. V., however, changes somewhat the sense of this verse, and reads: "I shall be satisfied, when I awake, with *beholding* thy form." See also Num. 12:8, R. V. It is fair to believe, however, that erectness of posture, intelligence of countenance, and a quick, glancing eye characterized the first man. We should also remember that the manifestations in the Old Testament and the incarnation must throw some light upon this subject (see p. 20).

127

b) NOR ARE THE EXPRESSIONS "IMAGE" AND "LIKE-NESS" EXHAUSTED WHEN WE SAY THAT THEY CONSISTED IN MAN'S DOMINION OVER NATURE, AND THE CREATION OF GOD IN GENERAL.

Indeed the supremacy conferred upon man presupposed those spiritual endowments, and was justified by his fitness, through them, to exercise it.

c) POSITIVELY, WE LEARN FROM CERTAIN SCRIP-TURES IN WHAT THIS IMAGE AND LIKENESS CON-SISTED.

Eph. 4:23, 24—"And be renewed in the spirit of your mind; and that ye put on the new man, which after God is created in righteousness and true holiness [R. V., holiness of truth]." Col. 3:10—"And have put on the new man, which is renewed in knowledge after the image of him that created him." It is clear from these passages that the image of God consists in knowledge, righteousness, and holiness; moral, not physical likeness.

d) THE ORIGINAL MAN WAS ENDOWED WITH IN-TELLECTUAL FACULTIES.

He had sufficient intelligence to give names to the animals as they were presented before him (Gen. 2:19, 20). Adam had not only the power of speech, but the power of reasoning and thought in connection with speech. He could attach words to ideas. This is not the picture, as evolution would have us believe, of an infantile savage slowly groping his way towards articulate speech by imi-tation of the sounds of animals.

e) THE ORIGINAL MAN POSSESSED MORAL AND SPIRITUAL FACULTIES.

Consider the moral test in Genesis 3. Adam had power to resist or to yield to moral evil. Sin was a volitional thing. Christ, the second Adam, endured a similar test (Matt. 4).

From all this it is evident that man's original state was not one of savagery. Indeed there is abundant evidence to show that man has been degraded from a very much higher stage. Both the Bible and science agree in making man the crowning work of God, and that there will be no higher order of beings here on the earth than man. We must not forget that while man, from one side of his nature, is linked to the animal creation, he is yet supra-natural—a being of a higher order and more splendid nature; he is in the image and likeness of God. Man has developed not *from* the ape, but *away from* it. He never was anything but potential man. "No single instance has yet been adduced of the transformation of one animal species into another, either by natural or artificial selection; much less has it been demonstrated that the body of the brute has ever been developed into that of the man. The links that should bind man to the monkey have not been found. Not a single one can be shown. None have been found that stood nearer the monkey than the man of today."—*Agassiz.*

II. THE FALL OF MAN

The doctrine of the fall of man is not peculiar to Christianity; all religions contain an account of it, and recognize the great and awful fact. Had there been no such. account as that found in Genesis 3, there would still have remained the problem of the fall and sin.

Yet, the doctrine of the fall has a relation to Christianity that it does not have to other religions, or religious systems. The moral character of God as seen in the Christian religion far surpasses the delineation of the Supreme Being set forth in any other religion, and thus heightens and intensifies its idea of sin. It is when men consider the very high character of God as set forth in Christianity, and then look at the doctrine of sin, that they find it hard to reconcile the fact that God, being the moral Being He is, should ever allow sin to come into the world. To some minds these two things seem incompatible.

1. *The Scriptural Account of the Fall of Man*

The third chapter of Genesis gives the fullest account of this awful tragedy in the experience of mankind. Other scriptures: Rom. 5:12-19; 1 Tim. 2:14; Gen. 6:5; 8:21; Psa. 14; Rom. 3:10-23.

The purpose of the Genesis narrative is not to give an account of the manner in which sin came into the *world,* but how it found its advent into the *human race.* Sin was already in the world, as the existence of Satan and the chaotic condition of things in the beginning strikingly testify.

The reasonableness of the narrative of the fall is seen in view of the condition of man after he had sinned, as compared with his condition when he was created. Compare Gen. 1:26 with 6:5, and Psa. 14. If the fall of man were not narrated in Genesis we should have to postulate some such event to account for the present condition in which we find man. In no part of the Scripture, save in the creation account as found in the first two chapters of Genesis, does man appear perfect and upright. His attitude is that of rebellion against God, of deepening and awful corruption.

2. Various Interpretations of the Narrative of the Fall of Man

Some look upon the whole narrative as being an *allegory*. Adam is the rational part of man; Eve, the sensual; the serpent, external excitements to evil. But the simplicity and artlessness of the narrative militates against this view.

Others, again, designate the narrative as being a *myth*. It is regarded as a truth invested in poetic form; something made up from the folklore of the times. But why should these few verses be snatched out of the chapter in which they are found and be called mythical, while the remaining verses are indisputably literal?

Then there is the *literal interpretation*, which takes the account as it reads, in its perfectly natural sense, just as in the case of the other parts of the same chapter. There is no intimation in the account itself that it is not to be regarded as literal history. It certainly is part of a historical book. The geographical locations in connection with the story are historic. The curse upon the man, upon the woman, and upon the ground are certainly literal. It is a fact that death is in the world as the wages of sin. Unquestionably Christ, and the other Scripture writers regard the event as historical and literal: cf. Matt. 19:4; Mark 10:6; 2 Cor. 11:3; 1 Tim. 2:13-15; 1 Cor. 15:56.

3. The Nature of the Fall

It must be kept in mind that Adam and Eve were free moral agents. That while they were sinless beings, it was yet possible for them to sin, just as it was possible for them not to sin. A careful reading of the narrative leads to the following remarks:

The sin of our first parents was purely volitional; it was an act of their own determination. Their sin was, like all other sin, a voluntary act of the will.

It came from an outside source, that is to say, it was instigated from without. There was no sin in the nature of the first human pair. Consequently there must have been an ungodly principle already in the world. Probably the fall of Satan and the evil angels had taken place already.

The essence of the first sin lay in the denial of the divine will; an elevation of the will of man over the will of God.

It was a deliberate transgressing of a divinely marked boundary; an overstepping of the divine limits.

In its last analysis, the first sin was what each and every sin committed since has been, a positive disbelief in the word of the living God. A belief of Satan rather than a belief in God.

It is helpful to note that the same lines of temptation that were presented to our first parents, were presented to Christ in the wilderness (Matt. 4:1-11), and to men ever since then (1 John 2:15-17). Satan's program is short and shallow after all.

4. The Results of the Fall

a) ON OUR FIRST PARENTS—ADAM AND EVE

The results of sin in the experience of our first parents were as follows:

The ground was cursed, so that henceforth it would not yield good alone (Gen. 3:17).

Sorrow and pain to the woman in child-bearing, and subjection of woman to the man (Gen. 3:16).

Exhausting physical labor in order to subsist (Gen. 3:19).

Physical and spiritual death (Gen. 3:19; 3:2; 5:5; Rom. 5:12).

Of course, with all this came also a fear of God, a shame because of sin, a hiding from God's presence, and finally, an expulsion from the garden (Gen. 3:8-11, 22-24).

b) ON THE RACE—VARIOUS THEORIES

There are three general views held with regard to the effect of Adam's sin upon the race. Before looking at the strictly Scriptural view in detail, let us briefly state these three theories:

That Adam's sin affected himself only; that every human being born into the world is as free from sin as Adam was. The only effect the first sin had upon the race was that of a bad example.

According to this theory man is well morally and spiritually. This view of the case is false because the Scriptures recognize all men as guilty and as possessing a sinful nature; because man, as soon as he attains the age of responsibility commits sinful acts, and there is no exception to this rule; because righteousness is impossible without the help of God, otherwise redemption would be by works of righteousness which we have done, and this the Scripture contradicts. According to this view man is perfectly well. (The Pelagian theory.)

That while Adam's sin, as guilt, is not imputed to man, he is yet destitute of original righteousness, and, without divine help is utterly unable to attain it. God, however, bestows upon each individual, at the dawn of consciousness, a special gift of His Spirit, which is sufficient to enable man to be righteous, if he will allow his will to co-operate with God's Spirit. According to this view man is only half sick, or half well. This view also is false because the Scriptures clearly state that man is utterly unable to do a single thing to save himself. (The Semi-Pelagian theory.)

That because of the unity of the race in Adam, and the organic unity of mankind, Adam's sin is therefore imputed to his posterity. The nature which man now possesses is like to the corrupted nature of Adam. Man is totally unable to do anything to save himself. According to this theory man is not only not well, nor half well, but totally dead. (The Augustinian theory.)

SCRIPTURAL TEACHING

(1) ALL MEN, WITHOUT RESPECT OF CONDITION OR CLASS, ARE SINNERS BEFORE GOD.

Rom. 3:9, 10, 22, 23; Psa. 14; Isa. 53:6. There may be a difference in the degree, but not in the fact of sin. All men, Jew and Gentile, have missed the mark, and failed to attain to God's standard. There is none righteous, no, not one.

(2) THIS UNIVERSAL SINFUL CONDITION IS VITALLY CONNECTED WITH THE SIN OF ADAM.

Rom. 5:12—"Wherefore, as by one man sin entered into the world, and death by sin; and so death passed upon all men, for that all have sinned." "For the judgment was by one to condemnation" (5:16). "For as by one man's disobedience many were made sinners" (5:19). All men were in Adam when he sinned; fallen he, fallen they. Herein lies the truth of the organic unity of the race. "In Adam all die." Two questions are raised here: How can man be held responsible for a depraved nature?—this touches the matter of *original sin*; and How can God justly impute Adam's sin to us?—this deals with the question of the *imputation of sin*.

(3) THE WHOLE WORLD RESTS UNDER CONDEMNATION, WRATH, AND CURSE.

Rom. 3:19—"That every mouth may be stopped, and all the world may become guilty before God." Gal. 3:10; Eph. 2:3. The law of God demands a perfect obedience; but no son of man can yield such obedience; hence the curse of a broken law rests upon those breaking it. The wrath of God abides on all not vitally united by faith to Jesus Christ (John 3:36).

(4) UNREGENERATE MEN ARE REGARDED AS CHILDREN OF THE DEVIL, AND NOT SONS OF GOD.

1 John 3:8-10; John 8:44—"Ye are of your father the devil." 1 John 5:19—"And we know that we are of God, and the whole world lieth in wickedness [in the wicked one, R. V.]."

(5) THE WHOLE RACE OF MEN ARE IN HELPLESS CAPTIVITY TO SIN AND SATAN.

Rom. 7, entire chapter; John 8:31-36; Eph. 2:3.

(6) THE ENTIRE NATURE OF MAN, MENTALLY, MORALLY, SPIRITUALLY, PHYSICALLY, IS SADLY AFFECTED BY SIN.

The *understanding* is darkened (Eph. 4:18; 1 Cor. 2:14); the *heart* is deceitful and wicked (Jer. 17:9, 10); the *mind and conscience* are defiled (Gen. 6:5; Titus 1:15); the *flesh and spirit* are defiled (2 Cor. 7:5); the *will* is enfeebled (Rom. 7:18); and we are utterly destitute of any Godlike qualities which meet the requirements of God's holiness (Rom. 7:18).

What does all this mean? A. H. Strong, in his *Systematic Theology,* explains the matter somewhat as follows: It does not mean the entire absence of conscience (John 8:9); nor of all moral qualities (Mark 10:21); nor that men are prone to every kind of sin (for some sins exclude others). It does mean, however, that man is totally destitute of love to God which is the all absorbing commandment of the law (John 5:42); that the natural man

has an aversion to God (Rom. 8:7); that all that is stated under
(6) above is true of man; that man is in possession of a nature that
is constantly on the downgrade, and from the dominion of which he
is totally unable to free himself (Rom. 7:18, 23).

THE DOCTRINES OF
SALVATION

THE DOCTRINES OF SALVATION

A. REPENTANCE

B. FAITH

C. REGENERATION

D. JUSTIFICATION

E. ADOPTION

F. SANCTIFICATION

G. PRAYER

THE DOCTRINES OF SALVATION

A. REPENTANCE

I. THE IMPORTANCE OF THE DOCTRINE

II. THE NATURE OF REPENTANCE

1. AS TOUCHING THE INTELLECT
2. AFFECTING THE EMOTIONS
3. WILL
   a) Confess Sin
   b) Forsake Sin
   c) Turn to God

III. HOW REPENTANCE IS PRODUCED
1. DIVINE GIFT
2. QUESTION OF MEANS

IV. RESULTS OF REPENTANCE
1. HEAVEN MADE GLAD
2. PARDON AND FORGIVENESS
3. HOLY SPIRIT POURED OUT

A. REPENTANCE

I. THE IMPORTANCE OF THE DOCTRINE

The prominence given to the doctrine of repentance in the Scriptures can hardly be overestimated. John the Baptist began his public ministry, as did Jesus also, with the call to repentance upon his lips (Matt. 3:1, 2; 4:17).

When Jesus sent forth the twelve and the seventy messengers to proclaim the good news of the kingdom of heaven, He commanded them to preach repentance (Luke 24:47; Mark 6:12).

Foremost in the preaching of the apostles was the doctrine of repentance: Peter (Acts 2:38); Paul (Acts 20:21).

The burden of the heart of God, and His one command to all men everywhere, is that they should repent (2 Pet. 3:9; Acts 17:30).

Indeed, failure on the part of man to heed God's call to repentance means that he shall utterly perish (Luke 13:3).

Does the doctrine of repentance find such a prominent place in the preaching and teaching of today? Has the need for repentance diminished? Has God lessened or changed the terms of admission into His kingdom?

II. THE NATURE OF REPENTANCE

There is a threefold idea involved in true repentance:

1. As Touching the Intellect

Matt. 21:29—"He answered and said, I will not: but afterward he repented, and went." The word here used for "repent" means to change one's mind, thought, purpose, views regarding a matter; it is to have another mind about a thing. So we may speak of it as a revolution touching our attitude and views towards sin and righteousness. This change is well illustrated in the action of the prodigal son, and of the publican in the well-known story of the pharisee and the publican (Luke 15 and 18). Thus, when Peter, on the day of Pentecost, called upon the Jews to repent (Acts 2:14-40), he virtually called upon them to change their minds and their views regarding Christ. They had considered Christ to be a mere man, a blasphemer, an impostor. The events of the few preceding days had proven to them that He was none other than the righteous Son of God, their Saviour and the Saviour of the world. The result of their repentance or change of mind would be that they would receive Jesus Christ as their long promised Messiah.

2. As Touching the Emotions

2 Cor. 7:9—"Now I rejoice, not that ye were made sorry, but that ye sorrowed to repentance; for ye were made sorry after a godly manner, that ye might receive damage by us in nothing." The context (vv. 7-11) shows what a large part the feelings played in true Gospel repentance. See also Luke 10:13; cf. Gen. 6:6. The Greek word for repentance in this connection means "to be a care to one afterwards," to cause one great concern. The Hebrew equiv-

alent is even stronger, and means to pant, to sigh, to moan. So the publican "beat upon his breast," indicating sorrow of heart. Just how much emotion is necessary to true repentance no one can definitely say. But that a certain amount of heart movement, even though it be not accompanied with a flood of tears, or even a single tear, accompanies all true repentance is evident from the use of this word. See also Psa. 38:18.

3. As Touching the Will and Disposition

One of the Hebrew words for repent means "to turn." The prodigal said, "I will arise . . . and he arose" (Luke 15:18, 20). He not only thought upon his ways, and felt sorry because of them, but he turned his steps in the direction of home. So that in a very real sense repentance is a crisis with a changed experience in view. Repentance is not only a heart broken *for* sin, but *from* sin also. We must forsake what we would have God remit. In the writings of Paul repentance is more of an experience than a single act. The part of the will and disposition in repentance is shown:

a) IN THE CONFESSION OF SIN TO GOD

Psa. 38:18—"For I will declare mine iniquity: I will be sorry for my sin." The publican beat upon his breast, and said, "God be merciful to me a sinner" (Luke 18:13). The prodigal said, "I have sinned against heaven" (Luke 15:21).

There must be confession to man also in so far as man has been wronged in and by our sin (Matt. 5:23, 24; James 5:16).

b) IN THE FORSAKING OF SIN

Isa. 55:7—"Let the wicked forsake his way, and the unrighteous man his thoughts; and let him return unto the Lord." Prov. 28:13; Matt. 3:8, 10.

c) IN TURNING UNTO GOD

It is not enough to turn away from sin; we must turn unto God; 1 Thess. 1:9; Acts 26:18.

III. HOW REPENTANCE IS PRODUCED

1. It Is a Divine Gift.

Acts 11:18—"Then hath God also to the Gentiles granted repentance unto life." 2 Tim. 2:25—"If God peradventure will give them repentance to the acknowledging of the truth." Acts 5:30, 31. Repentance is not something which one can originate within himself, or can pump up within himself as one would pump water out of a well. It is a divine gift. How then is man responsible for not having it? We are called upon to repent in order that we may feel our own inability to do so, and consequently be thrown upon God and petition Him to perform this work of grace in our hearts.

2. Yet this Divine Gift Is Brought About Through the Use of Means.

Acts 2:37, 38, 41. The very Gospel which calls for repentance produces it. How well this is illustrated in the experience of the people of Nineveh (Jonah 3:5-10)! When they heard the preaching of the word of God by Jonah they believed the message and turned unto God. Not any message, but the Gospel is the instrument that God uses to bring about this desired end. Furthermore, this message must be preached in the power of the Holy Spirit (1 Thess. 1:5-10).

Rom. 2:4—"Or despisest thou the riches of his goodness and forbearance and long-suffering; not knowing that the goodness of God leadeth thee to repentance?" Also 2 Pet. 3:9. Prosperity too often leads away from God, but it is the divine intention that it should lead to God. Revivals come mostly in times of panic.

Rev. 3:19; Heb. 12:6, 10, 11. The chastisements of God are sometimes for the purpose of bringing His wandering children back to repentance.

2 Tim. 2:24, 25. God oftentimes uses the loving, Christian reproof of a brother to be the means of bringing us back to God.

IV. THE RESULTS OF REPENTANCE

1. All Heaven Is Made Glad.

Luke 15:7, 10. Joy in heaven, and in the presence of the angels of God. Makes glad the heart of God, and sets the bells of heaven ringing. Who are those "in the presence of the angels of God"? Do the departed loved ones know anything about it?

2. It Brings Pardon and Forgiveness of Sin.

Isa. 55:7; Acts 3:19. Outside of repentance the prophets and apostles know of no way of securing pardon. No sacrifices, nor religious ceremonies can secure it. Not that repentance merits forgiveness, but it is a condition of it. Repentance qualifies a man for a pardon, but it does not entitle him to it.

3. The Holy Spirit Is Poured Out Upon the Penitent.

Acts 2:38—"Repent . . . and ye shall receive the gift of the Holy Ghost." Impenitence keeps back the full incoming of the Spirit into the heart.

B. FAITH

B. FAITH

I. THE IMPORTANCE OF THE DOCTRINE

Faith is fundamental in Christian creed and conduct. It was the one thing which above all others Christ recognized as the paramount virtue. The Syrophoenician woman (Matt. 15) had perserverance; the centurion (Matt. 8), humility; the blind man (Mark 10), earnestness. But what Christ saw and rewarded in each of these cases was faith. Faith is the foundation of Peter's spiritual temple (2 Pet. 1:5-7); and first in Paul's trinity of graces (1 Cor. 13:13). In faith all the other graces find their source.

II. THE DEFINITION OF FAITH

Faith is used in the Scriptures in a general and in a particular sense.

1. Its General Meaning

a) KNOWLEDGE

Psa. 9:10—"And they that know thy name will put their trust in thee " Rom. 10:17—"So then faith cometh by hearing, and hearing by the word of God." Faith is not believing a thing without evidence; on the contrary faith rests upon the best of evidence, namely, the Word of God. An act of faith denotes a manifestation of the intelligence: "How shall they believe in him of whom they have not heard?" Faith is no blind act of the soul; it is not a leap in the dark. Such a thing as believing with the heart without the head is out of the question. A man may believe with his head without believing with his heart; but he cannot believe with his heart without believing with his head too. The heart, in the Scriptures, means the whole man—intellect, sensibilities, and will. "As a man *thinketh* in his heart." "Why *reason* ye these things in your hearts?"

b) ASSENT

Mark 12:32—"And the scribe said unto him, Well, Master, thou hast said the truth." So was it with the faith which Christ demanded in His miracles: "Believe ye that I am able to do this?" "Yea, Lord." There must not only be the knowledge that Jesus is able to save, and that He is the Saviour of the world; there must be also an assent of the heart to all these claims. Those who, *receiving* Christ to be all that He claimed to be, *believed* in Him, became thereby sons of God (John 1:12).

c) APPROPRIATION

John 1:12; 2:24. There must be an appropriation of the things which we know and assent to concerning the Christ and His work. Intelligent perception is not faith. A man may know Christ as divine, and yet aside from that reject him as Saviour. Knowledge affirms the reality of these things but neither accepts nor rejects them. Nor is assent faith. There is an assent of the mind which does not convey a surrender of the heart and affections.

Faith is the consent of the will to the assent of the understanding. Faith always has in it the idea of action—movement towards its object. It is the soul leaping forth to embrace and appropriate the Christ in whom it believes. It first says: "My Lord and my God," and then falls down and worships.

A distinction between believing about Christ and on Christ is made in John 8:30, 31, R. V.—"Many believed *on* him . . . Jesus therefore said to those Jews that had believed *him.*"

2. *The Meaning of Faith in Particular*

a) WHEN USED IN CONNECTION WITH THE NAME OF GOD

Heb. 11:6—"But without faith it is impossible to please him; for he that cometh to God must believe that he is, and that he is a rewarder of them that diligently seek him." Also Acts 27:22-25; Rom. 4:19-21 with Gen. 15:4-6. There can be no dealings with the invisible God unless there is absolute faith in His existence. We must believe in His reality, even though He is unseen. But we must believe even more than the fact of His existence; namely, that He is a rewarder, that He will assuredly honor with definite blessing those who approach unto Him in prayer. Importunity will, of course, be needed (Luke 11:5-10).

There must be confidence in the Word of God also. Faith believes all that God says as being absolutely true, even though circumstances seem to be against its fulfillment.

b) WHEN USED IN CONNECTION WITH THE PERSON AND WORK OF CHRIST

Recall the three elements in faith, and apply them here.

First, there must be a *knowledge* of the claims of Christ as to His person and mission in the world: As to His person—that He is Deity, John 9:35-38; 10:30; Phil. 2:6-11. As to His work—Matt. 20:28; 26:26-28; Luke 24:27, 44.

Second, there must be an *assent* to all these claims, John 16:30; 20:28; Matt. 16:16; John 6:68, 69.

Third, there must be a personal *appropriation* of Christ as being all that He claims to be, John 1:12; 8:21, 24; 5:24. There must be surrender to a person, and not mere faith in a creed. Faith in a doctrine must lead to faith in a person, and that person Jesus

Christ, if salvation is to be the result of such belief. So Martha was led to substitute faith in a doctrine for faith in a person (John 11:25).

It is such faith—consisting of knowledge, assent, and appropriation—that saves. This is believing with the heart (Rom. 10:9, 10).

c) WHEN USED IN CONNECTION WITH PRAYER

Three passages may be used to set forth this relationship: 1 John 5:14, 15; James 1:5-7, Mark 11:24. There must be no hesitation which balances between belief and unbelief, and inclines toward the latter—tossed one moment upon the shore of faith and hope, the next tossed back again into the abyss of unbelief. To "doubt" means to reason whether or not the thing concerning which you are making request can be done (Acts 10:20; Rom. 4:20). Such a man only conjectures; he does not really believe. Real faith thanks God for the thing asked for, if that thing is in accord with the will of God, even before it receives it (Mark 11:24). Note the slight: "that man."

We must recognize the fact that knowledge, assent, and appropriation exist here also. We must understand the promises on which we base our prayer; we must believe that they are worth their full face value; and then step out upon them, thereby giving substance to that which, at the moment may be unseen, and, perchance, nonexistent, so far as our knowledge and vision are concerned, but which to faith is a splendid reality.

d) WHEN USED IN CONNECTION WITH THE WORD AND PROMISE OF GOD

First, we should know whether the particular promise in question is intended for us in particular. There is a difference in a promise being written *for* us and *to* us. There are dispensational aspects to many of the promises in the Bible, therefore we must rightly divide, apportion, and appropriate the Word of God (cf. 1 Cor. 10:32).

Second, when once we are persuaded that a promise is *for* us, we must believe that God means all He says in that promise; we must assent to all its truth; we must not diminish nor discount it. God will not, cannot lie (Titus 1:2).

Third, we must appropriate and act upon the promises. Herein lies the difference between belief and faith. Belief is mental; faith adds the volitional; we may have belief without the will, but not faith. Belief is a realm of thought; faith is a sphere of action. Belief lives in the study; faith comes out into the market-places and the streets. Faith substantiates belief—gives substance, life, reality, activity to it (Heb. 11:1). Faith puts belief into active service, and connects possibilities with actualities. Faith is acting upon what you believe; it is appropriation. Faith counts every promise valid, and gilt-edged (Heb. 11:11); no trial can shake it (11:35); it is so absolute that it survives the loss of anything (11:17). For illustration, see 1 Kings 18:41-43.

3. The Relation of Faith to Works

There is no merit in faith alone. It is not mere faith that saves, but faith in Christ. Faith in any other saviour but Christ will not save. Faith in any other gospel than that of the New Testament will not save (Gal. 1:8, 9).

There is no contradiction between Paul and James touching the matter of faith and works (cf. James 2:14-26; Rom. 4:1-12). Paul is looking at the matter from the Godward side, and asserts that we are justified, in the sight of God, *meritoriously,* without absolutely any works on our part. James considers the matter from the manward side, and asserts that we are justified, in the sight of man, *evidentially,* by works, and not by faith alone (2:24). In James it is not the *ground* of justification. as in Paul, but the *demonstration.* See under Justification, p. 159.

III. THE SOURCE OF FAITH

There are two sides to this phase of the subject—a divine and a human side.

1. It Is the Work of the Triune God.

God the Father: Rom. 12:3; 1 Cor. 12. This is true of faith both in its beginning (Phil. 1:29) and its development (1 Cor. 12). Faith, then, is a gift of His grace.

God the Son: Heb. 12:2—"Looking unto Jesus the author and finisher of our faith." (Illustration, Matt. 14:30, 31—Peter taking his eyes off Christ.) 1 Cor. 12; Luke 17:5.

God the Spirit: Gal. 5:22; 1 Cor. 12:9. The Holy Spirit is the executive of the Godhead.

Why then, if faith is the work of the Godhead, are we responsible for not having it? God wills to work faith in all His creatures, and will do so if they do not resist His Holy Spirit. We are responsible, therefore, not so much for the lack of faith, but for resisting the Spirit who will create faith in our hearts if we will permit Him to do so.

2. There Is Also a Human Side to Faith.

Rom. 10:17—"So then faith cometh by hearing, and hearing by the word of God." (cf. the context, vv. 9-21.)   Acts 4:4—"Howbeit many of them which heard the word believed." In this instance the *spoken* word, the Gospel, is referred to; in other cases the written Word, the Scriptures, is referred to as being instrumental in producing faith. See also Gal. 3:2-5. It was a looking unto the promises of God that brought such faith into the heart of Abraham (Rom. 4:19).

Prayer also is an instrument in the development of faith. Luke is called the *human* Gospel because it makes so much of prayer, especially in connection with faith: 22:32—"But I have prayed for thee that thy faith fail not." 17:5—"And the apostles said unto the Lord, Increase our faith." See also Mark 9:24; Matt. 17:19-21.

Our faith grows by the use of the faith we already have. Luke 17:5, 6; Matt. 25:29.

IV. SOME RESULTS OF FAITH

1. We Are Saved By Faith.

We, of course, recall that the saving power of faith resides not in itself, but in the Almighty Saviour on whom it rests; so that, properly speaking, it is not so much faith, as it is faith in Christ that saves.

The whole of our salvation—past, present, and future, is dependent upon faith. Our acceptance of Christ (John 1:12); our justification (Rom. 5:1); our adoption (Gal. 3:26); our sanctification (Acts 26:18); our keeping (1 Pet. 1:5), indeed our whole salvation from start to finish is dependent upon faith.

2. Rest, Peace, Assurance, Joy

Isa. 26:3; Phil. 4:6; Rom. 5:1; Heb. 4:1-3; John 14:1; 1 Pet. 1:8. Fact, faith, feeling—this is God's order. Satan would reverse this order and put feeling before faith, and thus confuse the child of God. We should march in accord with God's order: Fact leads, Faith with its eye on Fact, following, and Feeling with the eye on Faith bringing up the rear. All goes well as long as this order is observed. But the moment Faith turns his back on Fact, and looks at Feeling, the procession wabbles. Steam is of main importance, not for sounding the whistle, but for moving the wheels, and if there is a lack of steam we shall not remedy it by attempting by our own effort to move the piston or blow the whistle, but by more water in the boiler, and more fire under it. Feed Faith with Facts, not with Feeling.—*A. T. Pierson*.

3. Do Exploits Through Faith

Heb. 11:32-34; Matt. 21:21; John 14:12. Note the wonderful things done by the men of faith as recorded in the eleventh chapter of Hebrews. Read vv. 32-40. Jesus attributes a kind of omnipotence to faith. The disciple, by faith, will be able to do greater things than his Master. Here is a mighty Niagara of power for the believer. The great question for the Christian to answer is not "What can I do?" but "How much can I believe?" for "all things are possible to him that believeth."

C. REGENERATION, OR THE NEW BIRTH

I. ITS NATURE
1. NOT BAPTISM
2. NOT REFORMATION
3. A SPIRITUAL QUICKENING
4. AN IMPARTATION OF A DIVINE NATURE
5. A NEW AND DIVINE IMPULSE

II. ITS NECESSITY
1. UNIVERSAL
2. THE SINFUL CONDITION OF MAN DEMANDS IT
3. THE HOLINESS OF GOD DEMANDS IT

III. THE MEANS
1. THE DIVINE SIDE
2. THE HUMAN SIDE
3. THE MEANS USED

C. REGENERATION, OR THE NEW BIRTH

It is of the utmost importance that we have a clear understanding of this vital doctrine. By regeneration we are admitted into the kingdom of God. There is no other way of becoming a Christian but by being born from above. The doctrine, then, is the door of entrance into Christian discipleship. He who does not enter here, does not enter at all.

I. THE NATURE OF REGENERATION

Too often do we find other things substituted by man for God's appointed means of entrance into the kingdom of heaven. It will be well for us then to look, first of all, at some of these substitutes.

1. Regeneration Is Not Baptism.

It is claimed that John 3:5—"Except a man be born of water and of the Spirit," and Titus 3:5—"The washing of regeneration," teach that regeneration may occur in connection with baptism. These passages, however, are to be understood in a figurative sense, as meaning the cleansing power of the Word of God. See also

Eph. 5:26—"With the washing of water by [or in] the word"; John 15:3—"Clean through the word." That the Word of God is an agent in regeneration is clear from James 1:18, and 1 Pet. 1:23.

If baptism and regeneration were identical, why should the Apostle Paul seem to make so little of that rite (1 Cor. 4:15, and compare with it 1 Cor. 1:14)? In the first passage Paul asserts that he had *begotten* them through the Gospel; and in 1:14 he declares that he *baptized none of them* save Crispus and Gaius. Could he thus speak of baptism if it had been the means through which they had been begotten again? Simon Magus was baptized (Acts 8), but was he saved? Cornelius (Acts 11) was saved even before he was baptized.

2. Reformation Is Not Regeneration.

Regeneration is not a natural forward step in man's development; it is a supernatural act of God; it is a spiritual crisis. It is not evolution, but involution—the communication of a new life. It is a revolution—a change of direction resulting from that life. Herein lies the danger in psychology, and in the statistics regarding the number of conversions during the period of adolescence. The danger lies in the tendency to make regeneration a natural phenomenon, an advanced step in the development of a human life, instead of regarding it as a crisis. Such a psychological view of regeneration denies man's sin, his need of Christ, the necessity of an atonement, and the regenerating work of the Holy Spirit.

3. Regeneration Is a Spiritual Quickening, a New Birth.

Regeneration is the impartation of a new and divine life; a new creation; the production of a new thing. It is Gen. 1:26 over again. It is not the old nature altered, reformed, or re-invigorated, but a new birth from above. This is the teaching of such passages as John 3:3-7; 5:21; Eph. 2:1, 10; 2 Cor. 5:17.

By nature man is dead in sin (Eph. 2:1); the new birth imparts to him new life—the life of God, so that henceforth he is as those that are alive from the dead; he has passed out of death into life (John 5:24).

4. It Is the Impartation of a New Nature—God's Nature.

In regeneration we are made partakers of the divine nature (2 Pet. 1:4). We have put on the new man, which after God is created in holiness and righteousness (Eph. 4:24; Col. 3:10). Christ now lives in the believer (Gal. 2:20). God's seed now abides in him (1 John 3:9). So that henceforth the believer is possessed of two natures (Gal. 5:17).

5. A New and Divine Impulse Is Given to the Believer.

Thus regeneration is a crisis with a view to a process. A new governing power comes into the regenerate man's life by which he is enabled to become holy in experience: "Old things are passed away; behold all things are become new" (2 Cor. 5:17). See also Acts 16:14, and Ezek. 36:25-27; 1 John 3:6-9.

II. THE IMPERATIVE NECESSITY OF THE NEW BIRTH

1. The Necessity Is Universal.

The need is as far-reaching as sin and the human race: "Except a man [lit. anybody] be born again, he cannot see the kingdom of God" (John 3:3, cf. v. 5). No age, sex, position, condition exempts anyone from this necessity. Not to be born again is to be lost. There is no substitute for the new birth: "Neither circumcision availeth anything, nor uncircumcision, but a new creature" (Gal. 6:15). The absolute necessity is clearly stated by our Lord: whatever is born of the flesh, must be born again of the Spirit (John 3:3-7).

2. The Sinful Condition of Man Demands It.

John 3:6—"That which is born of the flesh is flesh"—and it can never, by any human process, become anything else. "Can the Ethiopian change his skin, or the leopard his spots? then may ye also do good that are accustomed to do evil" (Jer. 13:23). "They that are in the flesh cannot please God" (Rom. 8:8); in our "flesh dwelleth no good thing" (Rom. 7:18). The mind is darkened so that we cannot apprehend spiritual truth; we need a renewing of the mind (Rom. 12:2). The heart is deceitful, and does not welcome God; we need to be pure in heart to see God. There is no thought of God before the eyes of the natural man; we need a change in nature that we may be counted among those who "thought upon his name." No education or culture can bring about such a needed change. God alone can do it.

3. The Holiness of God Demands It.

If without holiness no man shall see the Lord (Heb. 12:14); and if holiness is not to be attained by any natural development or self-effort, then the regeneration of our nature is absolutely necessary. This change, which enables us to be holy, takes place when we are born again.

Man is conscious that he does not have this holiness by nature; he is conscious, too, that he must have it in order to appear before God (Ezra 9:15). The Scriptures corroborate this consciousness in man, and, still further, state the necessity of such a righteousness with which to appear before God. In the new birth alone is the beginning of such a life to be found. To live the life of God we must have the nature of God.

III. THE MEANS OF REGENERATION

1. Regeneration Is a Divine Work.

We are "born, not of blood, nor of the will of the flesh, nor of the will of man, *but of God"* (John 1:13). It was of His own will he begat us (Jas. 1:18): Our regeneration is a creative act on the part of God, not a reforming process on the part of man. It is not brought about by natural descent, for all we get from that is "flesh." It is not by natural choice, for the human will is impotent. Nor is it by self-effort, or any human generative principle. Nor is it by the blood of any ceremonial sacrifices. It is not by pedigree or natural generation. It is altogether and absolutely the work of God. Practically speaking, we have no more to do with our second birth, than we had to do with our first birth.

The Holy Spirit is the Divine Agent in our regeneration. For this reason it is called the "renewing of the Holy Ghost" (Tit. 3:5). We are "born of the Spirit" (John 3:5).

2. And Yet There Is a Human Side to the Work.

John 1:12 and 13 bring together these two thoughts—the divine and the human in regeneration: Those who *received* Him (i. e., Christ) . . . were born *of God*. The two great problems connected with regeneration are the efficiency of God and the activity of man.

a) MAN IS REGENERATED BY MEANS OF THE ACCEPTANCE OF THE MESSAGE OF THE GOSPEL.

God begat us by "the word of truth" (James 1:18). We are "born again," says Peter (1 Peter 1:23), "of incorruptible seed, by the word of God." We are "begotten through the gospel" (1 Cor. 4:15). These scriptures teach us that regeneration takes place in the heart of man when he reads or hears the Word of God, or the Gospel message, or both, and, because of the Spirit working in the Word as well as in the heart of man, the man opens his heart and receives that message as the Word of life to his soul. The truth is illuminated, as is also the mind, by the Spirit; the man yields to the truth, and is born again. Of course, even here, we must remember that it is the Lord who must open our hearts just as He opened the heart of Lydia (Acts 16:14). But the Word must be believed and received by man. 1 Pet. 1:25.

b) MAN IS REGENERATED BY THE PERSONAL ACCEPTANCE OF JESUS CHRIST.

This is the clear teaching of John 1:12, 13 and Gal. 3:26. We become "children of God by faith in Christ Jesus." When a man, believing in the claims of Jesus Christ receives Him to be all that He claimed to be—that man is born again.

"Man therefore is not wholly passive at the time of his regeneration. He is passive only as to the change of his ruling disposition. With regard to the exercise of this disposition he is active. A dead man cannot assist in his own resurrection, it is true; but he may, and can, like Lazarus, obey Christ's command, and 'Come forth!' "

Psa. 90:16, 17 illustrates both the divine and human part: "Let *thy* work appear unto thy servants," and then "the work of *our* hands establish thou it." God's work appears first, then man's. So Phil. 2:12, 13.

D. JUSTIFICATION

I. ITS MEANING
1. RELATIVELY
2. SCRIPTURALLY
3. PARDON—RIGHTEOUSNESS

II. ITS METHOD
1. NOT BY LAW
2. BY GOD'S FREE GRACE
3. THE BLOOD OF CHRIST
4. FAITH

D. JUSTIFICATION

I. THE MEANING OF JUSTIFICATION

1. Relatively

It is a change in a man's relation or standing before God. It has to do with relations that have been disturbed by sin, and these relations are personal. It is a change from guilt and condemnation to acquittal and acceptance. Regeneration has to do with the change of the believer's nature; justification, with the change of his standing before God. Regeneration is subjective; justification is objective. The former has to do with man's state; the latter, with his standing.

2. According to the Language and Usage of the Scriptures

According to Deut. 25:1 it means to declare, or to cause to appear innocent or righteous; Rom. 4:2-8: to reckon righteous; Psa. 32:2: not to impute iniquity. One thing at least is clear from these verses, and that is, that to justify does not mean to *make* one righteous. Neither the Hebrew nor Greek words will bear such meaning. To justify means to set forth as righteous; to declare righteous in a legal sense; to put a person in a right relation. It does not deal, at least not directly, with character or conduct; it is a question of relationship. Of course both character and conduct will be conditioned and controlled by this relationship. No real righteousness on the part of the person justified is to be asserted, but that person is declared to be righteous and is treated as such. Strictly speaking then, justification is the judicial act of God whereby those who put faith in Christ are declared righteous in His eyes, and free from guilt and punishment.

3. Justification Consists of Two Elements

a) THE FORGIVENESS OF SIN, AND THE REMOVAL OF ITS GUILT AND PUNISHMENT

It is difficult for us to understand God's feeling towards sin. To us forgiveness seems easy, largely because we are indifferent towards sin. But to a holy God it is different. Even men sometimes find it hard to forgive when wronged. Nevertheless God gladly forgives.

Micah 7:18, 19—"Who is a God like unto thee, that pardoneth iniquity, and passeth by the transgression of the remnant of his heritage? he retaineth not his anger forever, because he delighteth in mercy . . . he will subdue our iniquities; and thou wilt cast all their sins into the depths of the sea." See also Psa. 130:4. What a wondrous forgiveness!

Forgiveness may be considered as the cessation of the moral anger and resentment of God against sin; or as a release from the guilt of sin which oppresses the conscience; or, again, as a remission of the punishment of sin, which is eternal death.

In justification, then, all our sins are forgiven, and the guilt and punishment thereof removed (Acts 13:38, 39; Rom. 8:1). God sees the believer as without sin and guilt in Christ (Num. 23:21; Rom. 8:33, 34).

b) THE IMPUTATION OF CHRIST'S RIGHTEOUSNESS, AND RESTORATION TO GOD'S FAVOR

The forgiven sinner is not like the discharged prisoner who has served out his term and is discharged from further punishment, but with no rights of citizenship. No, justification means much more than acquittal. The repentant sinner receives back in his pardon, the full rights of citizenship. The Society of Friends called themselves Friends, not because they were friends one to another but because, being justified, they counted themselves friends of God as was Abraham (2 Chron. 20:7, James 2:23). There is also the imputation of the righteousness of Jesus Christ to the sinner. His righteousness is "unto all and upon all them that believe" (Rom. 3:22). See Rom. 5:17-21; 1 Cor. 1:30. For illustration, see Philemon 18.

II. THE METHOD OF JUSTIFICATION

1. Negatively: Not By Works of the Law

Rom. 3:20—"Therefore by the deeds of the law there shall no flesh be justified in his sight; for by the law is the knowledge of sin." "Therefore" implies that a judicial trial has taken place and a judgment pronounced. At the bar of God no man can be counted righteous in His sight because of his obedience to law. The burden of the Epistle to the Romans is to set forth this great truth. As a means of establishing right relations with God the law is totally insufficient. There is no salvation *by* character. What men need is salvation *from* character.

The reason why the law cannot justify is here stated: "For by the law is the knowledge of sin." The law can open the sinner's eyes to his sin, but it cannot remove it. Indeed, it was never intended to remove it, but to intensify it. The law simply defines sin, and makes it sinful, yea, exceedingly sinful, but it does not emancipate from it. Gal. 3:10 gives us a further reason why justification cannot take place by obedience to the law. The law demands perfect and continual obedience: "Cursed is every one that continueth not in all things which are written in the book of the law to do them." No man can render a perfect and perpetual obedience, therefore justification by obedience to the law is impossible. The only thing the law can do is to stop the mouth of every man, and declare him guilty before God (Rom. 3:19, 20).

Gal. 2:16, and 3:10, Rom. 3:28, are very explicit in their denial of justification by law. It is a question of Moses or Christ, works or faith, law or promise, doing or believing, wages or a free gift.

2. Positively: By God's Free Grace—The Origin or Source of Justification

Rom. 3:24—"Being justified freely by his grace through the redemption that is in Christ Jesus." "Freely" denotes that it is granted without anything done on our part to merit or deserve it.

From the contents of the epistle up to this point it must be clearly evident that if men, sinful and sinning, are to be justified at all, it must be "by his free grace."

3. By the Blood of Jesus Christ—The Ground of Justification

Rom. 3:24—"Being justified . . . through the redemption that is in Christ Jesus." 5:9—"Much more then, being now justified by his blood." 2 Cor. 5:21 (R. V.)—"Him who knew no sin he made to be sin on our behalf; that we might become the righteousness of God in him." The bloodshedding of Christ is here connected with justification. It is impossible to get rid of this double idea from this passage. The sacrifices of the Old Testament were more than a meaningless butchery—"Without shedding of blood is no remission" of sin (Heb. 9:22). The great sacrifice of the New Testament, the death of Jesus Christ, was something more than the death of a martyr—men are "justified by his blood" (Rom. 5:9).

4. By Believing in Jesus Christ—The Condition of Justification

Gal. 2:16—"Knowing that a man is not justified by the works of the law, but by the faith of Jesus Christ," or as the Revised Version margin has it: "But only through faith in Jesus Christ." Rom. 3:26—"To declare, I say, at this time his righteousness; that he might be just, and the justifier of him which believeth in Jesus." "Him that believeth in Jesus" is contrasted with "as many as are of the works of the law" (Gal. 3:10). When Paul in Romans 4:5 says: "Now to him that worketh not, but believeth on him that justifieth the ungodly," he gives the deathblow to Jewish righteousness. "His faith is counted for righteousness"; that pictures the man who, despairing of all dependence upon his works, casts himself unreservedly upon the mercy of God, as set forth in Jesus Christ, for his justification. Thus it comes to pass that "all that believe are justified from all things, from which ye could not be justified by the law of Moses" (Acts 13:39). The best of men need to be saved by faith in Jesus Christ, and the worst need only that. As there is no difference in the need, neither is there in the method of its application. On this common ground all saved sinners meet, and will stand forever. The first step, then, in justification is to despair of works; the second, to believe on him that justifieth the ungodly.

We are not to slight good works, for they have their place, but they follow, not precede justification. The workingman is not the justified man, but the justified man is the workingman. Works are not meritorious, but they meet with their reward in the life of the justified. The tree *shows* its life by its fruits, but it was alive before the fruit or even the leaves appeared. (See under Faith, p. 148, for further suggestions regarding the relation between faith and works.)

Summing up we may say that men are justified *judicially* by God (Rom. 8:33); *meritoriously* by Christ (Isa. 53:11); *mediately* by faith (Rom. 5:1); *evidentially* by works (James 2:14, 18-24).

E. ADOPTION

I. THE MEANING OF ADOPTION
1. ETYMOLOGICALLY
2. SCRIPTURALLY

II. THE TIME OF ADOPTION
1. ETERNAL
2. WHEN ONE BELIEVES
3. COMPLETE AT RESURRECTION

III. THE BLESSINGS OF ADOPTION
1. FILIAL
2. EXPERIMENTAL

IV. SOME EVIDENCES OF SONSHIP
1. GUIDANCE
2. CONFIDENCE
3. ACCESS
4. LOVE FOR THE BRETHREN
5. OBEDIENCE

E. ADOPTION

Regeneration begins the new life in the soul; justification deals with the new attitude of God towards that soul, or perhaps better, of that soul towards God; adoption admits man into the family of God with filial joy. Regeneration has to do with our change in nature; justification, with our change in standing; sanctification, with our change in character; adoption, with our change in position. In regeneration the believer becomes a child of God (John 1:12, 13); in adoption, the believer, already a child, receives a place as an adult son; thus the child becomes a son, the minor becomes an adult (Gal. 4:1-7).

I. THE MEANING OF ADOPTION

Adoption means *the placing of a son*. It is a legal metaphor as regeneration is a physical one. It is a Roman word, for adoption was hardly, if at all, known among the Jews. It means the taking by one man of the son of another to be his son, so that that son has the same position and all the advantages of a son by birth. The word is Pauline, not Johannine. The word is never once used of Christ. It is used of the believer when questions of rights, privileges, and heirship are involved. It is peculiarly a Pauline word (Gal. 4:5; Rom. 8:15, 23; 9:4; Eph. 1:5). John uses the word "children," not "sons," because he is always speaking of sonship from the standpoint of nature, growth, and likeness (cf. 1 John 3:1, R. V.).

Exodus 2:10 and Heb. 11:24 furnish two splendid illustrations of the Scriptural sense and use of adoption.

II. THE TIME WHEN ADOPTION TAKES PLACE

1. In a Certain Sense It Is Eternal in Its Nature

Eph. 1:4, 5—Before the foundation of the world we were predestinated unto the adoption of children. We need to distinguish between the foreordaining to adoption, and the actual act of adoption which took place when we believed in Christ. Just as the incarnation was foreordained, and yet took place in time; and just as the Lamb was slain from before the foundation of the world, and yet actually only on Calvary. Why then mention this eternal aspect of adoption? To exclude works and to show that our salvation had its origin solely in the grace of God (Rom. 9:11; 11:5, 6). Just as if we should adopt a child it would be a wholly gracious act on our part.

2. It Takes Place the Moment One Believes in Jesus Christ

1 John 3:2—"Beloved, now are we the sons of God." Gal. 3:26—"For ye are all the children of God by faith in Christ Jesus." See also John 1:12. Sonship is now the present possession of the believer. Strange as it may be, inconceivable as it may seem, it is nevertheless true. The world may not think so (I John 3:1), but God says so, and the Christian believing it, exclaims, "I'm a child of the King." Formerly we were slaves; now we are sons.

3. Our Sonship Will Be Completed at the Resurrection and Coming Again of Our Lord Jesus Christ.

Rom. 8:23—"Waiting for the adoption, to wit, the redemption of our body." Here in this world we are *incognito;* we are not recognized as sons of God. But some day we shall throw off this disguise (2 Cor. 5:10). It doth not appear, it hath not yet appeared what we shall be; the revelation of the sons of God is reserved for a future day. See also 1 John 3:1-3.

III. THE BLESSINGS OF ADOPTION

The blessings of adoption are too numerous to mention save in the briefest way. Some of them are as follows:

Objects of God's peculiar love (John 17:23), and His fatherly care (Luke 12:27-33).

We have the family name (1 John 3:1; Eph. 3:14, 15), the family likeness (Rom. 8:29); family love (John 13:35; 1 John 3:14); a filial spirit (Rom. 8:15; Gal. 4:6); a family service (John 14:23, 24; 15:8).

We receive fatherly chastisement (Heb. 12:5-11); fatherly comfort (Isa. 66:13; 2 Cor. 1:4), and an inheritance (1 Pet. 1:3-5; Rom. 8:17).

IV. SOME EVIDENCES OF SONSHIP

Those who are adopted into God's family:
Are led by the Spirit (Rom. 8:4; Gal. 5:18).
Have a childlike confidence in God (Gal. 4:5, 6).
Have liberty of access (Eph. 3:12).
Have love for the brethren (1 John 2:9-11; 5:1).
Are obedient (1 John 5:1-3).

F. SANCTIFICATION

I. ITS MEANING
1. NEGATIVELY—SEPARATION FROM EVIL
2. POSITIVELY—DEDICATION UNTO GOD
3. USED OF THE DIVINE NATURE

II. WHEN IT TAKES PLACE
1. INSTANT
2. PROGRESSIVE
3. COMPLETE

III. THE MEANS
1. DIVINE
2. HUMAN
3. MEANS USED

F. SANCTIFICATION

If regeneration has to do with our nature, justification with our standing, and adoption with our position, then sanctification has to do with our character and conduct. In justification we are declared righteous in order that, in sanctification, we may become righteous. Justification is what God does for us, while sanctification is what God does in us. Justification puts us into a right relationship with God, while sanctification exhibits the fruit of that relationship—a life separated from a sinful world and dedicated unto God.

I. THE MEANING OF SANCTIFICATION

Two thoughts are prominent in this definition: separation from evil, and dedication unto God and His service.

1. Separation From Evil

2 Chron. 29:5, 15-18—"Sanctify now yourselves, and sanctify the house of the Lord God . . . and carry forth the filthiness out of the holy places. . . . And the priests went into the inner part of the house of the Lord, to cleanse it, and brought out all the

uncleanness. . . . Then they went in to Hezekiah the king, and said, We have cleansed all the house of the Lord." 1 Thess. 4:3—"For this is the will of God, even your sanctification, that ye should abstain from fornication." See also Heb. 9:3; Exod. 19:20-22; Lev. 11:44.

It is evident from these scriptures that sanctification has to do with the turning away from all that is sinful and that is defiling to both soul and body.

2. Separation or Dedication Unto God

In this sense whatever is set apart from a profane to a sacred use, whatever is devoted exclusively to the service of God, is sanctified. So it follows that a man may "sanctify his house to be holy unto the Lord," or he may "sanctify unto the Lord some part of a field of his possession" (Lev. 27:14, 16). So also the first-born of all the children were sanctified unto the Lord (Num. 8:17). Even the Son of God Himself, in so far as He was set apart by the Father and sent into the world to do God's will, was sanctified (John 10:36). Whenever a thing or person is separated from the common relations of life in order to be devoted to the sacred, such is said to be sanctified.

3. It Is Used of God.

Whenever the sacred writers desire to show that the Lord is absolutely removed from all that is sinful and unholy, and that He is absolutely holy in Himself they speak of Him as being sanctified: "When I shall be sanctified in you before their eyes" (Ezek. 36:23).

II. THE TIME OF SANCTIFICATION

Sanctification may be viewed as past, present, and future; or instantaneous, progressive, and complete.

1. Instantaneous Sanctification

1 Cor. 6:11—"And such were some of you: but ye are washed, but ye are sanctified, but ye are justified in the name of the Lord Jesus, and by the Spirit of our God." Heb. 10:10, 14—"By the

which will we are sanctified through the offering of the body of Jesus Christ once for all. . . . For by one offering he hath perfected forever them that are sanctified." By the death of Jesus Christ the sanctification of the believer takes place at once. The very moment a man believes in Christ he is sanctified, that is, in this first sense: he is separated from sin and separated unto God. For this reason all through the New Testament believers are called saints (1 Cor. 1:2, R. V.; Rom. 1:7, R. V.). If a man is not a saint he is not a Christian; if he is a Christian he is a saint. In some quarters people are canonized after they are dead; the New Testament canonizes believers while they are alive. Note how that in 1 Cor. 6:11 "sanctified" is put before "justified." The believer grows *in* sanctification rather than *into* sanctification out of something else. By a simple act of faith in Christ the believer is at once put into a state of sanctification. Every Christian is a sanctified man. The same act that ushers him into the state of justification admits him at once into the state of sanctification, in which he is to grow until he reaches the fulness of the measure of the stature of Christ.

2. Progressive Sanctification

Justification differs from sanctification thus: the former is an instantaneous act with no progression; while the latter is a crisis with a view to a process—an act, which is instantaneous and which at the same time carries with it the idea of growth unto completion.

2 Pet. 3:18—"But grow in [the] grace, and in the knowledge of our Lord and Saviour Jesus Christ." 2 Cor. 3:18—We "are transformed into the same image from glory to glory, even as from the Lord the Spirit." The tense is interesting here: We are being transformed from one degree of character, or glory, to another. It is because sanctification is progressive, a growth, that we are exhorted to "increase and abound" (1 Thess. 3:12), and to "abound more and more" (4:1, 10) in the graces of the Christian life. The fact that there is always danger of contracting defilement by contact with a sinful world, and that there is, in the life of the true Christian, an ever increasing sense of duty and an ever-deepening consciousness of sin, necessitates a continual growth and development in the graces and virtues of the believer's life. There is such a thing as "perfecting holiness" (2 Cor. 7:1). God's gift to the church of pastors and teachers is for the purpose of the perfecting

of the saints in the likeness of Christ *until,* at last, they attain unto the fulness of the divine standard, even Jesus Christ (Eph. 4:11-15). Holiness is not a mushroom growth; it is not the thing of an hour; it grows as the coral reef grows: little by little, degree by degree. See also Phil. 3:10-15.

3. Complete and Final Sanctification

1 Thess. 5:23, R. V.—"And the God of peace himself sanctify you wholly; and may your spirit and soul and body be preserved entire, without blame at the coming of our Lord Jesus Christ." "Wholly" means complete in every part, perfect in every respect, whether it refers to the Church as a whole, or to the individual believer. Some day the believer is to be complete in all departments of Christian character—no Christian grace missing. Complete in the "spirit" which links him with heaven; in the "body" which links him with earth; in the "soul" as being that on which heaven and earth play. Maturity in each separate element of Christian character: body, soul, and spirit.

This blessing of entire and complete sanctification is to take place when Christ comes: 1 Thess. 3:13—"To the end that he may establish your hearts unblameable in holiness before God, even our Father, at the coming of our Lord Jesus Christ with all his saints." It is when we shall see Him that we shall be like Him (1 John 3:2). How explicitly Paul puts the matter in Phil. 3:12-14, R. V. —"Not that I have already obtained, or am already made perfect: but I press on, if so be that I may lay hold on that for which also I was laid hold on by Christ Jesus. Brethren, I count not myself yet to have laid hold: but one thing I do, forgetting the things which are behind, and stretching forward to the things which are before, I press on toward the goal unto the prize of the high calling of God in Christ Jesus."

III. THE MEANS OF SANCTIFICATION

How are men sanctified? What means are used, and what agencies employed to make men holy and conform them into the likeness of Christ? The agencies and means are both divine and human: both God and man contributing and co-operating towards this desired end.

1. From the Divine Side: It Is the Work of the Triune God.

a) GOD THE FATHER

1 Thess. 5:23, 24, R. V.—"And the God of peace himself sanctify you wholly. . . . Faithful is he that calleth you, who will also do it." God's work is here contrasted with human efforts to achieve the preceding injunctions. Just as in Hebrews 12:2, and Philippians 1:6, the Beginner of faith is also the Finisher; so is it here; consequently the end and aim of every exhortation is but to strengthen faith in God who is able to accomplish these things for us. Of course there is a sense in which the believer is responsible for his progress in the Christian life (Phil. 3:12, 13), yet it is nevertheless true that, after all, it is the divine grace which works all in him (Phil. 2:12, 13). We cannot purify ourselves, but we can yield to God and then the purity will come. The "God of peace," He who reconciles us—is the One who sanctifies us. It is as if the apostle said: "God, by His mighty power will do for you what I, by my admonitions, and you by your own efforts, cannot do." See also John 17:17—"Sanctify them through thy truth." Christ addresses God as the One who is to sanctify the disciples.

b) JESUS CHRIST THE SON

Heb. 10:10, R. V.—"By which will we have been sanctified through the offering of the body of Jesus Christ once for all." The death of Jesus Christ separates the believer from sin and the world, and sets him apart as redeemed and dedicated to the service of God. This same truth, namely, the sanctification of the Church as based on the sacrificial death of Christ, is set forth in Eph. 5:25, 27 —"Christ loved the church, and gave himself up for it; that he might sanctify it." Christ is "made unto us . . . sanctification" (1 Cor. 1:30). See also Heb. 13:12, R. V.

c) THE HOLY SPIRIT SANCTIFIES.

1 Pet. 1:2—"Elect according to the foreknowledge of God the Father, through sanctification of the Spirit." 2 Thess. 2:13—" . . . because God hath from the beginning chosen you to salvation through sanctification of the Spirit and belief of the truth." The Holy Spirit seals, attests, and confirms the work of grace in the soul by producing the fruits of righteousness therein. It is the

Spirit of life in Christ Jesus who gives us freedom from the law of sin and death (Rom. 8:2). He is called the *Holy* Spirit, not only because He is absolutely holy Himself, but also because He produces that quality of soul-character in the believer. The Spirit is the executive of the Godhead for this very purpose. It is the Spirit's work to war against the lusts of the flesh and enable us to bring forth fruit unto holiness (Gal. 5:17-22). How wonderfully this truth is set forth in the contrast between the seventh and eighth chapters of Romans. Note the unsuccessful struggle of the former, and the victory of the latter. Note also that there is no mention of the Holy Spirit in the seventh, while He is mentioned about sixteen times in the eighth chapter. Herein lies the secret of failure and victory, sin and holiness.

2. From the Human Side

a) FAITH IN THE REDEMPTIVE WORK OF JESUS CHRIST

1 Cor. 1:30, R. V.—"But of him are ye in Christ Jesus, who was made unto us wisdom from God, and righteousness, and sanctification, and redemption." Christ is indeed all these things to us, but, in reality, He becomes such only as we appropriate Him for ourselves. Only as the believer, daily, yea, even momentarily, takes by faith the holiness of Jesus, His faith, His patience, His love, His grace, to be his own for the need of that very moment, can Christ, who by His death was made unto him sanctification in the instantaneous sense, become unto him sanctification in the progressive sense—producing in the believer His own life moment by moment. Herein lies the secret of a holy life—the momentary appropriation of Jesus Christ in all the riches of His grace for every need as it arises. The degree of our sanctification is the proportion of our appropriation of Christ. See also Acts 26:18.

b) THE STUDY OF THE SCRIPTURES AND OBEDIENCE THERETO

John 17:17—"Sanctify them through thy truth: thy word is truth." Eph. 5:26—"That he might sanctify and cleanse it [i. e., the Church] with the washing of water by the word." John 15:3— "Now ye are clean through the word which I have spoken unto you." Our sanctification is limited by our limitation in the knowledge of and our lack of obedience to the Word of God. How does the Word of God sanctify? By revealing sin; by awakening conscience; by revealing the character of Christ; by showing the example of Christ; by offering the influences and powers of the Holy Spirit, and by setting forth spiritual motives and ideals. There is no power like that of the Word of God for detaching a man from the world, the flesh and the devil.

c) VARIOUS OTHER AGENCIES

Heb. 12:14, R. V.—"Follow after . . . the sanctification without which no man shall see the Lord." To "follow after" means to pursue, to seek out, as Saul of Tarsus pursued and followed the early Christians. One cannot become a saint in his sleep. Holiness must be the object of his pursuit. The lazy man will not be the holy man.

Heb. 12:10, 11: God chastens us "for our profit, that we might be partakers of his holiness." Chastisement ofttimes is intended to "produce the peaceable fruit of righteousness."

Rom. 6:19-22; 2 Cor. 6:17; 7:1. Sanctification is brought about in the life of the believer by his separating himself deliberately from all that is unclean and unholy, and by presenting, continually and constantly, the members of his body as holy instruments unto God for the accomplishment of His holy purposes. Thus by these single acts of surrender unto holiness, sanctification soon becomes the habit of the life.

G. PRAYER

I. ITS IMPORTANCE

II. ITS NATURE
1. AS SEEN IN ITS HISTORIC DEVELOPMENT
2. SCRIPTURAL TERMS

III. ITS POSSIBILITY
1. THE REVELATION OF GOD
2. THE WORK OF THE SON
3. THE ASSISTANCE OF THE SPIRIT
4. THE PROMISES
5. CHRISTIAN TESTIMONY

IV. ITS OBJECTS
1. GOD THE FATHER
2. CHRIST THE SON
3. THE HOLY SPIRIT

V. ITS METHOD
1. POSTURE
2. TIME AND PLACE

VI. HINDRANCES AND HELPS
1. HINDRANCES
2. HELPS—ESSENTIALS

G. PRAYER

I. THE IMPORTANCE OF PRAYER

Even a cursory perusal of the Scriptures will reveal the large and important place which the doctrine of prayer finds therein. The Christian life cannot be sustained without it; it is the Christian's vital breath. Its importance is seen when we recall:

That the neglect of prayer is grievous to the Lord (Isa. 43:21, 22; 64:6, 7, R. V.).

That many evils in life are to be attributed to the lack of prayer (Zeph. 1:4-6; Dan. 9:13, 14; cf. Hosea 7:13, 14; 8:13, 14).

That it is a sin to neglect prayer (1 Sam. 12:23).

That to continue in prayer is a positive command (Col. 4:2, R. V.; 1 Thess. 5:17; we are commanded to take leisure or a vacation for prayer: 1 Cor. 7:5).

That it is God's appointed method of our obtaining what He has to bestow (Dan. 9:3; Matt. 7:7-11; 9:24-29; Luke 11:13).

That the lack of the necessary blessings in life comes from failure to pray (James 4:2).

That the apostles regarded prayer as the most important employment that could engage their time or attention (Acts 6:4; Rom. 1:9; (Col. 1:9).

II. THE NATURE OF PRAYER

It is interesting to trace the development of prayer in the Scriptures.

In the life of the patriarch Abraham prayer seems to have taken the form of a dialogue—God and man drawing near and talking to each other (Gen. 18; 19); developing into intercession (Gen. 17:18; 18:23, 32), and then into personal prayer (Gen. 15:2; 24:12); cf. Jacob (Gen. 28:20; 32:9-12, 24; Hosea 12:4). The patriarchal blessings are called prayers (Gen. 49:1; Deut. 33:11).

During the period of the Law. Not very much prominence is given to formal prayer during this period. Deut. 26:1-15 seems to be the only one definitely recorded. Prayer had not yet found a stated place in the ritual of the law. It seems to have been more of a personal than a formal matter, and so while the Law may not afford much material, yet the life of the lawgiver, Moses, abounds with prayer (Exod. 5:22; 32:11; Num. 11:11-15).

In the Books of Joshua (7:6-9; 10:14) and Judges (chap. 6) we are told that the children of Israel "cried unto the Lord."

Under Samuel prayer seems to have assumed the nature of intercession (1 Sam. 7:5, 12; 8:16-18); personal (1 Sam. 15:11, 35; 16:1). In Jeremiah (15:1) Moses and Samuel are represented as offering intercessory prayer for Israel.

David seems to regard himself as a prophet and priest, and prays without an intercessor (2 Sam. 7:18-29).

The prophets seem to have been intercessors, e. g., Elijah (1

Kings 18). Yet personal prayers are found among the prophets (Jer. 20—both personal and intercessory; 33:3; 42:4; Amos 7).

In the Psalms prayer takes the form of a pouring out of the heart (42:4; 62:8; 100:2, title). The psalmist does not seem to go before God with fixed and orderly petitions so much as simply to pour out his feelings and desires, whether sweet or bitter, troubled or peaceful. Consequently the prayers of the psalmist consist of varying moods: complaint, supplication, confession, despondency, praise.

True prayer consists of such elements as adoration, praise, petition, pleading, thanksgiving, intercession, communion, waiting. The closet into which the believer enters to pray is not only an oratory —a place of prayer, it is an observatory—a place of vision. Prayer is not "A venture and a voice of mine; but a vision and a voice divine." Isa. 63:7 and 64:12 illustrate all essential forms of address in prayer.

III. THE POSSIBILITY OF PRAYER

This possibility consists in five things:

1. The Revelation of God Which Christ Has Brought to Us

John 1:18—"No man hath seen God at any time; the only-begotten Son, which is in the bosom of the Father, he hath declared him." Matt. 11:27—". . . Neither knoweth any man the Father, save the Son, and he to whomsoever the Son will reveal him."

Christ reveals God as a *personal* God, as a Being who sees, feels, knows, understands, and acts. Belief in the personality of God is absolutely necessary to true prayer (Heb. 11:6).

Christ reveals God as a *sovereign* God (Matt. 19:26)—"With God all things are possible." God is sovereign over all laws; He can make them subservient to His will, and use them in answering the prayers of His children. He is not bound by any so-called unchangeable laws.

Christ revealed God as a *Father* (Luke 11:13). In every instance in the life of Christ whenever He addresses God in prayer it is always as Father. The fact of the fatherhood of God makes prayer possible. It would be unnatural for a father not to commune with his child.

2. The Sacrificial Work of Jesus Christ

Heb. 10:19-22, R. V.—"Having therefore, brethren, boldness to enter into the holy place by the blood of Jesus by the way which he dedicated for us, a new and living way, through the veil, that is to say, his flesh; and having a great priest over the house of God; let us draw near with a true heart in fulness of faith." It is because of the death of Christ, which removed the barrier that stood between God and us so that He could not consistently hear and answer our prayers, that He can now hear and answer the petitions of His children.

3. The Inspiration of the Holy Ghost

Rom. 8:26—"Likewise the Spirit also helpeth our infirmities: for we know not what we should pray for as we ought: but the Spirit himself maketh intercession for us with groanings which cannot be uttered." See also Jude 20. The thought is this: Even though we are assured that there is a personal God to hear us, and although we have the confidence that the barrier of sin which stood between us and God has been removed, so that we now desire to pray, we often are hindered because we either do not know what to say or what to ask for. We may ask too ardently for wrong things, or too languidly for the things we most need. And so we are afraid to pray. The assurance that this verse gives us is that the Holy Spirit will pray within us, and will indite the petition, helping us in our prayer life.

4. The Many Promises of the Bible

We are told that there are over 3300 of them. Each promise is "yea and amen in Jesus Christ"; He is the guarantee and the guarantor of them all. They are not given to mock but to encourage us: "Hath he said and shall he not do it? Hath he spoken and shall he not make it good?" See John 14:13; 15:7; 1 John 5:14, 15; Luke 11:9, etc.

5. The Universal Christian Testimony

Christians, by the millions, the world over, can and do testify to the fact that God both hears and answers prayer. The credibility, character, and intelligence of the vast number of witnesses make their testimony indisputable and incontrovertible.

IV. THE OBJECTS OF PRAYER—TO WHOM TO PRAY

1. To God

Neh. 4:9; Acts 12:5—"Prayer was made without ceasing of the church unto God for him": God is holy—hence there must be no impurity in the life of the one praying; righteous, hence no crookedness; truthful, hence no lying or hypocrisy; powerful, hence we may have confidence; transcendent, hence reverence in our approach.

2. To Christ

Acts 7:59—"Lord Jesus, receive my spirit." 2 Cor. 12:8, 9; 2 Tim. 2:22.

3. The Holy Spirit

Rom. 8:15, 16 sets forth the relation of the Holy Spirit and prayer, as do also Zech. 12:10; Eph. 6:18; Jude 20. The Holy Spirit is God (Acts 5:3, 4; Matt. 28:19; 2 Cor. 13:14), hence is to be worshipped (Matt. 4:10; Rev. 22:9).

The normal mode of prayer is prayer in the Spirit, on the ground of the merits of the Son, to the Father: In the Spirit, through the Son, to the Father.

V. THE METHOD OR MANNER OF PRAYER

1. With Regard to the Posture of the Body

The soul may be in prayer no matter what is the attitude of the body. The Scriptures sanction no special bodily posture. Christ stood and prayed (John 17:1), knelt (Luke 22:41), He also fell on his face on the ground (Matt. 26:39); Solomon knelt (1 Kings 8:54); Elijah prayed with his elbows on his knees and his face buried in his hands; David prayed lying on his bed (Psa. 63:6); Peter prayed on the water (Matt. 14:30); the dying thief, on the cross (Luke 23:42).

2. Time and Place

Time: *Stated times* (Dan. 6:10; Psa. 55:16, 17; Acts 3:1; 2:46; 10:9, 30). *Special occasions*: Choosing the twelve (Luke

6:12, 13). Before the cross (Luke 22:39-46). After great successes (John 6:15, cf. Mark 6:46-48). *Early in the morning* (Mark 1:35). *All night* (Luke 6:12). *Times of special trouble* (Psa. 81:7, cf. Exod. 2:23; 3:7; 14:10, 24). *At meals* (Matt. 14:19; Acts 27:35; 1 Tim. 4:4, 5).

Place of Prayer: Inner chamber (Matt. 6:6); amid nature (Matt. 14:23; Mark 1:35). In the church (John 17:1; Psa. 95:6). Before the unsaved (Acts 16:25; 27:35). In all places (1 Tim. 2:8, R. V.).

VI. HINDRANCES AND HELPS TO PRAYER

1. Hindrances

Indulged known sin (Psa. 66:18; Isa. 59:1, 2). Wilful disobedience to known commandments (Prov. 28:9). Selfishness (James 4:3). Unforgiving spirit (Matt. 5:22, 23; 6:12). Lack of faith (Heb. 11:6; James 1:6). Idols in the heart (Ezek. 8:5-18; 14:1-3).

2. Helps—Essentials to Prevailing Prayer

Sincerity (Psa. 145:18; Matt. 6:5). Simplicity (Matt. 6:7, cf. 26:44). Earnestness (James 5:17; Acts 12:5; Luke 22:44). Persistence (Luke 18:1-8; Col. 4:2; Rom. 12:12, R. V.). Faith (Matt. 21:22; James 1:6). Unison with others (Matt. 18:19, 20). Definiteness (Psa. 27:4; Matt. 18:19). Effort (Exod. 14:15). In the name of Jesus (John 16:23; 14:13, 14). With fasting (Acts 13:2, 3; 14:23).

THE DOCTRINE OF THE CHURCH

THE DOCTRINE OF THE CHURCH

I. DEFINITION; DISTINCTIONS
    1. OLD TESTAMENT
    2. NEW TESTAMENT
    3. THE CHURCH; CHRISTENDOM; KINGDOM

II. THE FOUNDING OF THE CHURCH
    1. IN PROPHECY AND PROMISE
    2. HISTORICALLY FOUNDED

III. MEMBERSHIP IN THE CHURCH
      Conditions of Entrance; Characteristics
    1. REPENTANCE AND BAPTISM
    2. FAITH IN THE DEITY OF JESUS CHRIST
    3. REGENERATION
    4. PUBLIC CONFESSION OF CHRIST—BAPTISM
    5. ADHERENCE TO THE APOSTLES' DOCTRINE
    6. CHARACTERISTICS

IV. FIGURES UNDER WHICH THE CHURCH IS PRESENTED
    1. THE BODY OF CHRIST
    2. THE TEMPLE OF GOD
    3. THE BRIDE OF CHRIST

V. THE ORDINANCES OF THE CHURCH
    1. BAPTISM
    2. THE LORD'S SUPPER

VI. THE VOCATION OF THE CHURCH
    1. TO WORSHIP GOD
    2. TO EVANGELIZE THE WORLD
    3. PERFECT EACH MEMBER
    4. TO WITNESS
    5. FUTURE GLORY

THE DOCTRINE OF THE CHURCH

There is great danger of losing sight of the Church in the endeavor to emphasize the idea of the Kingdom of Heaven or Christendom. We are prone to think it a small thing to speak of the Church; the Kingdom and Christendom seem so large in comparison. We are tempted to distinguish and contrast Churchianity, as it is sometimes called, and Christianity, to the disparagement of the former. It is well to remember that Jesus Christ positively identifies Himself with the Church (Acts 9) and not with Christendom; He gave up His life that He might found the Church (Eph. 5:25). The Apostle Paul sacrificed himself in his endeavors to build up the Church, not Christendom. He speaks of his greatest sin as consisting in persecuting the Church of God (1 Cor. 15:9). The supreme business of God in this age is the gathering of the Church. Some day it will be complete (Eph. 4:12), and then the age will have served its purpose.

I. DEFINITIONS; DISTINCTIONS

1. Old Testament Use of the Word

Lev. 4:13—"And if the whole congregation of Israel sin through ignorance, and the thing be hid from the eyes of the assembly . . ." The Hebrew word for *assembly* means to *call* or *assemble*, and is used not only for the act of calling itself, but also for the assembly of the called ones. In this sense Israel is called a "church," an assembly, because it was called out from among the nations to be a holy people (Acts 7:38, "the church in the wilderness"). There is always a religious aspect associated with this particular call.

2. The New Testament Use of the Word

It is from the New Testament primarily, if not really exclusively, that the real meaning and idea of the Church is derived. The Christian Church is a New Testament institution, beginning with Pentecost, and ending, probably, with the rapture. Two words are of special importance in this connection:

a) "ECCLESIA," FROM TWO GREEK WORDS MEANING "TO CALL OUT FROM"

This word is used in all about 111 times in the New Testament. It is used in a secular sense in Acts 19:39—"It shall be determined in a lawful assembly"; of Israel in the wilderness (Acts 7:38), and of the assembly of believers in Christ (Matt. 16:18; 18:17; 1 Cor. 1:2; Eph. 5:25-27). In keeping with this idea the saints are said to be the "called-out" ones (Rom. 8:30; 1 Cor. 1:2; cf. 2 Cor. 6:17).

b) "KURIAKON"—THAT WHICH BELONGS TO THE LORD

So we have "the supper of the Lord" (1 Cor. 11:20); the "day of the Lord" (Rev. 1:10). See also Luke 22:25 and Rom. 14:8, 9, as illustrating that over which the Lord has dominion and authority.

To sum up then: The Church is composed of the body of believers who have been called out from the world, and who are under the dominion and authority of Jesus Christ.

c) THE GROWTH OF THE CHURCH IDEA IN THE NEW TESTAMENT

At first there was but one Church at Jerusalem. The meetings may have been held in different houses, yet there was but one Church with one roster: so we read of the total membership consisting at one time of 120 (Acts 1:15), again of 3,000 (2:41), and still again of 5,000 (4:4), to which there were daily additions (2:47). The apostles were at the head of the Church (2:41-47). See Acts, chaps. 1 and 2, for a fuller account of the first Church.

The second stage in the growth of the Church was its spread throughout Judea and Samaria, as recorded in Acts 8.

Antioch, in Syria, then became the head of the Gentile church (Acts 13:1), as Jerusalem was the head of the Jewish church (Acts 15); Paul representing the church at Antioch, and Peter and James at Jerusalem. The assembly at Antioch was called "the church" just as truly as was the assembly at Jerusalem (11:22; 13:1).

Because of the missionary activities of the apostles, especially Paul, churches sprang up in different cities, especially in Asia Minor, e. g., Corinth, Galatia, Ephesus, and Philippi.

In view of all this the term "church" came to be used of the Church *universal,* that is, the complete body of Christ as existing in every place (1 Cor. 15:9; Gal. 1:2, 13; Matt. 16:18); of *local* churches in any one place (Col. 4:16; Phil. 4:15; 1 Cor. 1:2, etc.); of *single meetings,* even where two or three met together (Matt. 18:19; Col. 4:15; Phil. 1:2; Rom. 16:5).

It is evident, then, from what has here been said, that by the term "church" is included all that is meant from the Church Universal to the meeting of the church in the house. Wherever God's people meet in the name of Christ to worship, there you have the Church.

3. Distinctions

a) THE CHURCH AND THE KINGDOM

The Church (which is the mystery) and the Kingdom in mystery are now contemporary. The Kingdom will be fully manifested at the coming of Christ. The Church is within the Kingdom; probably the regenerate are "the children of the kingdom." The Kingdom is comprised of both good and bad (Matt. 13); the Church, of real saints only. The Jews rejected the Kingdom under Christ and the apostles. That Kingdom, now rejected, will be set up again when the Messiah comes. This conception will help us to understand the parables of Matthew 13, as well as the Sermon on the Mount. The tares are sown not in the Church, but in the field, which is the world. The Church may be looked upon as part of the Kingdom of God, just as Illinois is part of the United States. The Kingdom is present, in a sense, just as the King is present in the hearts of his own people. There is a difference between the Church and Christendom, just as there is a difference between possessing and professing Christians. Baptized Christendom is one thing, and the Church of Christ is another.

b) THE CHURCH VISIBLE AND INVISIBLE: ACTUAL AND IDEAL

The Church *Visible* is composed of all those whose names are enrolled upon its roster; *Invisible,* of those whose names are written in the Lamb's book of life; *Actual,* people imperfect, yet aiming after perfection, alive here on the earth; *Ideal,* departed saints who are now triumphant in heaven (Heb. 12:23). There is a Church in heaven just as there is one upon the earth; indeed, it is but a part of the one Church; called the Church *militant* while upon the earth, and the Church *triumphant* in heaven.

c) THE CHURCH LOCAL AND UNIVERSAL

By the first is meant the Church in any particular place, such as "the church at Corinth"; by the latter, the Church as found in every place (1 Cor. 1:2).

II. THE FOUNDING OF THE CHURCH

1. Foretold By Christ

Matt. 16:16-18—". . . On this rock I will build my church." Here is the Church in prophecy and promise; the first mention of the Church in the New Testament. Note the distinction here recognized between the "Kingdom" and the "Church."

The Church is to be founded on Peter's confession of Jesus Christ as the Son of the living God. No supremacy is here given to Peter, as a comparison of these verses with John 20:19-23 and Matt. 18:18—in which the same privilege of the binding and loosing is given to the whole Church and to all the apostles—will show.

In Matthew 18:15-20 our Lord recognizes the fact of the Church, and also that it has the divine seal and sanction in the exercising of the power of the keys.

2. Historically Founded By the Apostles

Acts 1—2:47. The promise and prophecy of Matt. 16:16-18 is here fulfilled. Here is the account of the first Christian Church in its glorious beginning, and as it actually existed in Jerusalem. When a man became regenerate by believing in Jesus Christ he was thereby constituted a member of the Church. There was no question as to whether he ought to join himself to the Church or not; that was a fact taken for granted. So we read that the Lord was adding to the Church daily such as were being saved. The Church was already a concrete institution to which every believer in Christ united himself.

"The apostles' doctrine" formed the standard of faith—a fulfillment of Christ's prophecy and promise in Matthew 16:16-18: "On this rock I will build my church," etc.

The Church had *stated places of meeting*: the upper room (Acts

1:13), the temple (5:12), the homes of members (2:46, 12:12), and the synagogue; *stated times of* meeting: daily (2:46), each Lord's Day (20:7), the *regular hours* of prayer (3:1; 10:9); a *regular church roll*: 120 (1:15), 3,000 (2:41), 5,000 (4:4); *daily additions* (2:47).

That there were definitely, regularly organized churches is clear from the fact that the Apostle Paul addressed many of his epistles to churches in different localities. The letters to the Corinthians (e. g., 1 Cor. 12-14) show that the churches had already recognized certain forms of service and liturgy; those to Timothy and Titus presume a regularly organized congregation of believers. That there is a Church in the world is clear from 1 Cor. 5:9-13. The Christian Church is as much an entity as the Gentile, or the Jew (1 Cor. 10:32). The existence of church officers proves the existence of the Church in an organized form: bishops and deacons (Phil. 1:1), elders (Acts 20:17), the presbytery (1 Tim. 4:14). Church letters were granted to members (Acts 18:27).

III. MEMBERSHIP IN THE CHURCH—ITS CONDITIONS AND CHARACTERISTICS

1. Repentance and Baptism Required of All Its Members

Acts 2:38-41—"Then Peter said unto them, Repent, and be baptized every one of you in the name of Jesus Christ for the remission of sins, and ye shall receive the gift of the Holy Ghost. Then they that gladly received his word were baptized: and the same day there were added unto them about three thousand souls."

2. Faith in the Lord Jesus Christ as the Divine Redeemer

Matt. 16:16-18; Acts 2:38, 39. Peter's entire sermon in Acts 2 illustrates this fact.

3. Saved—Regenerated

Acts 2:47—". . . And the Lord added to the church such as should be saved." Cf. John 3:3, 5. It was essential that the members of the early Church should be "added unto the Lord" before they were added to the Church (5:14; 11:24).

4. Baptism in the Name of the Triune God as an Open Confession of Christ

Matt. 28:19—"Go ye therefore, and teach all nations, baptizing them in the name of the Father, and of the Son, and of the Holy Ghost." Acts 2:38-41; 10:47, 48; 22:16; cf. Rom. 10:9, 10.

5. Adherence to the Apostolic Doctrine

Acts 2:42—"And they continued steadfastly in the apostles' doctrine and fellowship." Cf. "On this rock I will build my church" (Matt. 16:16-18); also Eph. 2:20.

6. Characteristics of Membership in the Early Church

The members were known as believers (Acts 4:32); brethren (11:29; 12:17; Rom. 1:13—the absolute equality of all believers, cf. Matt. 23:8-10); Christians (Acts 11:26; 26:28); saints (9:13; 1 Cor. 1:2; Rev. 13:7); elect (Mark 13:27; Rom. 8:33; Eph. 1:4).

IV. FIGURES UNDER WHICH THE CHURCH IS SET FORTH IN THE SCRIPTURES

1. The Body, of Which Christ Is the Head

Two ideas are contained in this symbol:

a) THE RELATION OF THE CHURCH TO CHRIST, WHO IS ITS HEAD

Eph. 1:22, 23; Col. 1:18; 2:19. The Church is an organism, not an organization. There is a vital relation between Christ and the Church, both partaking of the same life, just as there is between the physical head and the body. We cannot join the Church as we would a lodge or any mere human organization. We must be partakers by faith of Christ's life before we can become members of Christ's Church, in the true sense. As the Head of the Church Christ is its Guardian and Director (Eph. 5:23, 24); the Source of its life, filling it with His fulness (Eph. 1:23); the Centre of its unity and the Cause of its growth (Eph. 4:15; Col. 2:19).

b) THE RELATION OF THE MEMBERS ONE TO ANOTHER

1 Cor. 12:12-27; Rom. 12:4, 5; Eph. 4:1-4, 15, 16.

2. A Temple, A Building, A Habitation, A Dwelling-Place for God's Spirit

Eph. 2:20, 21; 1 Cor. 3:9-17; 1 Tim. 3:15; 1 Pet. 2:4-8; Rev. 21:3; 1 Cor. 6:19. Of this building Christ is the cornerstone, and the prophets and apostles the foundation. In 1 Cor. 3:9-17, Christ is the chief cornerstone and the apostles the builders; the whole building is held in place by Christ.

3. The Bride of Christ

2 Cor. 11:2; Eph. 5:25-27; Rev. 19:7; 22:17. Christ is the Bridegroom (John 3:29). This is a great mystery (Eph. 5:32). The Bride becomes the wife of the Lamb (Rev. 21:2).

V. THE ORDINANCES OF THE CHURCH

1. Baptism

Matt. 28:19, 20; Mark 16:16; Acts 2:38, 41; 8:36-40; 10:47, 48.

2. The Lord's Supper

Acts 2:42, 46; 20:7—"And upon the first day of the week, when the disciples came together to break bread, Paul preached unto them, ready to depart on the morrow; and continued his speech until midnight." 1 Cor. 11:20-34.

VI. THE VOCATION OF THE CHURCH

1. To Worship God and to Glorify Him on the Earth

Eph. 1:4-6—"According as he hath chosen us in him before the foundation of the world, that we should be holy and without blame before him in love: Having predestinated us unto the adoption of children by Jesus Christ to himself, according to the good pleasure of his will, to the praise of the glory of his grace, wherein he hath made us accepted in the beloved."

2. To Evangelize the World With the Gospel

Matt. 28:19, 20—"Go ye therefore, and teach all nations, baptizing them in the name of the Father, and of the Son, and of the Holy Ghost." Acts 2; 5:42; 6:5-8; Eph. 3:8; Acts 15:7.

3. To Develop Each Individual Christian Until He Attains Unto the Fulness of the Stature of Christ

Eph. 4:11-15. Hence the gift of pastors, teachers, etc. Herein lies the value of church attendance—it promotes growth; failure to attend leads to apostasy (Heb. 10:25-28), cf. 1 Thess. 5:11; 1 Cor. 12.

4. A Constant Witness for Christ and His Word

Acts 1:8—"But ye shall receive power, after that the Holy Ghost is come upon you: and ye shall be witnesses unto me both in Jerusalem, and in all Judea, and in Samaria, and unto the uttermost part of the earth." 8:1, 4.

5. The Future Glory of the Church

Eph. 3:10, 21; Rev. 21:9-27.

THE DOCTRINE OF THE SCRIPTURES

THE DOCTRINE OF THE SCRIPTURES

I. NAMES AND TITLES
1. THE BIBLE
2. THE TESTAMENTS
3. THE SCRIPTURES
4. THE WORD OF GOD

II. INSPIRATION

1. DEFINITION

2. DISTINCTIONS
   a) Revelation
   b) Illumination
   c) Reporting

3. VIEWS
   a) Natural Inspiration
   b) Christian Illumination
   c) Dynamic Theory
   d) Concept Theory
   e) Verbal Inspiration
   f) Partial Inspiration
   g) Plenary Inspiration

4. THE CLAIMS OF THE SCRIPTURES THEMSELVES
   a) The Old Testament
   b) The New Testament

5. THE CHARACTER (OR DEGREES) OF INSPIRATION
   a) Actual Words of God Himself
   b) Actual Words Communicated by God to Men
   c) Individual Freedom in Choice of Words—To What Extent?

THE DOCTRINE OF THE SCRIPTURES

I. THE BIBLE—ITS NAMES AND TITLES

1. "The Bible"

Our English word *Bible* comes from the Greek words *biblos* (Matt. 1:1) and *biblion* (diminutive form) (Luke 4:17), which mean "book." Ancient books were written upon the biblus or papyrus reed, and from this custom came the Greek name *biblos,* which finally came to be applied to the sacred books. See Mark 12:26; Luke 3:4; 20:42; Acts 1:20; 7:42.

The Bible is not merely *a* book, however. It is THE BOOK—the Book that from the importance of its subjects, the wideness of its range, the majesty of its Author, stands as high above all other books as the heaven is high above the earth.

2. "The Old and New Testaments"

See Luke 22:20; 1 Cor. 11:25; 2 Cor. 3:6, 14; Heb. 9:15; 12:24.

The word *Testament* means *Covenant,* and is the term by which God was pleased to designate the relation that existed between Himself and His people. The term *Covenant* was first of all applied to the relation itself, and afterward to the books which contained the record of that relation.

By the end of the second century we find the "Old Covenant" and the "New Covenant" as the established names of the Jewish and Christian Scriptures; and Origen, in the beginning of the third century, mentioned "the divine Scriptures, the so-called Old and New Covenants."

The Old Testament deals with the record of the calling and history of the Jewish nation, and as such it is the Old Covenant. The New Testament deals with the history and application of the redemption wrought by the Lord Jesus Christ, and as such it is the New Covenant.

3. "The Scripture," and "The Scriptures"

The Bible is also called "The Scripture" (Mark 12:10; 15:28; Luke 4:21; John 2:22; 7:38; 10:35; Rom. 4:3; Gal. 4:30; 2 Pet. 1:20), and "The Scriptures" (Matt. 22:29; Mark 12:24; Luke 24:27; John 5:39; Acts 17:11; Rom. 1:2; 2 Tim. 3:15; 2 Pet. 3:16). These terms mean that the Scriptures are "Holy Writings." By the early Christians the most common designation for the whole Bible was "The Scriptures."

4. "The Word of God"

Of all the names given to the Bible, "The Word of God" (Mark 7:13; Rom. 10:17; 2 Cor. 2:17; Heb. 4:12; 1 Thess. 2:13) is doubtless the most significant, impressive, and complete. It is sufficient to justify the faith of the weakest Christian. It gathers up all that the most earnest search can unfold. It teaches us to regard the Bible as the utterance of divine wisdom and love—as God speaking to man.

II. THE INSPIRATION OF THE BIBLE

1. What Is Meant by the Term "Inspiration"

This question is best answered by Scripture itself. It defines its own terms. Let us turn, then, "to the Law and to the Testimony."

In 2 Tim. 3:16—"All Scripture is given by inspiration of God."

The word "inspired" means literally "God-breathed." It is composed of two Greek words—*theos=God;* and *pnein=to breathe.* The term "given by inspiration" signifies, then, that the writings of the Old Testament, of which Paul is here speaking, are the result of a certain influence exerted by God upon their authors.

The meaning of the word "breathed," as here used, is brought out very forcibly by the comparison of two other words translated in the same way. The one is the Greek word *psuchein=to breathe gently,* while in 2 Tim. 3:16 the term denotes a forcible respiration. The other is the Hebrew word *ah-ayrh=to breathe unconsciously,* while 2 Tim. 3:16 denotes a conscious breathing.

Inspiration, then, as defined by Paul in this passage, is the *strong, conscious inbreathing of God into men, qualifying them to give utterance to truth. It is God speaking through men, and the Old Testament is therefore just as much the Word of God as though*

God spake every single word of it with His own lips. The Scriptures are the result of divine inbreathing, just as human speech is uttered by the breathing through a man's mouth.

2 Pet. 1:21—"For not by the will of man was prophecy brought at any time, but being borne by the Holy Spirit, the holy men of God spoke." (This is a literal rendering, and brings out the sense more clearly.)

The participle "moved," AV, may be translated "when moved," so this passage teaches that holy men of God wrote the Scripture *when* moved to do so by the Holy Spirit.

Further, the participle is passive, and denotes "to be moved upon." This distinctly teaches that the Scripture was not written by mere men, or at their suggestion, but by men *moved upon,* prompted, yea indeed, driven by the promptings of the Holy Spirit.

This declaration of Peter may be said to intimate that the Holy Ghost was especially and miraculously present with and in the writers of the Scriptures, revealing to them truths which they did not know before, and guiding them alike in their record of these truths, and of the transactions of which they were eye and ear witnesses, so that they were enabled to present them with accuracy to the minds of others.

The statements of the Scriptures regarding inspiration may be summed up as follows: Holy men of God, qualified by the infusion of the breath of God, wrote in obedience to the divine command, and were kept from all error, whether they revealed truths previously unknown or recorded truths already familiar. In this sense, "all Scripture is given by inspiration of God," the Bible is indeed and in truth the very Word of God, and the books of the Bible are of divine origin and authority.

2. The Distinction Between Inspiration, Revelation, Illumination, and Verbatim Reporting

a) THE DISTINCTION BETWEEN INSPIRATION AND REVELATION

It is of the greatest importance, in considering the theme of inspiration, to distinguish it clearly from revelation.

The most cursory perusal of the Scriptures reveals the fact that they consist of two different kinds of records: first, records of truth directly revealed and imparted to the mind of the writer by

God, and which he could have learned in no other manner (such, for example, as the story of creation); and second, records of events that occurred within the writer's own observation, and of sayings that fell upon his own ears (such as Moses' account of the Exodus, Paul's account of his interview with Peter at Antioch). In the one case, the writer records things that had not been revealed to man before; in the other case, he records facts which were as well known to others as to himself.

Now, revelation is that act of God by which He directly communicates truth not known before to the human mind. Revelation discovers new truth, while inspiration superintends the communicating of that truth.

All that is in the Bible has not been "directly revealed" to man. It contains history, and the language of men, even of wicked men. But there is absolutely no part of the Bible record that is not inspired. The history recorded in the Bible is true. The sacred writers were so directed and influenced by the Spirit that they were preserved, in writing, from every error of fact and doctrine. The history remains history. Things not sanctioned by God, recorded in the Bible, are to be shunned (2 Tim. 3:16). Nevertheless, all these things were written under the guidance of the Holy Spirit. This is inspiration.

This distinction should be definitely and clearly understood, for many of the most plausible arguments against the full inspiration of the Scriptures have arisen from the fact that this has been either unrecognized or ignored.

Though all Scripture is inspired, it does not stamp with divine authority every sentiment which it reports as uttered by the men of whom it speaks, nor does it mark with divine approval every action which it relates as performed by those with whose biographies it deals. In the book of Job, for example, inspiration gives with equal accuracy the language of Jehovah, the words of Satan, and the speeches of Job and his three friends; but it does not therefore place them all on the same level of authority. Each speaker is responsible for his own utterances. Neither Satan, Job, nor his three friends spoke by inspiration of God. They gave utterance to their own opinions; and all that inspiration vouches for is that no one of them is misrepresented, but that each one spoke the sentiments that are attributed to him in Scripture. So, again, the fact that David's cruelty to the Ammonites is recorded in the book of Kings does not imply that God approved it any more than He approved the king's double crime of murder and adultery, which "displeased Him." The inspiration of the Book vouches only for the accuracy of the record.

b) THE DISTINCTION BETWEEN INSPIRATION AND ILLUMINATION

Spiritual illumination refers to the influence of the Holy Ghost, common to all Christians. No statement of a truth about God or spiritual things can be understood by a man unless the Holy Spirit takes it and reveals it to him. It is only the spiritual man who can understand spiritual things. "The natural man receiveth not the things of the Spirit" (1 Cor. 2:14). No learning of the schools can lead him to know God. Flesh and blood cannot reveal God to men (Matt. 16:17).

There is a vast difference between "a divine revelation of the mind of God" and "a divine action on the mind of man." The former is revelation; the latter is spiritual illumination.

Those who hold to the illumination theory to account for the origin of the Bible revelation claim that there is in every man an intuitive faculty that grasps the supernatural, that lays hold of God and spiritual things; and that whatever insight into the nature and being of God is given man, is produced by the divine Spirit playing upon this spiritual faculty in man, illuminating and irradiating it, so that it sees the perfection of God and is enabled to penetrate into His will.

According to this view, the Bible is the result of the meditations of godly men whose minds were acted upon by God. Any revelation of divinity of which man is the recipient comes in this manner. Subjective illumination God has carried on since the world began, and is still carrying on by a great variety of methods. The Scriptures are not in any way the oracles of God, nor do they come to us as direct, logical utterances of the divine mind. The patriarchs, prophets and apostles of old so deeply meditated on God and the things of God that their spiritual faculties were enlarged and illuminated to such a degree that they conceived of these visions of God, His nature, His will, etc., as recorded in the Scriptures.

Now, it is true, doubtless, that a man may be granted a very deep insight into the nature and being of God by spiritual meditation. That a fire does burn in the Bible, we do not deny. Throughout all ages of the Jewish and Christian churches men have lit their spiritual torches at this fire, and in their light they have seen Him who is invisible. This fire still burns, and to-day the devout student may catch its flame if, with uncovered head, with shoeless feet, and with humble spirit, he stands before the bush that ever burns and yet is never consumed. But this working of the truth of God on the mind of man is not God's revelation of His mind to man which the Bible professes to be. The Bible must of necessity be not merely a repository or receptacle of spiritual influences fitted to act upon the mind; it must be—it is—God making Himself known to men. It is God speaking to man through men.

In contradistinction to the illumination theory we have instances in the Bible in which God made revelations of Himself, His truth, and His will to men who were by no means at the time meditating upon God. See e. g.:

John 11:49-52—"And one of them, named Caiaphas, being the high priest that same year, said unto them, Ye know nothing at all, nor consider that it is expedient for us, that one man should die for the people, and that the whole nation perish not. And this spake he not of himself: but being high priest that year, he prophesied that Jesus should die for that nation; and not for that nation only, but that also He should gather together in one the children of God that were scattered abroad." See also Num. 22:34, 35.

c) THE DISTINCTION BETWEEN INSPIRATION AND VERBATIM REPORTING

Inspiration is not necessarily verbatim reporting.

It is not absolutely necessary to make such a claim to prove the inspiration of the Scriptures. Verbatim reporting is, in a sense, a mere mechanical operation. It would have robbed the writers of their individuality, and made them mere machines. But no; the Holy Spirit used the memories, the intuitions, the judgments, and indeed the idiosyncrasies of the writers, so that while each recorded that part of the event or discourse which (as we may express it) adhered to himself, he was enabled to give it with accuracy.

3. *Various Theories of Inspiration*

It will be in order here to note briefly various theories of inspiration; for it must be known that all students do not agree as to the degree of inspiration that characterized the writers of the Scripture. When a man says, "I believe in the inspiration of the Bible," it will be quite in place in these days to ask him what he means by inspiration. Following are some of the views of inspiration held at the present day.

a) NATURAL INSPIRATION

This theory identifies inspiration with genius of a high order. It denies that there is anything supernatural, mysterious, or peculiar in the mode of the Spirit's operation in and upon the Scripture writers. It claims that they were no more inspired than were Milton, Shakespeare, Muhammad, or Confucius.

Such a theory we absolutely reject. For if such be the character of the inspiration possessed by the Scripture writers, there is nothing to assure us that they were not liable to make the same errors, to teach the same false views of life, to give expression to the same uncertainties concerning the past, the present, and the future as did these shining lights of mere human genius.

When David said, "The Spirit of the Lord spake by me, and His word was in my tongue," he meant something more than the prayer which forms the gem of *Paradise Lost*. When Isaiah and his brethren said, "Thus saith the Lord," they claimed something higher than that they were speaking under the stirrings of poetic rapture. When Paul said to the Corinthians, "Which things also we speak, not in the words which man's wisdom teacheth, but which the Holy Ghost teacheth" (1 Cor. 2:13), he used the language to which you will find no parallel in the literature of mere human genius. And no man of candor or intelligence can pass from the writings even of the unapproachable Shakespeare into the perusal of the Bible without feeling that the difference between the two is not one simply of degree, but of kind; he has not merely ascended to a loftier outlook in the same human dwelling, but he has gone into a new region altogether. There is a certain "unknown quality" in this Book which clearly distinguishes it from all others; and if we may take its own explanation of the matter, that unknown quality is its divine inspiration.

b) UNIVERSAL CHRISTIAN INSPIRATION, OR ILLUMINATION

According to this theory, the inspiration of the Bible writers was the same as has characterized Christians of every age; the ordinary Christian of to-day is inspired as much as was the Apostle Paul.

If this be the true view, there seems to be no plausible reason why a new Bible should not be possible to-day. And yet no individual, however extreme his claims to inspiration may be, has even ventured such a task.

c) MECHANICAL, OR DYNAMIC INSPIRATION (See Verbatim Reporting, page 198.)

This theory ignores the human instrumentality in the writing of the Scriptures altogether, and claims that the writers were passive instruments, mere machines, just as insensible to what they were accomplishing as is the string of the harp or lyre to the play of the musician.

How, then, do we account for the differences in style of the various writers, the preservation of their individualities, their idiosyncrasies?

It seems evident that Scripture cannot be made to harmonize with the application of this theory.

d) CONCEPT, OR THOUGHT INSPIRATION

This theory claims that only the concepts, or thoughts, of men were given by inspiration. It will be examined more fully later. Concept inspiration is opposed by

e) VERBAL INSPIRATION

Here it is claimed that the very words of Scripture were given by the Holy Spirit; that the writers were not left absolutely to themselves in the choice of words they should use. (See page 205.)

f) PARTIAL INSPIRATION

The favorite way of expressing this theory is, "The Bible *contains* the Word of God."

This statement implies that it contains much that is *not* the Word of God, that is, that is not inspired. A serious question at once arises: Who is to decide what is and what is not inspired? Who is to be the judge of so vital a question? What part is inspired, and what part is not? Who can tell?

Such a theory leaves man in awful and fatal uncertainty.

g) PLENARY, OR FULL, INSPIRATION

This is the opposite of partial inspiration. It holds all Scripture to be equally inspired, as stated on page 195. It bases its claim on 2 Tim. 3:16.

The Revised Version translation of 2 Tim. 3:16 is erroneous. The reader might infer from it that there is some Scripture that is not inspired.

If Paul had said, "All Scripture that is divinely inspired is also profitable, etc.," he would virtually have said, "There is *some* Scripture, *some* part of the Bible, that is *not profitable, etc.,* and therefore is not inspired." This is what the spirit of rationalism wants, namely, to make human reason the test and judge and measure of what is inspired and what is not. One man says such and such a verse is not profitable to him, another says such and such a verse is not profitable to him; a third says such and such is not profitable to him. The result is that no Bible is left.

Is it possible that anyone need be told the flat and sapless tautology that all divinely-inspired Scripture is *also* profitable? Paul dealt in no such meaningless phrases. The word translated *also* does not mean *also* here. It means *and*. Its position in the sentence shows this.

Again, the Revised rendering is shown to be openly false because the revisers refused to render the same Greek construction elsewhere in the same way, which convicts them of error.

In Hebrews 4:13 we read: "All things are naked and laid open before the eyes of him with whom we have to do." The form and construction of this verse is identical with that of 2 Tim. 3:16. Were we, however, to translate this passage as the revisers translated the passage in Timothy, it would read: "All naked things are also open to the eyes of Him with whom we have to do." All naked things are also open things! All uncovered things are also exposed things! There is no *also* in the case.

Again, 1 Tim. 4:4: "Every creature of God is good and nothing is to be rejected." According to the principles the revisers adopted in rendering 2 Tim. 3:16, this passage would read: "Every good creature of God is also nothing to be rejected."

The Greek language has no such meaningless syntax. The place of the verb *is,* which must be supplied, is directly before the word "inspired," and not after it.

The great rationalistic scholar, DeWette, confessed candidly that the rendering the revisers here adopted cannot be defended. In his German version of the text, he gave the sense thus: "Every sacred writing, i. e., of the canonical Scriptures, is inspired of God and is useful for doctrine, etc." Bishops Moberly and Wordsworth, Archbishop Trench, and others of the Revision committee, disclaimed any responsibility for the rendering. Dean Burgon pronounced it "the most astonishing as well as calamitous literary blunder of the age." It was condemned by Dr. Tregelles, the only man ever pensioned by the British government for scholarship.

In accordance with this weight of testimony, therefore, we hold to the rendering of the Authorized Version, and claim that all Scripture is equally and fully inspired of God.

4. The Claims of the Scriptures to Inspiration

That the writers of the Scriptures claimed to write under the direct influence of the Spirit of God there can be no doubt. The *quality* or *degree* of their inspiration may be called into question, but surely not the *fact* of it. Let us examine the testimony of the writers themselves.

a) THE CLAIMS OF OLD TESTAMENT WRITERS TO INSPIRATION (WE USE THE WORD INSPIRATION HERE AS INCLUDING REVELATION.)

Compare and examine the following passages:

Exod. 4:10-15—"And Moses said unto the Lord, O my Lord, I am not eloquent, neither heretofore, nor since thou hast spoken unto thy servant; but I am slow of speech, and of a slow tongue. And the Lord said unto him, Who hath made man's mouth? or who maketh the dumb, or deaf, or the seeing, or the blind? have not I the Lord? Now therefore go, and I will be with thy mouth, and teach thee what thou shalt say. And he said, O my Lord, send, I pray thee, by the hand of him whom thou wilt send. And the anger of the Lord was kindled against Moses, and he said, Is not Aaron the Levite thy brother? I know that he can speak well. And also, behold, he cometh forth to meet thee; and when he seeth thee, he will be glad in his heart. And thou shalt speak unto him, and put words in his mouth, and I will be with thy mouth, and with his mouth, and will teach you what ye shall do."

Deut. 4:2—"Ye shall not add unto the word which I command you, neither shall ye diminish ought from it, that ye may keep the commandments of the Lord your God which I command you."

Jer. 1:7-9—"But the Lord said unto me, Say not, I am a child: for thou shalt go to all that I shall send thee, and whatsoever I command thee thou shalt speak. Be not afraid of their faces; for I am with thee to deliver thee, saith the Lord. Then the Lord put forth his hand, and touched my mouth. And the Lord said unto me, Behold, I have put my words in thy mouth." Also Ezek. 3:4; Micah 3:8.

These are but a few of the many passages in which the inspiration of the writers is affirmed and claimed.

Note further that the words "God said" occur ten times in the first chapter of Genesis. It is claimed that such expressions as "The Lord said," "The Lord spake," "The word of the Lord came," are found 3,808 times in the Old Testament. These writers, claiming to be the revealers of the will of God, almost always commenced their messages with the words, "Thus saith the Lord." That they were not deceived in their claims is evident from the minuteness and detail as to names, times and places which characterized their messages, and from the literal fulfillment of these oracles of God.

b) THE CLAIMS OF THE NEW TESTAMENT WRITERS TO INSPIRATION

It is worthy of note here to observe that inspiration is claimed by New Testament writers for Old Testament writers as well as for themselves. Read and compare the following passages:

2 Pet. 1:20, 21—"Knowing this first, that no prophecy of the Scripture is of any private interpretation. For the prophecy came not in old time by the will of man; but holy men of God spake as they were moved by the Holy Ghost."

1 Pet. 1:10, 11—"Of which salvation the prophets have inquired and searched diligently, who prophesied of the grace that should come unto you: searching what, or what manner of time the Spirit of Christ which was in them did signify, when it testified beforehand the sufferings of Christ, and the glory that should follow."

Acts 1:16—"Men and brethren, this scripture must needs have been fulfilled, which the Holy Ghost by the mouth of David spake before concerning Judas, which was guide to them that took Jesus."

Acts 28:25—"And when they agreed not among themselves,

they departed, after that Paul had spoken one word, Well spake the Holy Ghost by Esaias the prophet unto our fathers."

1 Cor. 2:13—"Which things also we speak, not in the words which man's wisdom teacheth, but which the Holy Ghost teacheth; comparing spiritual things with spiritual."

1 Cor. 14:37—"If any man think himself to be a prophet, or spiritual, let him acknowledge that the things that I write unto you are the commandments of the Lord."

1 Thess. 2:13—"For this cause also thank we God without ceasing, because, when ye received the word of God which ye heard of us, ye received it not as the word of men, but, as it is in truth, the word of God, which effectually worketh also in you that believe."

2 Peter 3:1, 2—"This second epistle, beloved, I now write unto you; in both which I stir up your pure minds by way of remembrance: that ye may be mindful of the words which were spoken before by the holy prophets, and of the commandment of us the apostles of the Lord and Saviour."

Matt. 10:20—"For it is not ye that speak, but the Spirit of your Father which speaketh in you."

Mark 13:11—"But when they shall lead you, and deliver you up, take no thought beforehand what ye shall speak, neither do ye premeditate; but whatsoever shall be given you in that hour, that speak ye, for it is not ye that speak, but the Holy Ghost."

See also Luke 12:12; 21:14, 15; Acts 2:4.

It is evident from these and many other passages of Scripture that the writers of both the Old and New Testaments were conscious of having received revelations from God, and considered themselves inspired of God to write the Scriptures. They felt while writing that they were giving expression to the infallible truth of God, and were conscious that the Holy Spirit was moving them to the work.

5. What Is the Nature of the Inspiration that Characterized the Writers of the Scriptures, and in What Degree Were They Under Its Influence?

Much has been said and written in answer to this question. Were the *thoughts* or *concepts* alone inspired, or were the *words* also inspired? Were the words dictated by the Holy Spirit, or were the writers left to choose their own words? These are the knotty questions current today regarding the inspiration of the Bible. We may say with certainty that

a) AT LEAST SOME OF THE WORDS OF SCRIPTURE ARE THE IDENTICAL WORDS WRITTEN OR SPOKEN BY GOD HIMSELF.

Note Exodus 32:16—"The writing was the writing of God"; Exodus 31:18—"Written with the finger of God." Compare also Deuteronomy 10:2, 4; 9:10; Exodus 24:12. See also 1 Chronicles 28:19 (R. V.)—"All this, said David, have I been made to understand in writing from the hand of Jehovah"; Daniel 5:5— There "came forth the finger of a man's hand and wrote . . ."

In the New Testament God is heard speaking both at the baptism and the transfiguration of Jesus, saying, "This is my beloved Son, in whom I am well pleased; hear ye him."

It is clearly evident from these passages that some part of the inspired record claims to be a record of the exact words of God.

b) IT IS ALSO VERY DEFINITELY STATED IN SCRIPTURE THAT GOD PUT INTO THE MOUTHS OF CERTAIN MEN THE VERY WORDS THEY SHOULD SPEAK, AND TOLD THEM WHAT THEY SHOULD WRITE.

Exod. 4:10-15—"And Moses said unto the Lord, O my Lord, I am not eloquent, neither heretofore, nor since thou has spoken unto thy servant: but I am slow of speech, and of a slow tongue. And the Lord said unto him, Who hath made man's mouth? or who maketh the dumb, or deaf, or the seeing, or the blind? have not I the Lord? Now therefore go, and I will be with thy mouth, and teach thee what thou shalt say. And he said, O my Lord, send, I pray thee, by the hand of him whom thou wilt send. And the anger of the Lord was kindled against Moses, and he said, Is not Aaron the Levite thy brother? I know that he can speak well. And also, behold, he cometh forth to meet thee: and when he seeth thee, he will be glad in his heart. And thou shalt speak unto him, and put words in his mouth: and I will be with thy mouth, and with his mouth, and will teach you what ye shall do."

Exod. 34:27—"And the Lord said unto Moses, Write thou these words: for after the tenor of these words I have made a covenant with thee and with Israel."

Num. 17:2, 3—"Speak unto the children of Israel, and take of every one of them a rod according to the house of their fathers, of all their princes according to the house of their fathers, twelve rods: write thou every man's name upon his rod. And thou shalt write Aaron's name upon the rod of Levi: for one rod shall be for the head of the house of their fathers."

Isa. 8:1, 11, 12—"Moreover the Lord said unto me, Take thee a great roll, and write in it with a man's pen concerning Maher-shalal-hash-baz. For the Lord spake thus to me with a strong hand, and instructed me that I should not walk in the way of this people, saying, Say ye not, A confederacy, to all them to whom this people shall say, A confederacy; neither fear ye their fear, nor be afraid."

Jer. 1:7—"But the Lord said unto me, Say not, I am a child: for thou shalt go to all that I shall send thee, and whatsoever I command thee thou shalt speak."

Jer. 7:27—"Therefore thou shalt speak all these words unto them; but they will not hearken to thee; thou shalt also call unto them; but they will not answer thee."

Jer. 13:12—"Therefore thou shall speak unto them this word: Thus saith the Lord God of Israel, Every bottle shall be filled with wine: and they shall say unto thee, Do we not certainly know that every bottle shall be filled with wine?"

Jer. 30:1, 2—"The word that came to Jeremiah from the Lord, saying, Thus speaketh the Lord God of Israel, saying, Write thee all the words that I have spoken unto thee in a book."

Jer. 36:1, 2, 4, 11, 27-32—"And it came to pass in the fourth year of Jehoiakim the son of Josiah king of Judah, that this word came unto Jeremiah from the Lord, saying, Take thee a roll of a book, and write therein all the words that I have spoken unto thee against Israel, and against Judah, and against all the nations, from the day I spake unto thee, from the days of Josiah, even unto this day. Then Jeremiah called Baruch the son of Neriah; and Baruch wrote from the mouth of Jeremiah all the words of the Lord, which he had spoken unto him, upon a roll of a book. When Michaiah the son of Gemariah, the son of Shaphan, had heard out of the book all the words of the Lord. . . . Then the word of the Lord came to Jeremiah, after that the king had burned the roll, and the words which Baruch wrote at the mouth of Jeremiah, saying, Take thee again another roll, and write in it all the former words that were in the first roll, which Jehoiakim the king of Judah hath burned. And thou shalt say to Jehoiakim king of Judah, Thus saith the Lord; Thou hast burned this roll, saying, Why hast thou written therein, saying, The king of Babylon shall certainly come and destroy this land, and shall cause to cease from thence man and beast? Therefore thus saith the Lord of Jehoiakim king of Judah; He shall have none to sit upon the throne of David: and his dead body shall be cast out in the day to the heat, and in the night to the frost. And I will punish him and his seed and his servants for their iniquity; and I will bring upon them, and upon the inhabitants of Jerusalem, and upon the men of Judah, all the evil that I have pronounced against them; but they hearkened not. Then took Jeremiah another roll, and give it to Baruch the scribe, the son of Neriah, who wrote therein from the mouth of Jeremiah all the words of the book which Jehoiakim king of Judah had burned in the fire; and there were added besides unto them many like words." Also Ezek. 2:7; 3:10, 11; 24:2; 37:16; Hab. 2:2; Zech. 7:8-12.

1 Cor. 14:37—"If any man think himself to be a prophet, or spiritual, let him acknowledge that the things that I write unto you are the commandments of the Lord."

Rev. 2:1, 8, 12, 18—"Unto the angel of the church of Ephesus write; These things saith he that holdeth the seven stars in his right hand, who walketh in the midst of the seven golden candlesticks . . . And unto the angel of the church in Smyrna write; These things saith the first and the last, which was dead, and is alive . . . And to the angel of the church in Pergamos write; These things saith he which hath the sharp sword with two edges . . . And unto the angel of the church in Thyatira write; These things saith the Son of God, who hath his eyes like unto a flame of fire, and his feet are like fine brass." Also 3:1, 7, 14.

Rev. 10:4—"And when the seven thunders had uttered their voices, I was about to write: and I heard a voice from heaven saying unto me, Seal up those things which the seven thunders uttered, and write them not."

To sum up these two arguments, then, let us say, regarding the nature of the inspiration of the sacred writings, that part of them claim to be the very words and writings of God Himself, spoken by His own mouth, or written by His own hand: that another part claim to be the record of words spoken to certain men who wrote them down just as they were spoken.

And yet if this is all that is involved in inspiration, shall we not be robbed of a very beautiful and helpful fact, namely, that the

Holy Spirit saw fit to preserve the characteristics of the writers? Do not the works of James, the faith of Paul, and the love of John appeal to us in their own peculiar way? This leads to the statement that

c) IN A CERTAIN SENSE, AND IN RESPECT TO SOME PARTS OF THE SCRIPTURE, THE AUTHORS WERE (HUMANLY SPEAKING) LEFT TO CHOOSE THEIR OWN WORDS IN RELATING DIVINE TRUTH.

This was by no means true of all the sacred writings. There are instances recorded of men who spoke without knowing what they were saying; and of men and animals speaking without knowledge of the substance of their message:

John 11:49-52—"And one of them, named Caiaphas, being the high priest that same year, said unto them, Ye know nothing at all, nor consider that it is expedient for us, that one man should die for the people, and that the whole nation perish not. And this spake he not of himself; but being high priest that year, he prophesied that Jesus should die for that nation; and not for that nation only, but that also he should gather together in one the children of God that were scattered abroad."

Num. 22:28-30—"And the Lord opened the mouth of the ass, and she said unto Balaam, What have I done unto thee, that thou hast smitten me these three times? And Balaam said unto the ass, Because thou hast mocked me: I would there were a sword in mine hand, for now would I kill thee. And the ass said unto Balaam, Am not I thine ass, upon which thou hast ridden ever since I was thine unto this day? was I ever wont to do so unto thee? And he said, Nay."

Dan. 12:8, 9—"And I heard, but I understood not: then said I, O my Lord, what shall be the end of these things? And he said, Go thy way, Daniel: for the words are closed up and sealed till the time of the end."

And yet the gift of inspiration admitted of personal, diligent, and faithful research into the facts recorded—Luke 1:1-4.

This fact allowed the expression of the same thought in different words, such differences (by no means discrepancies) between the accounts of inspired men as would be likely to arise from the different standpoint of each. Examples:

Matt. 26:26, 27—"And as they were eating, Jesus took bread, and blessed it, and brake it, and gave it to the disciples, and said,

Take, eat; this is my body. And he took the cup, and gave thanks, and gave it to them, saying, Drink ye all of it."

Luke 22:19, 20—"And he took bread, and gave thanks, and brake it, and gave unto them, saying, This is my body which is given for you; this do in remembrance of me. Likewise also the cup after supper, saying, This cup is the new testament in my blood, which is shed for you."

1 Cor. 11:24, 25—"And when he had given thanks, he brake it, and said, Take, eat; this is my body, which is broken for you; this do in remembrance of me. After the same manner also he took the cup, when he had supped, saying, This cup is the new testament in my blood; this do ye, as oft as ye drink it, in remembrance of me."

Matt. 3:17—"And lo a voice from heaven, saying, This is my beloved Son, in whom I am well pleased."

Mark 1:11—"And there came a voice from heaven, saying, Thou art my beloved Son, in whom I am well pleased."

Luke 3:22—"And the Holy Ghost descended in a bodily shape like a dove upon him, and a voice came from heaven, which said, Thou art my beloved Son; in thee I am well pleased."

The Spirit employed the attention, the investigation, the memory, the fancy, the logic, in a word, all the faculties of the writer, and wrought through them. He guided the writer to choose what narrative and materials, speeches of others, imperial decrees, genealogies, official letters, state papers or historical matters he might find necessary for the recording of the divine message of salvation. He wrought in, with, and through their spirits, so as to preserve their individuality to others. He used the men themselves, and spoke through their individualities. "The gold was His; the mould was theirs."

DID INSPIRATION AFFECT THE WORDS USED?

If the question be asked whether or not inspiration affected the words, it must be answered in the affirmative. It is hardly possible that inspiration could insure the correct transmission of thought without in some way affecting the words. Yet it affected the words not directly and immediately by dictating them in the ears of the writers, but mediately, through working on their minds and producing there such vivid and clear ideas of thoughts and facts that the writers could find words fitted to their purposes.

We must conclude, therefore, that while from the divine side the Holy Spirit gave through men clearly and faithfully that which He wished to communicate, from the human side that communication came forth in language such as men themselves would naturally have chosen.

This may seem to some to be an impossibility, and they would allege that if the words were affected by inspiration at all, there must have been dictation. But the must is a *non sequitur*. It is admitted that God works His purposes in the world through the ordinary actions of men, while yet no violence is done to their freedom. It is admitted, also, that God, through the gracious operations of His Holy Spirit, works in the hearts of His people so as to develop in each of them the new man, while yet the individuality of each is preserved; and the type of piety is just as distinct in each Christian as the style is in each of the sacred writers. These cases are so nearly parallel as to suggest that all denials of the possibility of inspiration without the destruction of the individual characteristics are as unphilosophical as they are unwarranted.

We may therefore safely say that in a very real sense the words as well as the thoughts have been given, whether mediately or immediately, under the influence of the divine Spirit. We claim that the Bible is in deed and in truth the very Word of God; that it is the Word of God in the language of men; truly divine, and at the same time truly human; that it is the revelation of God to His creatures; that infallible guidance was given to those who wrote it, so as to preserve them from error in the statement of facts; that what the writers of the Scriptures say or write under this guidance is as truly said and written by God as if their instrumentality were not used at all; that the ideas expressed therein are the very ideas the Holy Ghost intended to convey; that God is in the fullest sense responsible for every word. This is what the Bible claims for itself.

THE DOCTRINE OF
ANGELS

THE DOCTRINE OF ANGELS

I. THEIR EXISTENCE

1. THE TEACHING OF JESUS

2. THE TEACHING OF THE APOSTLES

II. THEIR NATURE

1. CREATED BEINGS

2. SPIRITUAL BEINGS

3. GREAT POWER AND MIGHT

4. VARIOUS GRADES

5. THE NUMBER OF ANGELS

III. THE FALL OF ANGELS

1. TIME AND CAUSE

2. THE WORK OF FALLEN ANGELS

3. THE JUDGMENT OF FALLEN ANGELS

IV. THE WORK OF ANGELS

1. THEIR HEAVENLY MINISTRY

2. THEIR EARTHLY MINISTRY

   a) In Relation to the Believer

   b) In Relation to Christ's Second Coming

THE DOCTRINE OF ANGELS

We are not to think that man is the highest form of created being. As the distance between man and the lower forms of life is filled with beings of various grades, so it is possible that between man and God there exist creatures of higher than human intelligence and power. Indeed, the existence of lesser deities in all heathen mythologies presumes the existence of a higher order of beings between God and man, superior to man and inferior to God. This possibility is turned into certainty by the express and explicit teaching of the Scriptures. It would be sad indeed if we should allow ourselves to be such victims of sense perception and so materialistic that we should refuse to believe in an order of spiritual beings simply because they were beyond our sight and touch. We should not thus shut ourselves out of a larger life. A so-called liberal faith may express unbelief in such beings. Does not such a faith (?) label itself narrow rather than liberal by such a refusal of faith? Does not a liberal faith mean a faith that believes *much*, not little—as much, not as little, as possible?

I. THEIR EXISTENCE

1. The Teaching of Jesus

Matt. 18:10—"For I say unto you, That in heaven their angels do always behold the face of my Father which is in heaven." Mark 13:32—"But of that day and that hour knoweth no man, no, not the angels which are in heaven." 8:38; Matt. 13:41; 26:53.

These are a sufficient number of passages, though they are by no means all, to prove that Jesus believed in the existence of angels. Jesus is not here speaking in any accommodative sense. Nor is He simply expressing a superstitious belief existing among the Jews at that time. This was not the habit of Jesus. He did not fail to correct popular opinion and tradition when it was wrong, e. g., His rebuke of the false ceremonialism of the Pharisees, and the unbelief of the Sadducees in the resurrection. See also the Sermon on the Mount (Matt. 5:20-37).

2. The Teaching of Paul, and Other Apostles

2 Thess. 1:7—"And to you who are troubled, rest with us, when the Lord Jesus shall be revealed from heaven with His mighty angels." Col. 2:18—"Let no man beguile you of your reward in a voluntary humility and worshipping of angels." Is not one of the principal reasons for the writing of the Epistle to the Colossians to correct the Gnostic theory of the worshipping of angels? See also Eph. 1:21; Col. 1:16. John believed in an angelic order of beings: John 1:51; Rev. 12:7; 22:9. Peter: 1 Pet. 3:22; 2 Pet. 2:11. See also Jude 9; Luke 22:43; Mark 8:38; Heb. 12:22. These and numerous other references in the Scriptures compel the candid student of the Word to believe in the existence of angels.

II. THE NATURE OF ANGELS

1. They Are Created Beings.

Col. 1:16—"For by him were all things created, that are in heaven, and that are in earth, visible and invisible, whether they be thrones, or dominions, or principalities, or powers; all things were created by him, and for him." Angels are not the spirits of the departed, nor are they glorified human beings (Heb. 12:22, 23). Neh. 9:6—"Thou, even thou, art Lord alone; thou hast made heaven, the heaven of heavens, with all their host."

2. They Are Spiritual Beings.

Heb. 1:14—"Are they not all ministering spirits?" Psa. 104:4—"Who maketh his angels spirits; his ministers a flaming fire." Although the angels are "spirits," they nevertheless ofttimes have appeared to men in visible, and even human form (Gen. 19; Judges 2:1; 6:11-22; Matt. 1:20; Luke 1:26; John 20:12). There seems to be no sex among the angels, although wherever the word "angel" is used in the Scriptures it is always in the masculine form.

3. They Are Beings of Great Might and Power.

2 Pet. 2:11—"Whereas angels, which are greater in power and might [than man]." Psa. 103:20—"Angels that excel in strength." One angel was able to destroy Sodom and Gomorrah, and other guilty cities; one angel smote the first-born, and rolled away the

great stone from the mouth of the tomb. One angel had power to lay hold of that old dragon, the devil (Rev. 20:2, 10); one angel smote a hundred and fourscore and five thousand Assyrians (Isa. 37:36). Their power is delegated; they are the angels of *His* might (2 Thess. 1:7), the ministers through whom God's might is manifested. They are mighty, but not almighty.

4. There Are Various Ranks and Orders of Angels.

We read of Michael, the archangel (Jude 9; 1 Thess. 4:16); angels, authorities, and powers—which are supposedly ranks and orders of angels (1 Pet. 3:22; Col. 1:16). In the Apocryphal books we find a hierarchy with seven archangels, including Michael, Gabriel, Raphael, Uriel. The fact that but one archangel is mentioned in the Scriptures proves that its doctrine of angels was not derived, as some supposed, from Babylonian and Persian sources, for there we find seven archangels instead of one.

5. The Number of Angels

Heb. 12:22, R. V.—"Innumerable hosts of angels." Cf. 2 Kings 6:17; Matt. 26:53; Job 25:3.

III. THE FALL OF ANGELS

Originally all angels were created good. The Scriptures speak of a fall of angels—"the angels that sinned"—who are now bound.

2 Pet. 2:4—"For if God spared not the angels that sinned, but cast them down to hell, and delivered them into chains of darkness, to be reserved unto judgment." Jude 6—"And the angels which kept not their first estate, but left their own habitation, he hath reserved in everlasting chains under darkness unto the judgment of the great day."

1. The Time of the Fall of Angels

Some maintain that it took place before the creation recorded in Genesis 1:2—between verses one and two; that it was this fall which made the original creation (Gen. 1:1) "waste and void." This view can neither be proven nor refuted, nevertheless the great and awful fact of a fall of angels remains.

2. The Cause of the Fall of Angels

Peter does not specify the sin. Jude says they "kept not their first estate, but left their own habitation." This, taken in connection with Deut. 32:8, which seems to indicate that certain territories or boundaries were appointed unto the angels, and Gen. 6:1-4, which speaks of the "sons of God" (which some suppose to refer to angels, which, however, is questionable), might seem to imply that the sin of the angels consisted in leaving their own abode and coming down to cohabit with the "daughters of men." Thus their sin would be that of lust. To some expositors the context in Jude would seem to warrant such a conclusion, inasmuch as reference is made to the sins of Sodom and Gomorrah. But this can hardly be true, for a close study of the text in Genesis 6 shows that by "the sons of God" are meant the Sethites. This would seem to be the true interpretation; if so, then the sin recorded in Genesis 6 would be (1) natural and not monstrous; (2) Scriptural, and not mythical (Num. 25; Judges 3:6; Rev. 2:14, 20-22 refer to sins of a similar description); (3) accords with the designations subsequently given to the followers of God (Luke 3:38; Rom. 8:14; Gal. 3:26); (4) has a historical basis in the fact that Seth was regarded by his mother as a (the) son of (from) God, (5) in the circumstance that already the Sethites had begun to call themselves by the name of Jehovah (Gen. 4:26); (6), finally, it is sufficient as a hypothesis, and is therefore entitled to the preference (after Lange).

There are still others who say that the sin of the angels was pride and disobedience. It seems quite certain that these were the sins that caused Satan's downfall (Ezek. 28). If this be the true view then we are to understand the words "estate" or "principality" as indicating that instead of being satisfied with the dignity once for all assigned to them under the Son of God, they aspired higher.

3. The Work of Fallen Angels Who Are Now Free

Scripture speaks of another company of angels who are associated with Satan and who are free to carry out his purposes (Matt. 25:41; Rev. 12:7-9). Nothing is revealed about the time or nature of their fall. Some students see in Rev. 12:4 a suggestion that they fell with Satan, and that they may have included one third of the heavenly host. These fallen angels are commonly believed to be identical with the demons mentioned throughout the New Testament.

They oppose God's purposes (Dan. 10:10-14); afflict God's

people (Luke 13:16; Matt. 17:15-18); execute Satan's purposes (Matt. 25:41; 12:26, 27); hinder the spiritual life of God's people (Eph. 6:12); try to deceive God's people (1 Sam. 28:7-20).

4. The Judgment of the Fallen Angels

Jude 6; 2 Pet. 2:4; Matt. 25:41, show that there is no hope of their redemption. Their final doom will be in the eternal fire. According to 1 Cor. 6:3 it would seem as though the saints were to have some part in the judgment of fallen angels.

IV. THE WORK OF ANGELS

1. Their Heavenly Ministry

Isa. 6; Rev. 5:11, 12; 8:3, 4—priestly service and worship.

2. Their Earthly Ministry

To the angels has been committed the administration of the affairs material to sense, e. g., showing Hagar a fountain; appearing before Joshua with a drawn sword; releasing the chains from Peter, and opening the prison doors; feeding, strengthening, and defending the children of God. To the Holy Spirit more particularly has been committed the task of imparting the truth concerning spiritual matters.

In general: Angels have a relation to the earth somewhat as follows: They are related to winds, fires, storms, pestilence (Psa. 103:20; 104:4; 1 Chron. 21:15, 16, 27). The nation of Israel has a special relationship to angels in the sense of angelic guardianship (Dan. 12:1; Ezek. 9:1; Dan. 11:1).

In particular: Angels have a special ministry with reference to the Church of Jesus Christ—the body of believers. They are the saints' "ministering servants" (Heb. 1:14)—they do service for God's people. Illustrations: To Abraham (Gen. 19); to Gideon (Judg. 6); to Mary (Luke 1); to the shepherds (Luke 2); to Peter (Acts 12); to Paul (Acts 27).

a) THEY GUIDE THE BELIEVER.

They guide the worker to the sinner (Acts 8:26), and the sinner to the worker (Acts 10:3). Note: The angel guides, but the Spirit instructs (8:29). Are angels interested in conversions? (Luke 15:10). How they watch our dealing with the unsaved!

b) THEY CHEER AND STRENGTHEN GOD'S PEOPLE.

1 Kings 19:5-8; Matt. 4:11; Luke 22:43; cf. Acts 27:4-35; 5:19.

c) THEY DEFEND, PROTECT, AND DELIVER GOD'S SERVANTS.

Dan. 6:22; Acts 5:19; 2 Kings 6:18; Gen. 19:11; Acts 12:8-11; 27:23, 24.

d) THEY ARE EYEWITNESSES OF THE CHURCH AND THE BELIEVER.

1 Tim. 5:21—in matters of preaching, the service of the church, and soul-saving, the angels look on—a solemn and appalling thought. 1 Cor. 4:9—the good angels are spectators while the church engages in fierce battle with the hosts of sin. This is an incentive to endurance. 1 Cor. 11:10—"Because of the angels." Is there intimated here a lack of modesty on the part of the women so shocking to the angels, who veil their faces in the presence of God when they worship?

e) THEY GUARD THE ELECT DEAD.

Luke 16:22; Matt. 24:31. Just as they guarded Christ's tomb, and as Michael guarded Moses' body (Jude 9).

f) THEY ACCOMPANY CHRIST AT HIS SECOND COMING.

Separating the righteous from the wicked (Matt. 25:31, 32; 2 Thess. 1:7, 8). Executing God's wrath upon the wicked (Matt. 13:39-42, R. V.) How this is done, no human pen can describe. The most fearful imagery of the Bible is connected with the judgment work of angels (cf. Revelation; fire, hail, blood, plague of locusts, poison of scorpions, etc.)—whether actual or symbolic, it is awful.

THE DOCTRINE OF
SATAN

THE DOCTRINE OF SATAN

I. HIS EXISTENCE AND PERSONALITY
  1. EXISTENCE
  2. PERSONALITY

II. HIS PLACE AND POWER
  1. A MIGHTY ANGEL
  2. PRINCE OF POWER OF THE AIR
  3. GOD OF THIS WORLD
  4. HEAD OF KINGDOM OF DARKNESS
  5. SOVEREIGN OVER DEATH

III. HIS CHARACTER
  1. ADVERSARY
  2. DIABOLOS
  3. WICKED ONE
  4. TEMPTER

IV. OUR ATTITUDE TOWARDS SATAN
  1. LIMITED POWER OF SATAN
  2. RESIST HIM

V. HIS DESTINY
  1. A CONQUERED ENEMY
  2. UNDER ETERNAL CURSE

VI. DEMONS

THE DOCTRINE OF SATAN

Throughout the Scriptures Satan is set forth as the greatest enemy of God and man. Too long has Satan been a subject of ridicule instead of fear. Seeing the Scriptures teach the existence of a personality of evil, man should seek to know all he can about such a being. Much of the ridicule attached to the doctrine of Satan comes from the fact that men have read their fancies and theories into the Scriptures; they have read Milton's *Paradise Lost* but have neglected the Book of Job; they have considered the experiences of Luther instead of the Epistles of Peter and Jude. To avoid skepticism on the one hand and ridicule on the other we must resort to the Scriptures to formulate our views of this doctrine.

I. THE EXISTENCE AND PERSONALITY OF SATAN

1. His Existence

To science the existence of Satan is an open question; it neither can deny nor affirm it. Satan's existence and personality can be denied therefore only on purely *a priori* grounds. The Bible, however, is very clear and positive in its teaching regarding the existence of a personality of evil called the devil. It is popular in some circles today to spell devil with the "d" left off, thus denying his real existence.

Matt. 13:19, 39—"Then cometh the wicked one. . . . The enemy that sowed them is the devil." John 13:2—"The devil having now put it into the heart of Judas Iscariot, Simon's son, to betray him." See also Acts 5:3; 2 Cor. 11:3, 14; 2 Pet. 2:4; Jude 6.

How Satan came to be is not quite as clear a fact as that he exists. In all probability he was once a good angel. It is claimed by scholarly and reliable interpreters that his fall is portrayed in Ezekiel 28:12-19; cf. Isa. 14:12-14. That he was once in the truth but fell from it is evident from John 8:44. His fall (Luke 10:18) was probably in connection with the fall of angels as set forth in such passages as 2 Pet. 2:4; Jude 6. Pride (?) was one of the causes (1 Tim. 3:6; Ezek. 28:15, 17). This fact may account for the expression "Satan and his angels" (Matt. 25:41). Paul doubtless refers to the fact that Satan was once an angel of light (2 Cor. 11:14). Whenever Satan is represented under the form of a serpent, we are to understand such expressions as describing him after his fall. There is certainly no ground for presenting the evil one as having horns, tail, and hoofs. This is only to bring into ridicule what is an exceedingly serious fact. A careful consideration of all the scriptures here given will assure the student that Satan is not a figment of the imagination, but a real being.

2. His Personality

John 8:44—"Ye are of your father the devil, and the lusts of your father ye will do. He was a murderer from the beginning, and abode not in the truth, because there is no truth in him. When he speaketh a lie, he speaketh of his own; for he is a liar, and the father of it." 1 John 3:8—"He that committeth sin is of the devil; for the devil sinneth from the beginning." Satan is here set forth as a murderer, a liar, a sinner—all elements of personality. He had the "power over death" (Heb. 2:14), and is the "prince of this world" (John 14:30).

The narrative of Satan in Job 1 and 2 strongly emphasizes his personality. He is as much a person as the "sons of God," Job, and even God himself. Zech. 3:1, 2; 1 Chron. 21:1; Psa. 109:6 also emphasize the fact of Satan's personality. Throughout all these Scriptures the masculine personal pronoun is used of Satan, and attributes and qualities of personality are ascribed to him. Unless we veto the testimony of the Scriptures we must admit that Satan is a real person. How can any one read the story of the temptation of Christ (Matt. 4:1-11) and fail to realize both parties in the wilderness conflict were persons—Christ, a person; Satan, a person?

Such offices as those ascribed to Satan in the Scriptures require an officer; such a work manifests a worker; such power implies an agent; such thought proves a thinker; such designs are from a personality.

Our temptations may be said to come from three sources: the world, the flesh, and the devil. But there are temptations which we feel sure come from neither the world nor the flesh, e. g., those which come to us in our moments of deepest devotion and quiet; we can account for them only by attributing them to the devil himself. "That old serpent, the devil, has spoken with fatal eloquence to every one of us no doubt; and I do not need a dissertation from the naturalist on the construction of a serpent's mouth to prove it. Object to the figure if you will, but the grim, damning fact remains."—*Joseph Parker*

There can scarcely be any doubt as to the fact that Christ taught the existence of a personality of evil. There can be but three explanations as to the meaning of His teaching: First, that He accommodated His language to a gross superstition, knowing it to be such. If this be true then what becomes of His sincerity? Second, that He shared the superstition not knowing it to be such. Then what becomes of His omniscience, of His reliability as a Teacher from God? Third, that the doctrine is not a superstition, but actual truth. This position completely vindicates Christ as to His sincerity, omniscience and infallibility as the Teacher sent from God.

II. THE PLACE AND POWER OF SATAN

1. *A Mighty Angel*

He was such, and probably is yet. Jude 8, 9—They "speak evil of dignities. Yet Michael the archangel, when contending with the devil he disputed about the body of Moses, durst not bring against him a railing accusation, but said, The Lord rebuke thee." Daniel 10 shows that Satan has power to oppose one of the chief angels (vv. 12, 13 in particular). In Luke 11:21 Christ calls Satan "a strong man armed." He is "the prince of this world" (John 14:30).

2. *Prince of the Power of the Air*

Eph. 2:2—"The prince of the power of the air, the spirit that now worketh in the children of disobedience." Cf. 6:11, 12. He is also prince of the demons or fallen angels, Matt. 12:24; 9:34; Luke 11:14-18. There is doubtless an allusion here to the fact that the world of evil spirits is organized, and that Satan is at its head.

3. *The God of This World*

2 Cor. 4:4—"In whom the god of this world hath blinded the minds of them which believe not." He is "the prince of this world" (John 12:31; 14:30; 16:11; cf. Eph. 2:1, 2; 1 John 5:19). Satan is not only the object of the world's worship, but also the moving spirit of its godless activities.

4. He Heads a Kingdom Which Is Hostile to the Kingdom of God and of Christ.

Acts 26:18—"To open their eyes, and to turn them from darkness to light, and from the power of Satan unto God." Col. 1:13—"Who hath delivered us from the power of darkness, and hath translated us into the kingdom of his dear Son." The kingdom of light is headed by a person—Jesus Christ; the kingdom of darkness, by a person—Satan. The one is a person equally with the other.

5. Has Sovereignty Over the Realm of Death.

Heb. 2:14—"That . . . he might destroy him that had the power of death, that is, the devil." It would seem as if the souls of the unregenerate dead are (or were) to some extent under Satan's dominion.

III. THE CHARACTER OF SATAN

We may judge of the nature and character of the evil one by the names and titles ascribed to him.

1. The Adversary, or Satan

Zech. 3:1—"And he showed me Joshua the high priest standing before the angel of the Lord, and Satan standing at his right hand to resist him." (See vv. 1-5.) 1 Pet. 5:8—"Your adversary the devil." Luke 10:18. See for use of the word: Num. 22:22. By adversary is meant one who takes a stand against another. Satan is the adversary of both God and man.

2. The Devil, Diabolos

Matt. 13:39—"The enemy . . . is the devil." John 8:44—"Ye are of your father the devil." This name is ascribed to Satan 33 times at least in the New Testament, and indicates an accuser or slanderer (Rev. 12:9). He slanders God to man (Gen. 3:1-7), and man to God (Job 1:9; 2:4).

3. The Wicked One

Matt. 13:19—"Then cometh the wicked one." Matt. 6:13 (R. V.); 1 John 5:19 (R. V.). This title suggests that Satan is not only wicked himself, but is also the source of all wickedness in the world.

4. The Tempter

Matt. 4:3—"And when the tempter came to him." See Gen. 3:1-6. None escape his temptations. He is continually soliciting men to sin.

In this connection we may speak of the cunning and malignity of Satan (Gen. 3:1). Satan transforms himself into an angel of light (2 Cor. 11:14). This phase of his work is well illustrated in the temptation of Christ (Matt. 4:1-11), and the temptation of Eve (Gen. 3). He fain would help Christ's faith, stimulate His confidence in the divine power, and furnish an incentive to worship. The Scriptures speak of the "wiles" or subtle methods of the devil (Eph. 6:11, 12). The "old serpent" is more dangerous than the "roaring lion."

Satan's subtlety is seen in tempting men in their weak moments (Matt. 4:1-11; Luke 22:40-46); after great successes (John 6:15, cf. vv. 1-14); by suggesting the use of right things in a wrong way (Matt. 4:1-11); in deluding his followers by signs and wonders (2 Thess. 2:9, 10).

IV. OUR ATTITUDE TOWARDS SATAN

1. So Far as the Believer Is Concerned His Power Is Limited.

Job. 1:9-12; 2:4-6. Satan had to ask leave of God to try Job. John 12:31; 16:11. Satan hath been already judged, i. e., his power and dominion over believers was broken at the cross, by reason of Christ's victory there. He had to ask permission to enter even swine (Matt. 8:30-32). Satan is mighty, but not almighty.

2. He Is to Be Resisted.

1 Pet. 5:8, 9—"Be sober, be vigilant; because your adversary the devil, as a roaring lion, walketh about seeking whom he may

devour; whom resist steadfast in the faith." James 4:7—"Resist the devil, and he will flee from you." This resistance is best accomplished by submitting to God (Rom. 6:17-23; James 4:7), and by putting on the whole armor of God (Eph. 6:10-20).

V. THE DESTINY OF SATAN

1. He Is a Conquered Enemy.

That is, so far as the believer is concerned; John 12:31; 16:9, 10; 1 John 3:8; Col. 2:15.

2. He Is Under a Perpetual Curse.

Gen. 3:14, cf. Isa. 65:25. There is no removal of the curse from Satan.

3. He Is Finally to Be Cast Alive Into the Lake of Fire, There to Be Tormented for Ever and Ever.

Matt. 25:41; Rev. 20:10—"And the devil that deceived them was cast into the lake of fire and brimstone, where the beast and the false prophet are, and shall be tormented day and night for ever and ever."

VI. DEMONS

The origin of demons is not revealed in the Bible. They are thought to be angels who fell with Satan (Matt. 25:41; Rev. 12:7, 9), not to be confused with the fallen angels who are now bound (2 Pet. 2:4; Jude 6). Satan is their prince (Matt. 12:22-28), ruling them through an evil hierarchy (Eph. 6:12).

Demons are evil, unclean, vicious spirits who seek to possess the bodies of men (Matt. 10:1; Mark 5:1-13). Demon possession is clearly distinguished from disease in Scripture (Matt. 8:16; 10:1). These wicked spirits can be cast out in Christ's name (Acts 16:18). They know He will some day judge and condemn them (Matt. 8: 29). In the last days they will delude men into holding false doctrine (1 Tim. 4:1), and they will have a part in Armageddon (Rev. 16:13-16).

THE DOCTRINES OF THE
LAST THINGS

THE DOCTRINES OF THE LAST THINGS

A. THE SECOND COMING OF CHRIST

B. THE RESURRECTION

C. THE JUDGMENT

D. THE DESTINY OF THE WICKED

E. THE REWARD OF THE RIGHTEOUS

THE DOCTRINES OF THE LAST THINGS

Under this caption are treated such doctrines as the second coming of Christ, the resurrection of both the righteous and wicked, the judgments, final awards, and eternal destiny.

A. THE SECOND COMING OF CHRIST

I. ITS IMPORTANCE
1. PROMINENCE IN THE SCRIPTURES
2. THE CHRISTIAN HOPE
3. THE CHRISTIAN INCENTIVE
4. THE CHRISTIAN COMFORT

II. ITS NATURE
1. PERSONAL AND VISIBLE COMING TO THE EARTH
2. DIFFERENT VIEWS
3. DISTINCTIONS

III. ITS PURPOSE
WITH REFERENCE TO—
1. THE CHURCH
2. THE UNREGENERATE
3. THE JEWS
4. THE ENEMIES OF GOD
5. THE MILLENNIUM

IV. ITS DATE
1. DAY AND HOUR UNKNOWN
2. RECOGNIZING THE "SIGNS"
3. IMMINENT

A. THE SECOND COMING OF CHRIST

I. ITS IMPORTANCE

1. Its Prominence in the Scriptures

It is claimed that one out of every thirty verses in the Bible mentions this doctrine; to every one mention of the first coming the second coming is mentioned eight times; 318 references to it are made in 216 chapters; whole books (1 and 2 Thess., e. g.) and chapters (Matt. 24; Mark 13; Luke 21, e. g.) are devoted to it.

It is the theme of the Old Testament prophets. Of course, they sometimes merge the two comings so that it is not at first sight apparent, yet the doctrine is there (1 Pet. 1:11).

Jesus Christ bore constant testimony to His coming again (John 14:3; Matt. 24 and 25; Mark 13; Luke 21; John 21:22).

The angels, who bore such faithful testimony to Christ's first advent, bear testimony to His second coming (Acts 1:11; cf. Heb. 2:2, for the faithfulness of their testimony).

The apostles faithfully proclaimed this truth (Acts 3:19, 20; 1 Thess. 4:16, 17; Heb. 9:28; 1 John 2:28; Jude 14, 15).

2. The Church of Christ Is Bidden to Look Forward to Christ's Second Coming as Its Great Hope.

Titus 2:13—"Looking for that blessed hope, and the glorious appearing of the great God and our Saviour Jesus Christ." 2 Pet. 3:12. The one great event, that which supersedes all others, towards which the Church is to look, and for which she is to ardently long, is the second coming of Christ.

3. It Is Set Forth as the Doctrine Which Will Prove to be the Greatest Incentive to Consistent Living.

Matt. 24:44-46; Luke 21:34-36—"And take heed to yourselves, lest at any time your hearts be overcharged with surfeiting, and drunkenness, and cares of this life, and so that day come upon you unawares. . . . Watch ye therefore, and pray always, that ye may be accounted worthy to escape all these things that shall come to pass, and to stand before the Son of man." 1 John 2:28; 3:3. The test which the church should apply to all questions of practice: Would I like to have Christ find me doing this when He comes?

4. It Is a Doctrine of the Greatest Comfort to the Believer.

1 Thess. 4:14-18. After stating that our loved ones who had fallen asleep in Christ should again meet with us at the coming of our Lord, the apostle says, "Wherefore comfort one another with these words."

Why then should such a comforting and helpful doctrine as this be spoken against? Many reasons may be suggested: the unreadiness of the church; preconceived views (2 Pet. 3:4); extravagant predictions as to time; lack of knowledge of the Scriptures. May not the guilt on our part for rejecting the second coming of Christ be as great if not greater than that of the Jews for rejecting His first coming?

II. WHAT IS MEANT BY THE SECOND COMING OF CHRIST

1. A Personal and Visible Coming

Acts 1:11—"Ye men of Galilee, why stand ye gazing up into heaven? This same Jesus, which is taken up from you into heaven, shall so come in like manner as ye have seen him go into heaven." 1 Thess. 4:16, 17—"For the Lord himself shall descend from heaven." Rev. 1:7. From these scriptures we learn that by the second coming of Christ is meant the bodily, personal, and visible coming of our Lord Jesus Christ to receive His saints and afterward to reign on the earth.

2. Erroneous Views Concerning the Second Coming of Christ

a) THAT THE SECOND COMING MEANS CHRIST'S COMING AT DEATH

This cannot be the meaning, because—

Death is not attended by the events narrated in 1 Thessalonians 4:16, 17. Indeed the second coming is here set forth as the opposite of death for "the dead in Christ shall rise" from the dead when Christ comes again.

According to John 14:3, Christ comes for us, and not we go to Him: "I will come again, and receive you unto myself."

John 21:21-23—"Peter seeing him [John] saith to Jesus, Lord, and what shall this man do? Jesus saith unto him, If I will that he tarry till I come, what is that to thee? Follow thou me. Then went this saying abroad among the brethren, that that disciple should not die; yet Jesus said not unto him, He shall not die; but, if I will that he tarry till I come, what is that to thee?"

1 Corinthians 15:50-57 declares that at the second coming of Christ we overcome, not succumb to, death. See John 8:51; Matt. 16:28.

The foolishness of such interpretation is seen if we substitute the word "death" for the second coming of Christ in such places where this coming is mentioned, e. g., Phil. 3:20; Matt. 16:28—"Verily I say unto you, There by some standing here, which shall not taste of death, till they see the Son of man coming in his kingdom."

b) THAT THE SECOND COMING MEANS THE COMING OF THE HOLY SPIRIT

There is no doubt but that the coming of the Holy Spirit is a coming (John 14:21-23), but it is by no means *the* second coming, and for the following reasons:

Many of the testimonies and promises of the second coming were given *after* Pentecost, e. g., Phil. 3:21; 2 Tim. 4:8; 1 Thess. 4:16, 17; 1 Cor. 15:51, 52.

Christ does not receive us unto Himself, but comes to us, at Pentecost. In the second coming He takes us, not comes to us.

The events of 1 Thessalonians 4:16, 17 did not occur on the day of Pentecost, nor do they occur when the believer receives the Holy Spirit.

c) THAT THE SECOND COMING REFERS TO THE DESTRUCTION OF JERUSALEM

Reply: The events of 1 Thessalonians 4:16, 17 did not take place then.

John 21:21-23 and Rev. 22:20 were written *after* the destruction of Jerusalem.

From all that has been said then, it seems clear that the second coming of Christ is an event still in the future.

3. The Need of Recognizing the Distinction Between Christ's Coming for His Saints and With His Saints

There is a distinction between the *presence* and the *appearing* of Christ: the former referring to His coming *for,* and the latter *with* His saints. We should remember, further, that the second coming còvers a period of time, and is not the event of a single moment. Even the first coming covered over thirty years, and included the events of Christ's birth, circumcision, baptism, ministry, crucifixion, resurrection, etc. The second coming will also include a number of events such as the rapture, the great tribulation, the millennium, the resurrection, the judgments, etc.

III. THE PURPOSE OF THE SECOND COMING

1. So Far as It Concerns the Church

1 Thess. 4:13-17; 1 Cor. 15:50-52; Phil. 3:20, 21, R. V.; 1 John 3:2. When Christ comes again He will first raise the righteous dead, and change the righteous living; simultaneously they shall be caught up to meet the Lord in the air to be with Him for ever.

Eph. 5:23, 32; 2 Cor. 11:2; Rev. 19:6-9; Matt. 25:1-10. The Church, the Bride of Christ, will then be married to her Lord.

Matt. 25:19; 2 Tim. 4:8; 1 Pet. 5:4; 1 Cor. 3:12-15; 2 Cor. 5:10. Believers will be rewarded for their faithfulness in service at His coming. (See under The Final Reward of the Righteous, page 266.)

2. So Far as It Concerns the Unconverted Nations and Individuals

Matt. 24:30; Rev. 1:7; Matt. 25:31, 32; Rev. 20:11, 12; Isa. 26:21; 2 Thess. 1:7-9. A distinction must be recognized between the judgment of the living nations, and that of the great white throne. These are not the same, for no resurrection accompanies the judgment of the living nations, as in the case of the throne judgment. Further, one thousand years elapse between these two judgments (Rev. 20:7-11). Again, one is at the beginning of the Millennium, and the other at its close.

3. With Reference to the Jews

The Jews will be restored to their own land (Isa. 11:11; 60), in an unconverted state; will rebuild the temple, and restore worship (Ezek. 40-48); will make a covenant with Antichrist for one week (seven years), in the midst of which they will break the covenant (Dan. 9:27; 2 Thess. 2); they will then pass through the great tribulation (Matt. 24:21, 22, 29; Rev. 3:10; 7:14); are converted (as a nation) at the coming of Christ (Zech. 12:10; Rev. 1:7); become great missionaries (Zech. 8:13-23); never more to be removed from the land (Amos 9:15; Ezek. 34:28).

4. With Regard to Antichrist, and the Enemies of God's People

2 Thess. 1:7-9; Rev. 19:20; 20:10. These shall be destroyed by the brightness of His coming; will be cast finally into the lake of fire and brimstone.

5. To Set Up the Millennial Reign on the Earth

The Millennium means the thousand years reign of Christ upon the earth (Rev. 20:1-4). Some think that it is the continuation of the Kingdom Age broken off by the unbelief of the Jews at the time of the apostles.

The Millennium begins with the coming of Christ with His saints; with the revelation of Christ after the great tribulation (Matt. 24:29, 30); at the close of the seventieth week of Daniel. For illustration, see Rev. 19:11-14; Dan. 7:21, 22; Zech. 14:3-9.

Then comes the destruction of Antichrist, the binding of Satan, and the destruction of the enemies of God's people (Rev. 19:20; 20:1-3, 10).

The judgment of the living nations (Matt. 25).

The conversion and missionary activity of the Jews (Zech. 8:13-23; cf. Acts 15:14-17). Then, we may have a converted world, but not now, nor in this age; Israel, not the Church, then concerned.

The nature of the Millennium:

It is a Theocracy: Jesus Christ Himself is the King (Jer. 23:5; Luke 1:30-33). The apostles will, doubtless, reign with Christ over the Jews (Isa. 66; Matt. 19:28); the Church, over the Gentile nations (Luke 19:11-19; Heb. 2:6, 7).

The capital city will be Jerusalem (Isa. 2:1-4). Pilgrimages will be made to the Holy City (Zech. 14:16).

The reign of Christ will be one of righteousness and equity (Isa. 11:4; Psa. 98:9).

A renovated earth (Rom. 8:19-21; Isa. 65:17; chap. 35).

The events closing the Millennium are apostasy and rebellion (Rev. 20:7-9); the destruction of Satan (Rev. 20:10); the great white throne judgment (Rev. 20:11-15); a new heaven and a new earth (Rev. 21 and 22).

IV. THE TIME OF CHRIST'S SECOND COMING

We need to carefully distinguish between Christ's coming *for* His saints—sometimes called the "rapture" or "parousia"; and His coming *with* His saints—the "revelation" or "epiphany."

In considering the matter of the "signs" of Christ's coming we need to pay particular attention to and distinguish between those signs which have been characteristic of and peculiar to many generations, and have, consequently, been repeated; and those which are to characterize specifically the near approach of the coming of Christ. Christians are not altogether in the dark concerning these facts: Luke 21:29-33—"So likewise ye, when ye see these things come to pass, know ye that the kingdom of God is nigh at hand" (v. 36). Also 1 Thess. 5:1-8—"But ye, brethren, are not in darkness, that that day should overtake you as a thief" (v. 4).

1. No One Knows the Day Nor the Hour.

Matt. 24:36-42—"But of that day and hour knoweth no man, no, not the angels of heaven, but my Father only" (v. 36). Mark 13:32, cf. Acts 1:7.

The Scriptures tell us enough regarding the time of Christ's coming to satisfy our faith, but not our curiosity. These statements of the Master should be sufficient to silence that fanaticism which is so anxious to tell us the exact year, month, and even the day when Christ will come. This day is hidden in the counsels of God. Jesus Himself, by a voluntary unwillingness to know, while in His state of humiliation, showed no curiosity to peer into the chronology of this event. We should not nor ought we to want to know more than Christ did on this point. The Revelation which Jesus gave to John would seem to teach that "that day," which was at one time hidden from Christ, is now, in His state of exaltation, known to Him.

2. Yet, We Must Not Forget That While We May Not Know the Exact Day or Hour of Christ's Coming, We May Know When It Is Near at Hand. (Matt. 24:36-42; 1 Thess. 5:1-5.)

There are certain "signs" which indicate its nearness:

General apostasy and departure from the faith (1 Tim. 4:1; 2 Tim. 3:1-5; Luke 18:8).

A time of great heaping up of wealth (James 5:1-9).

A time of great missionary activity (Mark 13:10; Rev. 5:9). Consider the missionary activity of the last century. Is it not marvellous? Is it a "sign" of His coming?

The return of the Jews to Palestine is associated with the Lord's return (Deut. 30:1-3; Zech. 14:1-4). A return in unbelief, Zech. 12:9-13, is to precede the promised divine regathering at the Lord's return (Jer. 31:10). The recovery of Jerusalem by the Jews after it was controlled by Gentiles for 2000 years is remarkable in view of Luke 21:24. Worldwide interest in the near east suggests the possible early fulfillment of Zech. 12:2, 3, when Jerusalem is to become a world problem.

It should not be forgotten in this connection that many of the signs mentioned refer primarily to the coming of Christ *with* His saints. But if that stage of the coming be near then surely the first stage of it must be. Other signs have reference to the first stage in the one great event of His coming, which is known as the "rapture" or Christ's coming *for* His saints.

3. It Seems Clear From the Teaching of the Scriptures That There Is Nothing to Prevent the Coming of Christ for His Saints at Any Moment.

By this is meant that there is nothing, so far as we can see from the teaching of the Scriptures and the signs of the times, to hinder the introduction of the Day of the Lord, or the second coming of Christ looked upon as a great whole—a series of events, by Christ's coming to take His own people unto Himself. In other words, there is nothing to hinder the "rapture" or "parousia"—the "epiphany," "manifestation," or "revelation" is something for a later day.

Some objections are offered to this view, the which it will be well to examine and answer eveh though briefly.

First, That the Gospel has not been preached in all the world (Matt. 24:14), therefore the coming of Christ is not imminent.

Reply: We must understand the emphatic words of the text: By "end" is meant the end of the age; but the rapture, or Christ's coming *for* His saints, of which we are here speaking as being imminent, is not the end of the age. By "world" is meant the inhabited earth; by "Gospel," good news; by "witness," not conversion but testimony. Even if these events are to precede the "rapture," have they not all been fulfilled? See Acts 2:5; 8:4; Rom. 10:18; Col. 1:6, 23, for the answer, which is certainly in the affirmative. We must give the same meaning to the word "world" in Romans and Colossians that we do to Matt. 24:14. Further, is the Church the *only* witness? See Rev. 14:6. If the rapture is not the end of the age, and if an angel can proclaim the Gospel, why cannot part of the work of witnessing be carried on after the rapture?

Second, Peter, James, and John were told that they should not taste of death until they had seen the coming of Christ's kingdom (Matt. 16:28; Mark 9:1; Luke 9:27).

Reply: True, but was not this fulfilled when they saw Christ on the Transfiguration Mount? Peter, who was there, in his second epistle (1:16-18) distinctly says it was thus fulfilled.

Third, The disciples were told that they shall not have gone over all the cities of Israel until the Son of Man be come (Matt. 10:23).

Reply: Mark 6:30, Luke 9:10 show that they did not finish all the cities, nor is there evidence anywhere that they ever did, for Israel rejected the message of the kingdom. May it not be that under the restoration of the Jews and the preaching of the "two witnesses" (Rev. 11) this shall be accomplished?

Fourth, Christ said "This generation shall not pass, till all these things be fulfilled." See Matt. 24:34; Luke 21:32; Mark 13:30.

Reply: What is meant by a "generation"? Some would say "forty years," consequently the Master referred to the destruction of Jerusalem, which event was the second coming of Christ. But this is not necessarily the case. The word "generation" may refer to the Jewish *race*; cf. the use of the same Greek word in Matt. 11:16; 16:4; Mark 8:38; Luke 7:31; 16:8; 17:25; Phil. 2:15; Psa. 22:30; 24:6. And in this connection consider carefully the wonderful preservation of the Jewish race. Other nations have passed away, having lost their identity; the Jew remains—that generation (race) has not yet passed away, nor will it "till all these things be fulfilled."*

Many students believe "this generation" refers to the generation living when these things are fulfilled.

Jesus Is Coming, by W. E. B., is heartily recommended as an exceedingly helpful book on this subject. The author is indebted thereto.

B. THE RESURRECTION OF THE DEAD

Under this caption is included the resurrection of both the righteous and the wicked, although, as will be seen later, they do not occur at the same time.

I. THIS DOCTRINE CLEARLY TAUGHT IN THE SCRIPTURES
1. IN THE OLD TESTAMENT
2. IN THE NEW TESTAMENT

II. THE NATURE OF THE RESURRECTION
1. LITERAL RESURRECTION OF THE BODIES OF ALL MEN
2. RESURRECTION OF THE BODY NECESSARY TO COMPLETE SALVATION
3. THE NATURE OF THE RESURRECTION BODY
   a) In General
   b) The Body of the Believer
   c) The Body of the Unbeliever

III. THE TIME OF THE RESURRECTION
1. OF THE RIGHTEOUS
2. OF THE WICKED

I. THE DOCTRINE OF A RESURRECTION CLEARLY TAUGHT IN THE SCRIPTURES

1. In the Old Testament

It is set forth in various ways:

In Word: Job 19:25-27—"For I know that my redeemer liveth, and that he shall stand at the latter day upon the earth; and though after my skin worms destroy this body, yet in my flesh shall I see God: whom I shall see for myself, and mine eyes shall behold, and not another; though my reins be consumed within me." Also Psa. 16:9; 17:15; Dan. 12:1-3.

In Figure: Gen. 22:5 with Heb. 11:19—"Accounting that God was able to raise him up, even from the dead; from whence also he received him in a figure."

In Prophecy: Isa. 26:19—"Thy dead men shall live, together with my dead body shall they arise. Awake and sing, ye that dwell in the dust." The words "men" and "together with" may be omitted —"Thy dead [ones] shall live." These words are Jehovah's answer to Israel's wail as recorded in vv. 17, 18. Even if they refer to resurrection of Israel as a nation, they yet teach a bodily resurrection. See also Hosea 13:14

In Reality: 1 Kings 17 (Elijah); 2 Kings 4:32-35 (Elisha and the Shunamite's son); 13:21 (Resurrection through contact with the dead bones of Elisha).

The Old Testament therefore distinctly teaches the resurrection of the body. Mark 9:10, which might seem to indicate that the apostles did not know of a bodily resurrection, is accounted for by their unwillingness to believe in a crucified Christ.

2. In the New Testament

In Word: Note the teaching of Jesus in John 5:28, 29; chap. 6, especially vv. 39, 40, 44, 54; Luke 14:13, 14; 20:35, 36. The teaching of the apostles: Paul—Acts 24:15; 1 Cor. 15; 1 Thess. 4:14-16; Phil. 3:11; John—Rev. 20:4-6, 13.

In Reality: The resurrection of saints (Matt. 27:52, 53); of Lazarus (John 11); of Jesus Christ (Matt. 28). Our Lord's resurrection assured them of what till then had been a hope imperfectly supported by Scriptural warrant, and contested by the Sadducees. It enlarged that hope (1 Pet. 1:3), and brought the doctrine of the resurrection to the front (1 Cor. 15).

II. THE NATURE OF THE RESURRECTION

1. A Literal Resurrection of the Bodies of All Men—a Universal Resurrection

John 5:28—"Marvel not at this: for the hour is coming, in the which all that are in the graves shall hear his voice, and shall come forth." 1 Cor. 15:22—"For as in Adam all die, even so in Christ shall all be made alive." The apostle is speaking of physical death in Adam, and physical resurrection in Christ.

Revelation 20:12 and 2 Corinthians 5:10 both show the necessity of the raising of the body in order that judgment may take place according to things done in the body. See also Job's hope (19:25-27); David's hope (Psa. 16:9).

An objection is sometimes made to the effect that we literalize these scriptures which are intended to be metaphorical and spiritual. To this we reply: While the exact phrase, "resurrection of the body," does not occur in the Bible, yet these scriptures clearly teach a physical rather than a spiritual resurrection. Indeed John 5:25-29 draws a sharp contrast between a spiritual (v. 25) and a literal (v. 28) resurrection. See also Phil. 3:21; 1 Thess. 4:13-17. 2 Tim. 2:18—"Who concerning the truth have erred, saying that the resurrection is past already," indicates that the early church believed in a literal resurrection. Surely there is no reference here to a spiritual resurrection such as we read of in Ephesians 5:14. Acts 24:15 speaks of a resurrection of the just and the unjust—this cannot refer to a spiritual resurrection surely. The term "spiritual body" describes, not so much the body itself, as its nature. The "spiritual body" is body, not spirit, hence should not be considered as defining body. By the term "spiritual body" is meant the body spiritualized. So there is a natural body—a body adapted and designed for the use of the soul; and there is a spiritual body—a body adapted for the use of the spirit in the resurrection day.

2. The Redemption of the Body Is Included in Our Complete Redemption.

Rom. 8:11-23—"And not only they, but ourselves also, which have the firstfruits of the Spirit, even we ourselves groan within ourselves, waiting for the adoption, to wit, the redemption of our body" (v. 23). See also 1 Cor. 6:13-20. In John 6:39 and Job 19:25-27 we are taught that the dust into which our bodies have decayed will be quickened, which indicates a physical resurrection.

This conception of the value of the body is doubtless what leads to the Christian's care for his dead loved ones and their graves. The believer's present body, which is called "the body of his humiliation" (Phil. 3:21) is not yet fitted for entrance into the kingdom (1 Cor. 15:50). Paul's hope is not for a deliverance from the body, but the redemption of it (2 Cor. 5:4).

3. The Nature of the Resurrection Body

a) IN GENERAL

Because the Scripture teaches a literal resurrection of the body it is not necessary to insist on the literal resurrection of the identical body—hair, tooth, and nail—that was laid under the ground. The idea that at the resurrection we are to see hands flying across the sea to join the body, etc., finds no corroboration in the Scriptures. Such an idea is not necessary in order to be true to the Bible teaching. Mere human analogy ought to teach us this (1 Cor. 15:36, 37)—"thou sowest not that body which shall be." The identity is preserved—that is all that we need to insist upon. What that identity tie is we may not yet know. After all it is not so much a question of material identity as of glorified individuality. The growth of the seed shows that there may be personal identity under a complete change of physical conditions.

Four things may be said about the resurrection body: first, it is not necessarily identical with that which descended into the grave; second, it will have some organic connection with that which descended into the grave; third, it will be a body which God, in His sovereignty, will bestow; fourth, it will be a body which will be a vast improvement over the old one.

b) THE BODY OF THE BELIEVER

Phil. 3:21 (R. V.)—"Who shall fashion anew the body of our humiliation, that it may be conformed to the body of his glory, according to the working whereby he is able even to subject all things unto himself." See also I John 3:2; 1 Cor. 15:49.

What was the nature and likeness of Christ's resurrection body which our resurrection body is to resemble? It was a real body (Luke 24:39); recognizable (Luke 24:31; John 20:16); powerful (John 20:19).

Summing up these passages, we may say that the resurrection body of the believer will be like the glorified body of Christ.

Characteristics of the believer's resurrection body as set forth in 1 Cor. 15:

It is not flesh and blood (vv. 50, 51; cf. Heb. 2:14; 2 Cor. 5:1-6; Luke 24:39)—"flesh and bones," so not pure spirit; a real body.

It is incorruptible (v. 42)—no decay, sickness, pain.

It is glorious (v. 43), cf. the Transfiguration (Matt. 17); Rev. 1:13-17. It has been said that Adam and Eve, in their unfallen state, possessed a glorious body. The face of Stephen was glorious in his death (Acts 6:15). 2 Cor. 3:18.

It is powerful (v. 43)—not tired, or weak; no lassitude; cf. now "spirit is willing, but the flesh is weak"; not so then.

It is a spiritual body (v. 44). Here the soul is the life of the body; there the spirit will be the life of the body.

It is heavenly (vv. 47-49).

c) THE RESURRECTION BODY OF THE UNBELIEVER

The Scriptures are strangely silent on this subject. It is worthy of note that in the genealogies of Genesis 5 no age is attached to the names of those who were not in the chosen line. Is there a purpose here to ignore the wicked? In the story of the rich man and Lazarus no name is given to the godless rich man; why?

III. THE TIME OF THE RESURRECTION

1. *The Resurrection of the Righteous*

John 6:39, 40, 44—"The last day." This does not mean a day of twenty-four hours, but a period of time. It will be safe, usually, to limit the word "day" to a period of twenty-four hours only where a numeral, ordinal or cardinal, occurs in connection therewith, like "fourth day," etc. When the "day of grace," "day of judgment," "this thy day," etc., are mentioned, they refer to periods of time either long or short, as the case may be.

1 Cor. 15:23—"But every man in his own order: Christ the firstfruits; afterwards they that are Christ's at his coming." 1 Thess. 4:14-17. In both these passages the resurrection of the believer is connected with the coming of Christ. This event ushers in the last day; it is treated as a separate and distinct thing.

2. *The Resurrection of the Wicked*

As there is a difference in the issue (John 5:28, 29; Dan. 12:2, cf. literal Hebrew rendering below) so there is as to time between the resurrection of the righteous and that of the wicked.

Phil. 3:11—"If by any means I might attain unto the resurrection of [lit. out of] the dead." It was no incentive to Paul simply to be assured that he would be raised from the dead; for he knew that all men would be thus raised. What Paul was striving for was to be counted worthy of that first resurrection—of the righteous from among the wicked. The resurrection "out from among" the dead is the resurrection unto life and glory; the resurrection "of" the dead is to shame and contempt everlasting.

1 Cor. 15:21-24. Note the expressions used, and their meaning: "Then," meaning the next in order, the Greek denoting sequence, not simultaneousness—each in his own cohort, battalion, brigade (cf. Mark 4:28—"First the blade, then the ear, after that the full corn in the ear"). Nineteen hundred years have already elapsed between "Christ the firstfruits" and "they that are Christ's." How many years will elapse between the resurrection of "they that are Christ's" and that of the wicked ("the end") we may not be able to definitely state, but certainly long enough for Christ to have "put all enemies under his feet" (v. 25). Three groups or ranks are here mentioned: "Christ," "they that are Christ's," "the end" (the resurrection of the wicked). (Cf. vv. 5, 6, 7—"Seen of Cephas, then of the twelve: after that . . . after that . . . then . . . and last of all he was seen of me also.") First Christ, afterwards (later than) "they that are Christ's," then (positively meaning afterwards, a new era which takes place after an interval) "cometh the end."

Dan. 12:2—"And many of them that sleep in the dust of the earth shall awake, some [lit. those who awake at this time] to everlasting life, and some [lit. those who do not awake at this time] to shame and everlasting contempt." Some of the most eminent Hebrew scholars translate this passage as follows: "And [at that time] many [of thy people] shall awake [or be separated] out from among the sleepers in the earth dust. These [who awake] shall be unto life eternal, but those [who do not awake at that time] shall be unto contempt and shame everlasting." It seems clear from this passage that all do not awake at one (this) time, but only as many as are written in the book (12:1).

Revelation 20:4-6 shows that at least a thousand years—whatever period of time may be thereby designated—elapses between the resurrection of the righteous and the wicked.

John 5:28, 29; Dan. 12:2; Rev. 20:12 all show that the resurrection of the wicked is always connected with the judgment, and that takes place at the close and not at the beginning of the Day of the Lord.

Whatever difficulties may present themselves in connection with the resurrection, whatever obstacles of a miraculous or supernatural nature may present themselves in connection therewith are to be met by remembering the truth enunciated by Christ in connection with this very subject: Matt. 22:29—"Ye do err, not knowing the scriptures, nor the power of God." (Cf. v. 23.—"The same day came to him the Sadducees, which say that there is no resurrection," etc., and the following verses for the setting of v. 29.)

C. THE JUDGMENT

I. THE FACT OF THE JUDGMENT
1. AS TAUGHT IN THE OLD TESTAMENT
2. AS TAUGHT IN THE NEW TESTAMENT
3. THE TESTIMONY OF CONSCIENCE
4. THE TESTIMONY OF CHRIST'S RESURRECTION

II. THE JUDGE—CHRIST

III. THE NATURE OF THE JUDGMENT
1. JUDGMENT AT THE CROSS
2. THE DAILY JUDGMENT
3. FUTURE JUDGMENT
a) Of the Saints
b) Of the Living Nations
c) Of the Great White Throne
d) Of the Fallen Angels
e) Of Israel

C. THE JUDGMENT

I. THE FACT OF THE JUDGMENT

1. Distinctly Taught in the Old Testament

Psa. 96:13—"For he cometh, for he cometh to judge the earth: he shall judge the world with righteousness, and the people with his truth." While this passage refers more particularly to the rewarding of the righteous, yet the idea of judgment is here. Both reward and punishment are involved in the idea of judgment.

2. The New Testament

Acts 17:31—"Because he hath appointed a day, in the which he will judge the world in righteousness by that man whom he hath ordained; whereof he hath given assurance unto all men, in that he hath raised him from the dead." Heb. 9:27. Just as it is "appointed unto men once to die" so it is appointed unto men to appear before the judgment. There is no more escape from the one than from the other.

It is part of the burden of both the Old and New Testament message that a day of judgment is appointed for the world. God's kingdom shall extend universally; but a judgment in which the wicked are judged and the righteous rewarded is necessary and in order that the kingdom of everlasting righteousness may be established upon the earth.

3. The Conscience of All Mankind Corroborates the Teaching of the Scripture With Regard to the Certainty of a Coming Judgment.

This is true of both the individual and universal conscience. The discoveries of tablets as well as the history of all peoples establish this fact. This is enforced by Eccl. 11:9; 12:14—a book which is in a very real sense a book of worldly philosophy, narrating, as it does, the experiences and observations of a man who judged all things from the viewpoint of "under the sun," i.e., without special reference to any revelation from above.

4. The Resurrection of Jesus Christ Is a Sure and Certain Proof Which God Has Given to Men of a Coming Judgment.

Acts 17:31 (quoted above). Here is "assurance" in the sense of proof or ground of evidence. The context is suggestive: God had long borne with the sins of men, and in a sense, overlooked them. Therefore men have thought that God would continue to do so. But no, this shall not be; there is a day of judgment coming, the evidence of which lies in the fact of the resurrection of Jesus Christ.

II. THE JUDGE—CHRIST

John 5:22, 23, 27; 2 Tim. 4:1; 2 Cor. 5:10; Acts 10:42; 17:31. The Man of the Cross is the Man of the throne. Note the expression "Because he is the Son of Man." That indicates His fitness to judge: He can sympathize. But He is equal with the Father. This too indicates His competency to judge, for it implies omniscience. The texts which speak of God as judging the world are to be understood as referring to God the Son. No appeal can be made from the Son to the Father.

III. THE NATURE OF THE JUDGMENT

The erroneous idea that there is to be one great general judgment which is to take place at the end of the world, when all mankind shall stand before the great white throne, is to be guarded against. The judgments of the Bible differ as to time, place, subjects, and results.

1. *There Is a Judgment That Is Already Past—the Judgment at the Cross.*

John 5:24; 12:31; 2 Cor. 5:21; Gal. 3:13; 1 Pet. 2:24. At this judgment bar Satan was judged and his power over the believer broken. Here also the sins of the believer were judged and put away.

2. *There Is a Present Judgment Which Is Taking Place Daily in the Life of the Believer.*

1 Cor. 11:31, 32; 5:5; 1 Tim. 1:20; cf., for illustration, 2 Sam. 7:14, 15; 12:13, 14. This continual judgment must be going on in the life of the believer or there will be judgment from God because of the consequent failure to grow in grace. There must be constant and continual judging of sin as it comes up in the believer's life (1 John 1:5-7).

3. *There Is a Future Judgment.*

a) OF THE SAINTS

1 Cor. 3:8-16; 2 Cor. 5:10; 1 Cor. 4:5. This is to be a judgment with reference to the works, not the salvation, of the believer. It is called "the judgment seat of Christ." That the saints are here referred to is clear from 2 Cor. 5:1, 5, 7, 9; also 1 Cor. 4:5 which says that those who are judged "shall have praise of God." This is not true of the wicked. This is a judgment, not for destiny, but for adjustment, for reward or loss according to our works, for position in the kingdom; every man according as his work shall be.

b) OF THE LIVING NATIONS

Matt. 25:31-46. This judgment will take place at the coming of Christ with His saints. Note three things in this chapter: first, the marriage supper of the Lamb (vv. 1-13); second, the judgment of the saints (vv. 14-30); third, the judgment of the living nations (vv. 31-46). This is not a general judgment of good and bad, for there are three classes here. "My brethren" can hardly refer to the saints, for then it would be "inasmuch as ye have done it unto yourselves, ye have done it unto me." Nor is the Church in this judgment, for she is already translated and rewarded as we have seen. The Church no more belongs to the nations than does Israel. The nations are those who deal with Israel through the great tribulation. The "brethren" are probably the Jewish remnant who have turned to Christ during the great tribulation and whom the Antichrist has severely persecuted as also have many of the wicked nations, like Russia today. This is a judgment of nations that are living; there is no mention of the dead.

c) OF THE GREAT WHITE THRONE

Rev. 20:11-15. It is called the final judgment and takes place at the close of the millennium, after the judgment of the living nations (Matt. 25). It is a judgment of "the dead"; no mention is made of the living in connection therewith.

Note the difference between the judgments of the living nations and of the great white throne: the former at the beginning, the latter at the close of the millennium; one deals with the living, the other with the dead; one deals with conduct towards "the brethren," the other with general sins recorded in the books.

d) OF ISRAEL

Ezek. 20:33-44; Psa. 50:16-22. Takes place probably at the end of the great tribulation.

e) OF THE FALLEN ANGELS

Jude 6; 2 Pet. 2:4. Believers are associated with Christ in this judgment (1 Cor. 6:3).

D THE FINAL DESTINY OF THE WICKED

I. PRELIMINARY CONSIDERATIONS
1. DIFFERENCE BETWEEN FUTURE OF THE RIGHTEOUS AND WICKED
2. DIFFICULTY OF FIGURATIVE LANGUAGE
3. DISPARITY IN NUMBER OF THE SAVED AND LOST
4. PROPHECY VS. HISTORY

II. THE WICKED DIE IN THEIR SINS

III. THE WICKED ARE NOT ANNIHILATED

IV. THE WICKED ARE TO BE PUNISHED.
1. ETERNAL
2. PUNISHMENT
3. FIRE
4. DARKNESS

D. THE FINAL DESTINY OF THE WICKED

"Every view of the world has its eschatology. It cannot help raising the question of the whither, as well as of the what and the whence? 'O, my Lord,' said Daniel to the angel, 'what shall be the end of these things?' (12:8). What is the end, the final destiny of the individual? Does he perish at death, or does he enter into another state of being; and under what conditions of happiness or woe does he exist there? What is the end, the final aim of the great whole, that far-off divine event towards which the whole creation moves? It is vain to tell man not to ask these questions. He will ask them, and must ask them. He will pore over every scrap of fact, or trace of law, which seems to give an indication of an answer. He will try from the experience of the past, and the knowledge of the present, to deduce what the future shall be. He will peer as far as he can into the unseen; and, where knowledge fails, will weave from his hopes and trusts pictures and conjectures.

"The Christian view of the world also has its eschatology. The Christian view, however, is positive, where that of science is negative; ethical, where it is material; human, where it is cosmogonic; ending in personal immortality, where this ends in extinction and death. The eschatology of Christianity springs from its character as a teleological religion—it seeks to grasp the unity of the world through the conception of an end or aim."—*James Orr.*

This is probably the hardest of all the doctrines of Christianity to be received. If we ask the reason why, we receive various answers. Some would tell us that this doctrine is unwelcome to many because they feel themselves guilty, and their conscience tells them that unless they repent and turn to God this awful doom awaits them. Others believe that it is because the thought of future punishment strikes terror to people's hearts, and therefore this doctrine is repulsive to them. To others again, the thought of future anguish seems utterly incompatible with the fatherly love of God. Yet it is acknowledged to be a remarkable fact that both Jesus and John, who more than any one else in the New Testament represent the element of love in their lives and teaching, speak most of the future anguish of the wicked.

That future punishment of the wicked holds a prominent place in the teachings of the Scriptures there can be no reasonable doubt. What is between the covers of the Bible is the preacher's message. Yet great care must be exercised in the teaching or proclamation of this doctrine. After all it is not the saying of hard things that pierces the conscience of people; it is the voice of divine love heard amid the thunder.

Yet there must be no consciousness of cowardice in proclaiming the doctrine of future retribution, however awful its delineation may be. Fear is a legitimate motive to which we may appeal, and while it may be classed among the lower motives, it is nevertheless true that it is the only motive that will effectively move some people to action.

SOME RECOGNIZED FACTS

There are certain preliminary facts which should be recognized in the discussion of this subject:

1. That it shall be well with the righteous, and woe to the wicked (Isa. 3:10, 11). That there is to be retribution for sin and a reward for the righteous must be held to be beyond question, and

must be recognized as an unchangeable law. One cannot very well meddle with that truth without serious danger. So long as a man persistently, willingly and knowingly continues in his sin he must suffer for it. That suffering the Bible calls eternal death.

2. We must recognize that much of the language of the Scripture dealing with this condition is couched in figurative terms. But the condition is none the less real because of that, for, generally speaking, the reality is more severe than the figure in which it is set forth. Yet we need caution here, and must distinguish between the things that are stated in clear unmistakable language and those that are set forth in words symbolic and figurative.

3. The disparity in the number of saved and lost. There is a danger lest we should be unmindful of the problems connected with this doctrine, such as that seeming fewness of the saved; the condition of the heathen who have not had a chance to hear the Gospel; and the difference in privilege and opportunity among those who live in so-called Christian lands.

4. Prophecy vs. History. We must recognize that it is more difficult to deal with facts which lie in the future than with those lying in the past. Prophecy is always more difficult to deal with than history. The past we may sketch in details, the future but in broad outlines.

"Our treatment of themes that deal with the future must, in the very nature of the case be very different than it would be were we dealing with the things of the past. History and prophecy must be handled differently. In dealing with the history of God's past revelations—with the ages before the Advent, with the earthly life and revelation of Jesus Christ, with the subsequent course of God's providence in the Church—we are dealing with that which has already been. It stands in concrete reality before us, and we can reason from it as a thing known in its totality and its details. But when the subject of revelation is that which is yet to be, especially that which is yet to be under forms and conditions of which we have no direct experience, the case is widely altered. Here it is at most outlines that we can look for; and even these outlines will be largely clothed in figure and symbol; the spiritual kernel will seek material investiture to body itself forth; the conditions of the future will require to be presented largely in forms borrowed from known relations. The outstanding thoughts will be sufficiently apparent, but the thoughts in which these thoughts are cast will partake of metaphor and image."—*James Orr.*

II. THE WICKED ARE SAID TO "DIE IN THEIR SINS."

John 8:21, 24—"Then said Jesus again unto them, I go my way, and ye shall seek me, and shall die in your sins: whither I go, ye cannot come. I said therefore unto you, that ye shall die in your sins: for if ye believe not that I am he, ye shall die in your sins." Rom. 6:23—"For the wages of sin is death." See Rev. 20:14, 15; 21:8.

The "death" spoken of here does not mean cessation of existence any more than eternal life means the beginning of existence. Eternal life does not mean merely to live for ever, but to live in a state of blessedness for ever. Eternal life deals not so much with quantity as with quality of existence. Just so with eternal death. It is a quality of existence, not cessation of being. Even in this life death can co-exist with life: "But she that liveth in pleasure is dead while she liveth" (1 Tim. 5:6); Eph. 2:1. What men call life God calls death. There are two things which the believer gets: at his regeneration, eternal life; at his resurrection, immortality; but in both instances he already has life and existence. So it is in the case of the wicked: the second death does not mean cessation of existence, for he is dead already, now in this life (1 Tim. 5:6; Eph. 2:1; John 5:24, 25). Rev. 21:8 describes what "death," as here used, means: "But the fearful, and the unbelieving . . . shall have their part in the lake which burneth with fire and brimstone: which is the second death."

III. THE WICKED ARE NOT ANNIHILATED.

The texts most strongly urged as teaching the annihilation theory, if rightly interpreted, will be seen to refer to removal from off the earth, and not to future retribution Here are the principal passages:

Psa. 37:20—"But the wicked shall perish, and the enemies of the Lord shall be as the fat of lambs: they shall consume; into smoke shall they consume away." This psalm is written for the encouragement of Israel and against her enemies and their power on the earth. This earthly power shall be utterly broken, and be of no more account than the smoke of a burnt sacrifice. The great truth taught here is that the earth is the inheritance of the saints, and that the wicked shall have no part in it.

Obadiah 16—". . . And they shall be as though they had not been." These words are taken from the vision regarding Edom, and refer to the destruction of the Edomites and their land, and not to the future of the wicked in the next life.

In speaking of the "everlasting punishment" with which the wicked will be visited, as recorded in 2 Thess. 1:9, the annihilationist would say that reference is made to the "results or consequences" of that punishment and not to the punishment itself. But the Scriptures state that it is the "punishment" itself, and not the consequences, that is everlasting.

No such interpretation as that put upon these passages by those holding the annihilation theory can be maintained by sound exegesis. What need is there of a resurrection if the wicked are to be annihilated at death, or why should they be raised from the dead if only to be at once extinguished for ever? Again, there is no such thing as "unconscious" punishment. You cannot punish anything that is unconscious. Can you punish a stone or a house? Punishment can take place only where there is consciousness on the part of the one suffering.

IV. THE WICKED ARE TO BE PUNISHED.

Rom. 2:8, 9—"But unto them that are contentious, and do not obey the truth, but obey unrighteousness, indignation and wrath, tribulation and anguish, upon every soul of man that doeth evil, of the Jew first, and also of the Gentile." "Wrath" indicates the settled mind of God towards the persistently wicked (John 3:36); "indignation," the outbreak of that wrath at the day of judgment; "tribulation," severe affliction (Matt. 13:21; 24:9; Rev. 7:14); "anguish," torturing confinement in a strait place without relief, as in a dungeon, or in stocks. God grant that we may never know what these terms fully mean.

Matt. 25:41, 46—"Then shall he say also unto them on the left hand, Depart from me, ye cursed, into everlasting fire, prepared for the devil and his angels. And these shall go away into everlasting punishment." 2 Thess. 1:7-9—"When the Lord Jesus shall be revealed from heaven with his mighty angels, in flaming fire taking vengeance on them that know not God, and that obey not the gospel of our Lord Jesus Christ: who shall be punished with everlasting destruction from the presence of the Lord, and from the glory of his power." See also Mark 9:43-50 which speaks of the wicked being cast into "hell, into the fire that never shall be quenched: where their worm dieth not, and the fire is not quenched."

There are certain important words in these scriptures which demand our attention, and which we need to understand in order to get right views of the doctrine we are now considering. They are as follows:

1. "Eternal"

We read of "eternal" or "everlasting" punishment, "everlasting" fire. It is objected that the word "eternal" or "everlasting" does not mean "forever." This may be true. But we are all willing to admit that when this word qualifies the condition of the righteous it means for ever, without end, e. g., the righteous shall go "into life eternal." The same word, however, qualifies the punishment of the wicked, e. g., "these shall go away into everlasting punishment." Fairness demands that we make the joy of the righteous and the punishment of the wicked—both qualified as they are by the same Greek word—of the same duration. If there is an end to the reward of the righteous, there is also to the penalty of the wicked. The one lasts as long as the other. If "destruction" means annihilation, then there is no need of the word "eternal" to qualify it. Further the Scriptures present the punishment of the wicked not only as "eternal" (or age-long) but as enduring "for ever and ever," or "unto the ages of the ages" (Rev. 19:3; 20:10; 14:11, R. V.). Here is a picture of ages tumbling upon ages in eternal succession.

2. "Punishment"

The meaning of this word will be found under the previous division (III) dealing with the subject of annihilation.

3. "Fire"

This is one of the most constant images under which the torment and misery of the wicked is represented. Fire is a symbol of the divine judgment of wrath (Matt. 5:22). In Matthew 3:10 the godless are represented as a tree hewn down and cast into the fire; in

3:12 the chaff (godless) is burned with unquenchable fire; in 13:42 the wicked are said to be cast into a furnace of fire.

Is the "fire" spoken of here *literal* fire? It is an accepted law of language that a figure of speech is less intense than the reality. If "fire" is merely a figurative expression, it must stand for some great reality, and if the reality is more intense than the figure, what an awful thing the punishment symbolized by fire must be.

It is contended that fire must necessarily consume; that nothing could continue to exist in fire. Is it not remarkable that the Baptist uses the word "unquenchable" (Greek, *asbestos*) when speaking of this fire? Is any light thrown on the question by the incident of the three Hebrew children in the fiery furnace? Did they consume, or did they withstand the fire? (Dan. 3:27). In the parable of the tares (Matt. 13:36-43) our Lord speaks of the tares being burned up. When Christ retired to the house after delivering the parable, his disciples asked Him to explain to them what He meant by the figures of speech He used in the parable. This request He granted. He explained the figurative language of the parable; every figurative word in it except that of "fire." He said: "The field is the world; the good seed are the children of the kingdom; but the tares are the children of the wicked one; the enemy that sowed them is the devil; the harvest is the end of the world; and the reapers are the angels. As therefore the tares are gathered and burned in the fire, so shall it be at the end of this world. . . . And they shall cast them into a furnace of fire: there shall be wailing and gnashing of teeth." Why did not the Master explain what he meant by the figurative word "fire"? He explained all the other figurative words, why not this one? Did He forget? Or did He intend that His disciples should have the impression that He was speaking of literal fire? Here was His opportunity to explain His use of words, for the disciples were asking for just that very thing. Was there any significance in the fact that Jesus did not explain the word "fire"? Whether we believe in literal fire or not, we certainly ought to ask for a reason for the Master's failure to literalize the figurative word "fire."

4. "Darkness"

This word is used to describe the condition of the lost: "Cast into outer darkness: there shall be weeping and gnashing of teeth." Seven times these terms are found together: Matt. 8:12;

13:42, 50; 22:13; 24:51; 25:30; Luke 13:28. The picture is that of a banquet which was usually held at night. The wicked are thrust out from the light, joy, and festivity into the darkness and gloom without, as into the remote gloom and anguish of a dungeon in which are found agony, wrath, and despair. Is this a description of hell—absence of spiritual light; separation from the company of the saved; lamentation; impotent rage?

E. THE FINAL REWARD OF THE RIGHTEOUS

I. THE BELIEVER NEVER DIES.

II. THE BELIEVER GOES TO BE WITH CHRIST.

III. THE BODY OF THE BELIEVER IS RAISED FROM THE DEAD.

IV. THE BELIEVER IS REWARDED.

V. THE NATURE OF THE BELIEVER'S REWARD
1. THE "CROWNS" OF SCRIPTURE
2. THE SEVEN "OVERCOMES" (REV. 2 AND 3)

VI. THE NEW CONDITION AND ABODE OF LIFE FOR THE SAINTS
1. NEW SPHERE OF LIFE
2. A NEW HOME
3. NEW CONDITIONS

E. THE FINAL REWARD OF THE RIGHTEOUS

If, says the Apostle Paul, in this present life we have a hope resting on Christ, and nothing more, we are more to be pitied than all the rest of the world (1 Cor. 15:19). The idea is that if this hope in Christ which the believer has is a delusive hope, with no prospect of fulfillment in the future, the Christian is indeed in a sad state. He has chosen a life of self-denial; he will not indulge in the pleasures of the world, and if there are no pleasures in the darkness into which he is about to enter, then he has miscalculated, he has chosen a life that shall end in self-obliteration. If he has no home to go to, no God to welcome him, no King to say, "Well done, exchange mortality for life," then he is indeed in a pitiable plight. But such is not the case. The hope of the Christian enters beyond the vail, into the very presence of God Himself, and endures throughout all the eternities.

I. THE CHRISTIAN NEVER DIES.

1 John 8:51—"Verily, verily, I say unto you, If a man keep my saying, he shall never see death." 11:25, 26—"Jesus said unto her, I am the resurrection, and the life: he that believeth in me, though he were dead, yet shall he live: and whosoever liveth and believeth in me shall never die. Believest thou this?"

What Jesus means here is not that the believer shall not pass through the experience that we call death, but that in reality it is not death, at least, not in the sense in which it is death to the unbeliever. Jesus has taken the sting out of death. How sharply the contrast between death and the experience through which the believer passes is presented in 1 Thess. 4:13, 14—"But I would not have you to be ignorant, brethren, concerning them which are asleep, that ye sorrow not, even as others which have no hope. For if we believe that Jesus died and rose again, even so them also which sleep in Jesus will God bring with him." Jesus "died"—He tasted the awfulness of death; the believer in Him "falls asleep." Cf. John 11:11—"Our friend Lazarus sleepeth." We have no ground in these words for the modern doctrine of soul-sleeping. Christ did not mean to say that the soul is unconscious between the time of death and the resurrection. For, when the disciples did not understand His *figurative* language, He told them *plainly,* "Lazarus is dead" (11:11-15). What Jesus meant was that death is something like that which takes place when we go to sleep. What takes place when we go to sleep? Surely the current of life does not cease, but flows on, and when we awake we feel better and stronger than before. There is a shutting out of all the scenes of the world and time. Just so it is in the case of the believer's death. Three ideas are contained in the word "sleep": continued existence—for the mind is active even though the body is still; repose—we lose our hold on and forget the things of the world; wakening—we always think of sleep as followed by awakening.

The word "see" in John 8:51 means that the believer shall not gaze at death protractedly, steadily, exhaustively. Death is not the objective of his gaze. The believer's outlook is that of life, not death. The death of the body is to be reckoned no more as death than the life of the body is life (1 Tim. 5:6). The believer's back is turned upon death; he faces and gazes upon life. The temporary separation of the soul and body does not even interrupt, much less impair, the eternal life given by Jesus.

II. THE BELIEVER GOES TO BE WITH CHRIST.

2 Cor. 5:6, R. V.—"Being therefore always of good courage, and knowing that, whilst we are at home in the body, we are absent from the Lord." Phil. 1:23, R. V.—"But I am in a strait betwixt the two, having the desire to depart and be with Christ; for it is very far better."

The experience (death-sleep) through which the believer passes ushers him at once into the presence of Christ. It takes him instantly to be "at home" with the Lord. Surely there can be no hint of unconsciousness or the sleeping of the soul in these words. It would seem from Paul's words in 2 Corinthians 5:1-5 that some kind of spiritual body is given to the believer during the period of his waiting for the resurrection body. What Paul longs for is not to be in a bodiless state, but to put on another body which shall not be subject to death. "At home with the Lord"—that is what "death" (?) means to the believer.

III. THE BODY OF THE BELIEVER IS RAISED FROM THE DEAD.

See under the Doctrine of the Resurrection, p. 245, for the full discussion of the believer's resurrection body, its characteristics, etc.

IV. THE BELIEVER SHALL RECEIVE HIS FINAL REWARD IN THE FUTURE.

1. Matt. 25:20-23—"And so he that had received five talents came and brought other five talents, saying, Lord, thou deliveredst unto me five talents: behold, I have gained beside them five talents more. His lord said unto him, Well done, thou good and faithful servant: thou hast been faithful over a few things, I will make thee ruler over many things: enter thou into the joy of thy lord. He also that had received two talents came and said, Lord, thou deliveredst unto me two talents: behold, I have gained two other talents beside them. His lord said unto him, Well done, good and faithful servant: thou hast been faithful over a few things, I will make thee ruler over many things: enter thou into the joy of thy lord."

Luke 19:12-19.—"He said therefore, A certain nobleman went into a far country to receive for himself a kingdom, and to return. And he called his ten servants, and delivered them ten pounds, and said unto them, Occupy till I come. But his citizens hated him, and sent a message after him, saying, We will not have this man to reign over us. And it came to pass, that when he was returned, having received the kingdom, then he commanded these servants to be called unto him, to whom he had given the money, that he might know how much every man had gained by trading. Then came the first, saying, Lord, thy pound hath gained ten pounds. And he said unto him, Well, thou good servant: because thou hast been faithful in a very little, have thou authority over ten cities. And the second came saying, Lord, thy pound hath gained five pounds. And he said likewise to him, Be thou also over five cities."

Matthew 24 exhorts us to watch and wait for Christ's coming; chapter 25 shows us how we may obey this exhortation. Chapter 25 illustrates to us, in the parable of the virgins (vv. 1-13), the necessity of caring for the inward spiritual life; while the parable of the talents (vv. 14-30), emphasizes the necessity of activity for Christ while awaiting His return.

While both parables deal with the matter of the rewarding of the saints, they nevertheless present the subject from different viewpoints. The parable of the pounds was delivered before the entry into Jerusalem; that of the talents, three days after; the pounds, to the multitudes; the talents, to the disciples. The pounds was given because the people thought that the kingdom would immediately appear, hence the idea of a long journey. In the pounds there is opposition to Christ; in the talents, none. In the talents unequal sums are multiplied in the same proportion; in the pounds equal sums in differed proportions. The parable of the pounds was uttered to repress impatience; that of the talents, to stimulate activity until Christ should return.

The talents are distributed not capriciously but according to each man's ability to handle them. He who had five talents was able to use five, and was therefore held responsible for the use of this number; so with the two, and the one. The question is not so much "How many talents have I received," but "To what use am I putting them?" The rewards for faithfulness are the same in each case—"Be thou ruler over many cities." In the parable of the pounds it is different. All start out with the same number of pounds. As men differ in their use of them, in their fidelity, zeal and labor, so they differ in spiritual gains and rewards (ten cities, five cities). The reward of the believer will be in proportion to the faithfulness of his service for God with the use of the talents with which God has endowed him. The rewards therefore will differ according to the faithfulness or unfaithfulness of our service and life.

Faith in Jesus Christ saves the believer, but his position in the future life together with the measure of his reward will depend upon his faithfulness in the use of the gifts with which he has been endowed by God. Thus it comes to pass that a man may be saved "yet so as by fire," i. e., saved because of his faith in Christ, but minus his reward. See 1 Cor. 3:10-15—"In discharge of the task which God graciously entrusted to me, I—like a competent master-builder—have laid a foundation, and others are building upon it. But let every one be careful how and what he builds. For no one can lay any other foundation in addition to that which is already laid, namely, Jesus Christ. And whether the building which anyone is erecting on that foundation be of gold or silver or costly stones, of timber or hay or straw—the true character of each individual's work will become manifest. For the day of Christ will disclose it, because that day is soon to come upon us clothed in fire, and as for the quality of every one's work—the fire is the thing which will test it. If any one's work—the building which he has erected—stands the test, he will be rewarded. If any one's work is burned up, he will suffer the loss of it; yet he will himself be rescued, but only, as it were, by passing through the fire." (Translation from *Weymouth's New Testament.*) While this passage has its primary reference, probably, to Christian teachers and preachers, and touches the matter of doctrines that are taught, it nevertheless has a fitting and true application to the life and work of every believer.

V. THE NATURE OF THE BELIEVER'S REWARD

1. He Shall Receive a Crown.

The Scriptures speak of a number of crowns: The crown of *Life* (James 1:12; Rev. 2:10, compare context which speaks of death); of *Glory* (1 Pet. 5:4; cf. John 17:22; Heb. 2:9); of *Righteousness* (2 Tim. 4:8), the full realization of the imputed and inwrought righteousness of Christ; of *Rejoicing* (1 Thess. 2:19) at the sight of converts that have been won by one's ministry for Christ; of *Gold* (Rev. 4:4); *Incorruptible* (1 Cor. 9:25), as compared with the perishable crowns of the Greek games; *Thy* crown (Rev. 3:11), that which is laid up for you, and which should not be lost by unfaithfulness; the summing up of all the previous expressions—all are characteristic of "thy" crown.

2. The Seven "Overcomes" in Revelation (chaps. 2, 3.)

a) 2:7—"EAT OF THE TREE OF LIFE, WHICH IS IN THE MIDST OF THE PARADISE OF GOD."

The tree of life, which has been practically unmentioned since Genesis 3, where it was lost through sin, is here restored in accordance with the restitution of all things in Christ. This figure expresses participation in life eternal—the believer shall die no more.

b) 2:11—"SHALL NOT BE HURT OF THE SECOND DEATH."

He who is born but once—"of the flesh"—dies twice: physically, and eternally. He (the believer) who is born twice—"of the flesh" and "of the spirit"—dies but once; that is, he passes through only that physical dissolution of soul and body which is called death. The "second death" means, to say the least, utter exclusion from the presence of God. To say that the believer shall not be hurt of the second death is equivalent to saying that he shall eternally behold the face of the Father which is in heaven.

c) 2:17—HE SHALL RECEIVE A "STONE WITH A NEW NAME WRITTEN" THEREON; TO THE BELIEVER ALSO WILL BE GIVEN TO EAT OF THE "HIDDEN MANNA."

This figure may mean that to the believer is given the white stone of acquittal. In courts of justice in those days a black stone was given to the condemned. Reference may here be made to the white stone (diamond?) which was not among the stones in the high priest's ephod, and thought by some to be the Urim and Thummim. The partaking of the hidden manna may refer to the fact that they who had resisted the eating of meat offered in sacrifice to idols would, as a reward, be allowed to feast on the bread of God, the divine food. The new name mentioned may stand for a new nature and character which the believer will possess in that new country.

d) 2:26, 27—AUTHORITY OVER THE NATIONS

There is doubtless a reference here to the reign of the saints with the Lord Jesus Christ on the millennial earth. Those that have suffered with Him shall also reign with Him.

e) 3:4, 5—HE SHALL BE "ARRAYED IN WHITE GARMENTS," AND HIS NAME SHALL IN NO WISE BE BLOTTED OUT OF THE BOOK OF LIFE.

"White garments" undoubtedly refers to the righteousness of the saints. In the Old Testament days to be blotted out of the book of life meant to forfeit the privileges of the Theocracy—to be shut out forever from God's favor. Here the certainty of the believer's eternal security is assured. Christ will rejoice over him and gladly confess that He knows him as one who belonged to Him and served and confessed Him on the earth.

f) 3:12—THE BELIEVER WILL BE A PILLAR IN THE TEMPLE OF GOD; HE SHALL GO OUT NO MORE; GOD WILL WRITE UPON HIM HIS OWN NEW NAME.

Philadelphia, the place in which was situated the church to whom these words were written, was subject to earthquakes, and quite frequently the massive pillars of the temple were shattered. It shall not be so with the believer—he shall never be moved. He will go in and out no more—no possibility of falling then. He will have the name of God written upon him—no danger of anyone else making claim to him. Then the believer's period of probation will have passed away; he shall have a permanent and eternal place in the kingdom of the Father.

g) 3:21, R. V.—"I WILL GIVE TO HIM TO SIT DOWN WITH ME IN MY THRONE."

Not "on" or "upon" but "in" my throne. Christ will exalt us *with* Himself. James and John wanted to sit by Christ's *side* in the coming kingdom. Here is something infinitely better—to sit with Him in His throne.

VI. THE BELIEVER WILL ENTER INTO A NEW CONDITION AND ABODE OF LIFE.

1. A New Sphere of Life for the Saints

New heavens and a new earth: Paradise regained; new spiritual environment; new physical conditions. Not surrounded by the temptations and defects of this mortal life. "No more sea"—to the Jew a symbol of unmixed peril, trouble, and restlessness.

2. A New Home for the Saints

Rev. 21–22:5—A picture of the holy city, the New Jerusalem, which is to be the final and eternal abode of the people of God.

Within the new heavens and on the new earth is the holy city. Note some characteristics of the holy city: Its *Name:* New Jerusalem—what music to the ear of the Jew, who for so long had been without a city of his own! Its *Walls* (21:17): high, secure, safe against all assaults. Its *Gates* (21:15, 21): guarded by angels; names on gates; only saints enter. Its *Foundations* (v. 14): the apostles of the Lamb; lustrous (18). Its *Citizens:* of the nations that are saved (citizens' characteristics 21:6, 7; 22:14, R. V.; contrast with 21:8, 27). Its *Magnitude:* 4800 stadia (the earthly Jerusalem being but 33 stadia). Its *Glory* (11–23): what costliness!

3. New Conditions of Life for the Redeemed

God's home is there (21:3); thus the believer has uninterrupted communion with God. Some things that used to be have all passed away: death, mourning, curse, tears, sorrow, night—all have gone. New created things appear: the river of life, the tree of life, new service, new relationships, new light (22:4).

"AND AFTER THESE THINGS I HEARD A GREAT VOICE OF MUCH PEOPLE IN HEAVEN, SAYING, ALLELUIA; SALVATION, AND GLORY, AND HONOUR, AND POWER, UNTO THE LORD OUR GOD:

"AND THE FOUR AND TWENTY ELDERS AND THE FOUR BEASTS FELL DOWN AND WORSHIPPED GOD THAT SAT ON THE THRONE, SAYING, AMEN; ALLELUIA.

"AND A VOICE CAME OUT OF THE THRONE, SAYING PRAISE OUR GOD, ALL YE HIS SERVANTS, AND YE THAT FEAR HIM, BOTH SMALL AND GREAT.

"AND I HEARD AS IT WERE THE VOICE OF A GREAT MUL-TITUDE, AND AS THE VOICE OF MANY WATERS, AND AS THE VOICE OF MIGHTY THUNDERINGS, SAYING, ALLELUIA: FOR THE LORD GOD OMNIPOTENT REIGNETH.

"LET US BE GLAD AND REJOICE, AND GIVE HONOUR TO HIM: FOR THE MARRIAGE OF THE LAMB IS COME, AND HIS WIFE HATH MADE HERSELF READY.

"AND TO HER WAS GRANTED THAT SHE SHOULD BE ARRAYED IN FINE LINEN, CLEAN AND WHITE: FOR THE FINE LINEN IS THE RIGHTEOUSNESS OF SAINTS."

PART TWO

EIGHTY ADDITIONAL ENTRIES
by
S. MAXWELL CODER

CONTENTS OF PART TWO

AGES

Among various periods or epochs in the history of mankind, most students distinguish an age of innocence before Adam sinned, Rom. 5:12; an age of law and an age of grace, Rom. 5:20, 21; a future kingdom age, Matt. 25:34; and "the ages to come," which follow other ages, Eph. 2:7; 3:5. Some would add an age of conscience, Gen. 3:7—8:22; an age of human government, Gen. 9:6; and an age of promise, Gen. 12:1—Ex. 19:4. The tribulation is sometimes regarded as a separate age, Matt. 24:21.

God's plan for His church was not made known in earlier ages, Eph. 3:4-6; Col. 1:26. One revealed purpose for the present offer of salvation by grace is to make it possible for God ultimately to show the riches of His grace in His kindness toward us through Christ Jesus, Eph. 2:4-7.

The Greek word for age is translated world some 29 times in the AV, as in Matt. 13:39; Rom. 12:2. The margin corrects this in many places. For example, Heb. 9:26, "now once in the end of the world hath he appeared," has been changed in the RV margin to state that He came "in the consummation of the ages."

The Bible doctrine of the ages during which the divine purposes unfold emphasizes the antiquity and variety of God's program, while revealing that it is to have an unending extension in eternity future.

ANTICHRIST

The brief prophecy, "antichrist shall come," 1 John 2:18, has taken hold of the imagination of so many that the name antichrist is more widely known than other Bible names given to a wicked being who darkens the horizon in the end time.

These include such expressions as the man of sin, the son of perdition, and that wicked one, 2 Thess. 2:3-8; the wicked king, Dan. 7:24, 25; the king of fierce countenance, Dan. 8:23-25; and the beast from the sea, Rev. 13:1-10.

If the word antichrist is taken to mean one who is against Christ, these names belong to him, but if the word means a false Christ, then it properly applies to the beast from the earth or the land, Rev. 13:11-18, who is the false prophet of Rev. 16:13; 19:20; 20:10.

The personal antichrist must be distinguished from the many antichrists of 1 John 2:18; 2 John 7; from those who have the spirit of antichrist, 1 John 4:3, and from the false Christs who are to deceive the people of Israel in the latter days, Matt. 24:24; John 5:43.

A considerable body of Scripture is devoted to this evil being. The beast king is given power over all nations for only three and a half years, Rev. 13:5. He will perish in the lake of fire, Rev. 19:20; 20:10.

APOSTASY

This difficult doctrine must be distinguished from heresy, which is simply a belief in false doctrine. Apostasy is a deliberate turning away from revealed truth after it has been tentatively received. There are a number of Bible descriptions of it. It is a claim that men know God which is denied by their actions, Tit. 1:16; abiding not in the doctrine of Christ, 2 John 9; a departure from the faith, 1 Tim. 4:1; an unwillingness to endure sound doctrine, 2 Tim. 4:3; a forsaking of the right way, 2 Pet. 2:15; a turning from the holy commandment, 2 Pet. 2:21.

Apostates are not saved persons, because they do not have the Spirit, Jude 19; Rom. 8:9. They are "rocky ground" hearers who receive the Word with joy, Luke 8:13; but afterward fall away, which is literally "apostatize." The "good ground" hearers receive the Word into their hearts, a much stronger word for receiving it, Mark 4:20, Gr.

Individual apostasy has occurred throughout history. Jude 11 cites three examples from the OT. Judas is the outstanding example in the NT. Corporate apostasy will overtake Christendom in the last days, 2 Thess. 2:3; Rev. 3:14-20. Christ foretold this, Luke 18:8. Jude describes apostates as ungodly men who pervert God's grace and deny our Lord, Jude 8, 16, 19.

ASSURANCE

The confident belief that one is truly saved, that he is already a child of God through faith in Jesus Christ, destined to eternal life in glory, is not to be confused with the doctrine of security. "Quietness and assurance forever" are the effect of righteousness, Isa. 32:17. The NT speaks of full assurance of hope and of faith, Heb. 6:11; 10:22. The gospel came to the believers in Thessalonica in much assurance, 1 Thess. 1:5. Assurance comes to Christians when they understand the revelation God has given, Col. 2:2; 2 Pet. 3:18.

Many of the occurrences of the word "know" in the NT emphasize the doctrine of assurance, Rom. 8:28; 1 Cor. 2:12; 15:58; 2 Cor. 5:1. It is normal for all Christians to know they are saved. 1 John was written so that believers may know they have eternal life, 1 John 5:13. The saints are exhorted to examine and prove to themselves that they are in the faith, 2 Cor. 13:5.

Among the revelations which provide a basis for assurance is 1 John 3:14, "We know that we have passed from death unto life, because we love the brethren," cf. 2:3, 5; 3:19, 24. Assurance is the work of the Holy Spirit. "The Spirit himself beareth witness with our spirit, that we are the children of God," Rom. 8:16. Assurance is therefore not presumption; it is faith.

BAPTISM

To many, *baptizo* means a ceremonial cleansing with water, carrying on the OT practice of sprinkling, Num. 8:7; Ezek. 36:25; Acts 22:16; Heb. 9:10; 19-22. It is regarded as a sign and seal of the baptism of the Spirit, 1 Cor. 12:13, who is shed forth or poured out on believers, Isa. 44:3; Acts 2:17, 33; 10:44-48. Many passages associate baptism with water and by the Spirit, Luke 3:16; John 1:33; Acts 11:15, 16. Texts cited to show baptism was by pouring or sprinkling include Mark 7:4; Luke 11:38; Acts 2:41; 10:47.

To others who believe that *baptizo* means to dip, the ritual is a symbolic burial and resurrection of believers by the use of water as a testimony that they died in Christ. Quoted in support are Rom. 6:4, "buried with him by baptism into death," and Col. 2:12, "buried with him in baptism, wherein also ye are risen with him," cf. 1 Pet. 3:20, 21. Texts cited to show early believers were immersed include Matt. 3:6, "baptized of him in Jordan," cf. Matt. 3:16; Mark 1:9; also John 3:23, "because there was much water there," and Acts 8:38, 39, "when they were come up out of the water," cf. Acts 16:13-15.

Infant baptism is based on a parallel with circumcision, Col. 2:11, 12, and the belief that a normal NT household would include children, Acts 16:15, 33; 1 Cor. 1:16.

BIBLE FACTS

A theme of Scripture often overlooked is what the Bible promises to do for God's people. The Word, under various synonyms, is said in Psa. 19:7, 8 to convert the soul, make wise the simple, rejoice the heart, and enlighten the eyes. These great rewards are given to all who keep the precepts of Scripture, v. 11.

Men are born again through the instrumentality of the Word, Jas. 1:18; 1 Pet. 1:23. Faith comes to believers as they hear the Word, Rom. 10:17. Spiritual growth results from the realized desire for the sincere milk of the Word, 1 Pet. 2:2; 2 Pet. 3:18. Great peace have they who love God's Word, Psa. 119:165. Those who obey it are promised divine blessings, Jas. 1:25. In the same way that Christ overcame the devil by using the written Word, Matt. 4:1-11, Christians are able to overcome the wicked one as the Word abides in them, 1 John 2:14.

Paul spoke of the Word as able to build us up, Acts 20:32. An entire book has been written to provide the assurance of salvation which is normal Christian experience, 1 John 5:13. It is the Word that sanctifies or cleanses, John 17:17, acting as a laver which reveals sin and provides cleansing as well, Eph. 5:25-27. The promise is given that those who honor the Word will find prosperity and success in all of God's will, Josh. 1:8; Psa. 1:3.

BLESSING

In popular usage the term is seldom defined, and its meaning is vague. Scripture reveals that the blessing of God is a specific, recognizable manifestation of divine favor, including such things as rain, Ezek. 34:26; peace, Psa. 29:11; enrichment, Prov. 10:22; and comfort, Matt. 5:4. The theme appears five hundred times.

It has a definite beginning, Hag. 2:19; it cannot be disannulled by man, Num. 23:20; it is visible, Deut. 28:10, and abounding, Prov. 28:20. Although it is conditional, God challenges men to secure it, Mal. 3:10.

The people of God who enjoy His blessing, Psa. 3:8, are described as righteous, Psa. 5:12; just, Prov. 3:33; faithful, Prov. 28:20; pure in heart, Psa. 24:4, 5. During the present age Christian blessings are primarily spiritual rather than physical, Eph. 1:3.

The blessings of God are secured by delighting in His Word, Josh. 1:8; Psa. 1:1-3, and obeying its precepts, Deut. 28:1, 2; Jas. 1:25. They may result from divine chastening which results in teaching from the Word, Psa. 94:12; Heb. 12:5-11. Other keys to God's blessing are kindness to the people of Israel, Gen. 12:3; Psa. 122:6; generosity, Prov. 11:26; Mal. 3:10; fearing God and walking in His ways, Psa. 128:1-4; and prayer, Gen. 32:26; Jas. 5:16.

BODY, SOUL, SPIRIT

Man consists of body, soul, and spirit, distinguished in 1 Thess. 5:23. The body is the material part of man, created by God, Gen. 2:7, as the instrument by which soul and spirit relate to the material universe and fulfill His will. Spiritual and physical death came to the body in the day man sinned, as God reckons time, 2 Pet. 3:8. Believers present their bodies to God for His use, Rom. 12:1, 2. Redeemed and transformed, Rom. 8:23; Phil. 3:21, the body will be resurrected for life in a new environment, 1 Cor. 15:35-54.

The soul is immaterial, intermediate between body and spirit. It is the seat of the will, affections, personality. Man is called a soul, Gen. 2:7, because he has a soul, Psa. 103:1; 2 Cor. 1:23. The body is now suited to the life of the soul. In resurrection it will be suited rather to the life of the spirit. The soul continues to live after the body is dead, Acts 2:31; Rev. 6:9.

The spirit is the immaterial part of man which is related to worship and communion with God. It gives man God-consciousness. We are to win souls, not spirits, Prov. 11:30. Men worship and serve God with the spirit, not the soul, John 4:24; Rom. 1:9. The spirit is distinguished from the soul in Heb. 4:12.

CHASTISEMENT

The corrective discipline by God of all whom He loves is the subject of an extended revelation. The clearest OT statement, Prov. 3:11, 12, is repeated and developed in Heb. 12:3-15, and restated in Rev. 3:19.

Chastisement at the hand of God is the experience of every Christian. Individuals who are not true children of God know nothing of it, Heb. 12:8; 1 Pet. 5:9. Scourging in Heb. 12:6 is understood to refer to the breaking of the stubborn human will. Chastening includes every form of discipline imposed by a loving Father as He prepares His children to reign with Christ.

Four possible attitudes toward chastening are suggested in Heb. 12. Some may despise divine discipline, that is, think lightly of it, v. 5. Others may faint or become disheartened, v. 5. It is possible simply to endure chastisement with stoical resignation, v. 7; but those who are exercised thereby reap great benefits, v. 11.

Everyone whom the Lord chastens is blessed and taught of

God, Psa. 94:12. Their lives are changed, and they bear fruit for Him, Heb. 12:11. Chastisement is never capricious. It comes only for a limited time, and only as Christians need it, 1 Pet. 1:6, 7. It is always for their profit, Heb. 12:10.

COMMANDMENTS

Each age has its divine law. God gave the Ten Commandments to Israel, Ex. 20:1-17; Rom. 10:4, with death as the penalty for disobedience, Num. 15:32-36; Heb. 10:28. That law, which "worketh wrath," Rom. 4:15, was given to bring men to Christ, Gal. 3:19-24.

For the present age Christ gave the new commandment that believers love one another, John 13:34. It is embedded in the church epistles and is contrasted with the law of Moses, Rom. 13:8-10. Although the law was never given to the church, nine of the commandments are repeated for the life under grace. Missing is the fourth, requiring observance of the Sabbath.

Christ used the term "my commandments" for the first time in John 14:15. Called "the law of Christ" in Gal. 6:2, they include all He taught for the new age, and all He has given by the Spirit since His ascension, John 16:12-15, 1 Cor. 14:37. Those who honor this rich body of truth receive assurance, and their prayers are answered, 1 John 2:3; 3:22-24. The mistranslation of Rev. 22:14 in the AV is corrected in the other versions.

An increase in the severity of the law during the kingdom age is seen in Matt. 5:21, 22, where Christ changed the law of Moses and made hatred as serious as murder.

CONDUCT

Believers have liberty in Christ, Gal. 5:1. This is limited by personal conviction, Rom. 14:5; by warnings against self indulgence, Gal. 5:13; by enslaving habits, 1 Cor. 6:12; and by anything which does not edify, 1 Cor. 10:23; which is hypocritical, 1 Pet. 2:16; or which tends to harm the weak, 1 Cor. 8:9. Three principles govern conduct.

1. Effect upon self. Conduct must be pure rather than lustful, 1 Tim. 5:22; 1 Pet. 2:11. It must not defile, 1 Cor. 3:17; Tit. 1:15, or result in self condemnation, Rom. 14:22. It is always to be in the category of good works, Tit. 3:8, rather than in the category of sin, Rom. 6:13.

2. Effect upon others, Rom. 14:7. It is to be a good example,

1 Tim. 4:12; worthy of our calling, Eph. 4:1; honest, 2 Cor. 8:21; free from the appearance of evil, 1 Thess. 5:22; helpful rather than offensive to a neighbor, Rom. 15:2; 1 Cor. 10:32; not a cause of stumbling, Rom. 14:13. It must honor parents, Col. 3:20; and government, Tit. 3:1; while it may not be an unequal yoke, 2 Cor. 6:14.

3. Relationship to God. Everything is to be done in the name of the Lord, 1 Tim. 6:1; as unto Him, Col. 3:23; and for His glory, 1 Cor. 10:31. It is to be worthy of God and His kingdom, 1 Thess. 2:12; 2 Thess. 1:5.

CONFESSION

The only reference in Scripture to a confession by one person to another is found in Jas. 5:16, "Confess your faults one to another, and pray for one another." However, believers are to confess Christ before others in testimony that they have received Him as Saviour, Matt. 10:32; Rom. 10:9; 1 John 4:15. This is not in order to be saved, but because they have been saved. It fulfills Acts 1:8, and it brings assurance, 1 John 3:18,19. On His part, Christ promises to confess before His Father in heaven the names of all who trust Him, Rev. 3:5.

When fellowship with the Father has been lost because of known sin, confession to Him results in the free granting of forgiveness and the restoration of fellowship, 1 John 1:9. This is in contrast with the popular notion that believers must ask God for forgiveness in fervent prayer.

In OT days also, the confession and forsaking of sins brought mercy from God, Prov. 28:13. David was forgiven after he confessed his sins to God, Psa. 32:5. Revival came in Ezra's time after he had confessed his sins and those of his people, Ezra 9:6; 10:1. While Daniel was confessing his sin and that of the nation Israel, the angel Gabriel came to him with a new revelation from God, Dan. 9:20-27. Confession led to blessing in Luke 15:21-24.

CONSCIENCE

Conscience is an inherent awareness of the difference between what is right and what is wrong, an inborn ability to "discern both good and evil," Heb. 5:14. It is a human characteristic as fallible as other human traits. It seems clear that it is neither an acquired attitude of mind nor the voice of God in the soul of man. The word appears only in the NT.

Conscience is found in the unsaved. It justified Paul's actions, Acts 23:1, and it convicted the scribes, John 8:9. It is said to bear witness, Rom. 2:15. It may be defiled, Tit. 1:15; or seared, 1 Tim. 4:2, implying insensitivity.

In saved persons it testifies, 2 Cor. 1:12; bears witness in the Holy Spirit, Rom. 9:1; leads to submission, 1 Pet. 2:19. It should be good, 1 Tim. 1:5, and pure, 1 Tim. 3:9. Its purity results from its having been purged by the blood of Christ, Heb. 9:14.

One illustration of the action of the conscience is found in 1 Cor. 8:1-13. Instructed Christians are to abstain from anything, even though right in itself, which may embolden the weak conscience of some brethren so they fall into that which is sin for them. On the other hand, no one with a weak conscience has the right to judge the actions of any other believer, 1 Cor. 10:27-30.

CURSE

A terrible revelation is found throughout Scripture about this word. The curse of God came upon the animal creation, Gen. 3:14; Isa. 11:6, 7. The ground itself was cursed so that it has brought forth thorns and thistles ever since, Gen. 3:17-19; Isa. 24:5, 6. The whole creation, including man, is involved, Rom. 8:22.

An important key to history is found in the fact that a special curse rests upon Israel's enemies, Gen. 12:3. The Jews themselves were cursed for turning away from God's Word, Deut. 28:15. It was further predicted that they would be a curse while scattered among the nations, but a blessing after God restores them to Palestine, Jer. 29:18; Zech. 8:13.

Everyone who has not perfectly kept God's law is cursed, Deut. 27:26; Gal. 3:10. "The curse of the LORD is in the house of the wicked," Prov. 3:33. Men are still called "ye cursed" when they are cast into everlasting fire, Matt. 25:41. However, Christ has redeemed from the curse all who believe on Him, being made a curse for them on the cross, Gal. 3:13. He bore the symbol of the curse when He wore the crown of thorns, Matt. 27:29. A curse rests upon anyone who preaches a false gospel, Gal. 1:8, 9, or who does not love the Lord, 1 Cor. 16:22. The curse is finally to be lifted, Rev. 21:1-5; 22:3.

DAY OF THE LORD

Expressions such as "the day of the Lord," Isa. 2:12, and "that great day," Rev. 16:14, refer to a major theme of prophecy. These terms, used some 100 times, deal with a wide panorama of world transforming events, extending over a vast period of time. They include the great tribulation, Christ's return and His kingdom, Matt. 24, 25, the final judgment of the wicked dead, Rev. 20, and the new creation which follows the burning up of the present heavens and earth, 2 Pet. 3:7-13.

God's wrath and judgment are often emphasized in OT prophecies of the day of the Lord, and the Revelation is largely devoted to them. Representative passages are Joel 2, 3; Zeph. 1; Rev. 16. This aspect of the day of the Lord is described as "great and very terrible," Joel 2:11. The question is raised as to whether the human race can survive it, Matt. 24:22. Other passages describing the joy of the kingdom during that day include Isa. 12, 35; Zeph. 3; Psa. 126, 145.

The day of the Lord must be distinguished from the day of Christ, 1 Cor. 1:7, 8; Phil. 1:10. This expression is used six times in the NT with reference to the destiny of the church when believers are taken away to be with Christ, rewarded for faithfulness during the present age, and united with Him forever at the marriage of the Lamb, Rev. 19:7, 8.

DESTINY OF BELIEVERS

When Christians die, they depart to be with Christ, Phil. 1:23. Absent from the body is present with the Lord, 2 Cor. 5:8, which is "far better," Phil. 1:22, 23, because in His presence there is fulness of joy, Psa. 16:11.

When the church is translated, living believers and the resurrected dead in Christ rise together to meet the Lord in the air, 1 Thess. 4:13-18. They will stand before the judgment seat of Christ, Rom. 14:10, not to be punished but to receive rewards for things done in the body, 2 Cor. 5:10. Their works will be tried by fire, but their salvation will not be affected, 1 Cor. 3:13-15.

After the Lord is united with His bride, the church, Rev. 19:7, 8, He returns to the earth, Luke 12:36, with all His saints, 1 Thess. 3:13. He sits on the throne of His glory judging the nations, Matt. 25:31. Christians are with Him, judging the world and angels, 1 Cor. 6:2, 3. At that time their knowledge will be vastly increased, 1 Cor. 13:12.

Eternal life will mean knowing the true God and Jesus Christ, John 17:3. The horizons of believers' minds will expand forever as they grow in the knowledge of the God who creates no two snowflakes alike. They are destined to sit with the Lord on His throne, Rev. 3:21, and to reign with Him forever, Rev. 22:5.

DESTINY OF THE UNGODLY

The fact that 37 Hebrew and Greek words are translated "destruction" in the AV emphasizes the awful destiny of the lost. The first reference to perishing men is found in Num. 16:31-33. The earth opened, and Korah and his company "went down alive into the pit," a subterranean prison called Sheol in the OT and Hades in the NT. They had rejected Moses, God's mediator. In Luke 16:19-31 a believer after death is found with Abraham, separated by a great gulf from an unsaved man who is in Hades, conscious but without hope.

After the church has been translated all living men who have heard and rejected the gospel are lost, 2 Thess. 2:10-12. They become the tormented earth dwellers of Revelation. Those who have never heard the truth are given opportunity to hear a message from God, Matt. 24:14. A great multitude will be saved and enter the kingdom, Rev. 7:1-14; Matt. 25:34.

At Christ's return in judgment, He will cast all the ungodly out of His kingdom, Matt. 13:41, 42. Haters of the Lord born during the millennium, Psa. 81:15, unite under Satan and are destroyed, Rev. 20:7-9. The ungodly dead of all ages appear before the great white throne for the final judgment, Rev. 20:11-15. They are cast into the lake of fire before eternity dawns, Rev. 21:1.

DISCIPLE

The word means simply a learner or pupil, which is doubtless the reason it is never used in the epistles. It occurs 270 times in the Gospels and Acts, where it sometimes refers to the disciples of John the Baptist, Matt. 9:14, and of the Pharisees, Matt. 22:15, 16. Disciples were not synonymous with apostles, because Christ chose the apostles from a larger number of disciples, Luke 6:13.

The great commission contains the words, "Go ye therefore and make disciples of all the nations," Matt. 28:19, RV. This is commonly regarded as equivalent to a call for evangelizing the lost during the present age.

Christians were called disciples at first, Acts 11:26, but references to disciples in the Gospels cannot always be applied to Christians. For example, to require that Christians forsake everything they have in order to become truly spiritual would contradict many passages addressed to the church. Luke 14:33, where this requirement is found, was not addressed to believers but to the multitudes, v. 25.

The word is applied to Christians for the last time in Acts 21:16. In the next verse they are called brethren, a word used 140 times in Scripture as the most common term to describe believers who form the church.

EDUCATION

There are some 70 references to instruction in the Bible, and 260 verses refer to teaching. At least 18 distinct Hebrew and Greek words are used in these passages.

One reason why God saved the people of Israel was so that He might instruct them, Deut. 4:36; 32:10. The Hebrew word here is the common OT word for the chastising of children. A similar reason is given for the salvation of men in the present age, Tit. 2:11, 12. The Greek word for teaching means discipline.

God teaches men by giving His Holy Spirit, who instructed Israel, Neh. 9:20, and who teaches Christians, John 14:26; 16:13; cf. Psa. 32:8. God also calls men as teachers, 1 Cor. 12:28; Eph. 4:11, and He leads in the establishing of schools, 2 Tim. 2:2; cf. 2 Ki. 2:3-18.

Believers are admonished to receive instruction from the Lord, Prov. 8:10; Jas. 1:21. For Israel, failure to do so carried the danger that the Lord would depart from them, Jer. 6:8; Prov. 5:7-13. God's people are to apply their hearts to what is taught, Prov. 23:12, and to put the teaching into action, Jas. 1:22.

Rewards promised to instructed believers include prudence and knowledge, Prov. 1:3-6. Instruction is better than riches, Prov. 8:10-12. It brings life and favor with God, Prov. 8:33-35; 9:11.

ELECTION AND PREDESTINATION

These profound and controversial words are not to be confused with each other. Election looks back to God's choice of certain individuals to be His children, predestination looks forward to the destiny He has planned for them. Neither word is ever used in Scripture of unsaved persons.

Christians were chosen by God before the foundation of the world, Eph. 1:4, in contrast with the people of Israel, who may be said to have been chosen on a particular day in time, Deut. 26:18, 19. Believers are chosen according to the foreknowledge of God the Father, 1 Pet. 1:2, but the Bible does not reveal what it was that God foreknew. The only way we may know that others are among the elect is on the basis of the way they receive the gospel, 1 Thess. 1:4-8.

Election is entirely by the grace of God; it is not related to human acts or works, Rom. 11:5, 6. Believers are said to be chosen by Christ, John 15:16, and given by the Father to the Son, John 17:6.

The theme of the predestination of Christians appears only four times in the Bible. They are predestined to be conformed to the image of Christ in glory, Rom. 8:29, 30; they are predestined to be adopted as sons and to receive an eternal inheritance, Rom. 8:15-23; Eph. 1:5, 11.

ENEMIES

Believers have three great enemies: the world, the flesh, and the devil, Matt. 13:19-22; Eph. 2:2, 3; Jas. 4:1-7. Three weapons have been provided for victory, and a different member of the Trinity is available to help the Christian in each case.

The world in this usage is not the material creation, given to us richly to enjoy, 1 Tim. 6:17, but the world of men, devoted to lust and pleasure, 1 John 2:15-17. The child of God has been given the weapon of faith so that he can overcome, 1 John 5:4, 5. God the Father has a special relationship to the world, 1 John 2:15; Jas. 4:4.

The enemy called the flesh is not the human body, but the old nature with its propensity to sin, in which dwelleth no good thing, Rom. 7:18. Walking in the Spirit is the means of victory, Gal. 5:16. God the Holy Spirit is set over against the flesh. They who are in the flesh cannot please God; they who are "in the Spirit" are not "in the flesh," Rom. 8:8, 9.

The devil is revealed in Scripture to be a person, exceedingly wise, Ezek. 28:11-18, the leader of the hosts of wickedness, Matt. 25:41. Christ overcame the devil by using the Word of God, Matt. 4:1-11. So may every believer, 1 John 2:14; Rev. 12:11. Christ and the devil are given a relationship in the Bible which suggests the believer's victory is in Christ, Gen. 3:15; Zech. 3:1-5.

ETERNITY PAST

"Before the world was," Christ was in glory with the Father, John 1:1, 2; 17:5, 24. A divine purpose was established within the

Godhead, by which sin was permitted to be fully manifested in a world of men before being banished forever from the universe, Heb. 9:26. The Son of God agreed to become incarnate so that He could destroy the works of the devil, 1 John 3:8, in whom iniquity had been found, Isa. 14:12-15; Ezek. 28:14, 15.

Before the foundation of the world, it was ordained that Christ should become the lamb of God and be slain for the ungodly, 1 Pet. 1:18-20; Heb. 10:5-10. The world was then created by Christ, Heb. 1:10, "to be inhabited," Isa. 45:18. Man was placed upon it as a stage on which the drama of sin and salvation was to be enacted before the universe, 1 Cor. 4:9, Gr.

Believers were chosen in Christ before the world was founded, Eph. 1:4. A book was written containing the names of every person who would survive the destruction of the still uncreated world, Phil. 4:3; Rev. 17:8; 20:15. Nothing could disannul this "purpose that is purposed upon the whole earth," Isa. 14:24-27; 46:10, 11. The Bible closes with its final fulfillment as the devil is destroyed, Rev. 20:10, and God brings many sons to glory, Heb. 2:10; Rev. 21:1-5.

ETERNITY TO COME

Revealed truth about the ages to come, Eph. 2:7, matches what has been written about past ages, Eph. 3:5. In bringing many sons to glory, Heb. 2:10, God has purposes for Israel, Isa. 66:22; for the nations; Rev. 21:23-26; and for the church, 2 Tim. 2:12. Believers are to be adopted as children of God, Eph. 1:5, and enjoy an eternal inheritance, which will never fade away, 1 Pet. 1:4. It is God's purpose to make His wisdom and the riches of His grace known by the church, Eph. 2:7; 3:10, 11.

All former things are going to pass away; God will make all things new. There will be no sea, no death, sorrow, crying or pain, no night, no need of the sun, Rev. 21:1-5, 23. The curse will be lifted, Rev. 22:3. All things in heaven and earth will be gathered together in one, Eph. 1:10. The present creation will be forgotten, Isa. 65:17.

A river of water of life and the tree of life will be seen in a new city which comes from heaven, Rev. 21:9—22:2. The Son of God will rule over an everlasting dominion, Dan. 2:44; 7:13, 14, 27. He will still be subject to the Father, John 10:29; 1 Cor. 15:28. The everlasting fire which has received the wicked will continue to exist in a visible form, Isa. 66:24. Such revelations as these belong to "the dispensation of the fulness of times," Eph. 1:9, 10.

EVANGELISM

The idea that the work of soul winning or evangelism is to be carried out by specialists like pastors and missionaries is not taught in Scripture. Every child of God bears some responsibility, 2 Cor. 5:18-20.

Early in His ministry, Christ promised to make His followers fishers of men, Matt. 4:19. At its close He said, "Ye are witnesses of these things," Luke 24:48. Each Gospel ends with an emphasis on personal testimony, Mark 16:15. The last words of Christ before His ascension dealt with witnessing, Acts 1:8, 9.

The gospel has not been proclaimed until people have been given good news from God to believe. That good news is defined in 1 Cor. 15:1-3. It is not related to anything men may do, Eph. 2:8, 9. The only acceptable response is to receive Christ, John 1:12; to believe, John 3:16; to call upon Him, Rom. 10:13; to confess Him, Rom. 10:9; to look unto Him, Isa. 45:22.

Faith comes by hearing the Word of God, Rom. 10:17. It is the Holy Spirit who convicts and regenerates, John 16:8-11; Tit. 3:5. God provides pastors and teachers to perfect the saints for their work of ministry, Eph. 4:11, 12. This can be done by anyone, at any time, anywhere, and in many ways. Wise believers will win souls, Prov. 11:30, and receive an eternal reward, Dan. 12:3.

FAITH AND WORKS

Faith is the confident assurance of things hoped for, a conviction of the reality of things not seen, Heb. 11:1. It is the basis for salvation, Gal. 3:26; 1 Pet. 1:5. Works are the deeds men do, whether good or evil, Gal. 2:16; Eph. 5:11. They are the basis for rewards or punishment when men are judged, 1 Cor. 3:11-15; Rev. 20:11-15. Men confuse these two concepts; Scripture never does.

A contradiction has been imagined between two passages. Paul wrote, "a man is justified by faith without the deeds of the law," Rom. 3:28. Wrote James, "by works a man is justified, and not by faith only," Jas. 2:24. There is no real problem. Paul was writing about justification before God, Rom. 4:2, while James wrote about justification before men. He was dealing with the question of the man who says he has faith, but has no works to demonstrate its reality, Jas. 2:14-20. He says nothing to discredit faith, nor to suggest that a man of faith may be lost. Paul speaks of the root of the Christian life; James its fruit.

Faith and works are put in their proper perspective in Eph. 2:8-

10. We are saved by faith, not by works, but we are saved "unto good works." This means we are to maintain good works, Tit. 3:8, being fruitful in them, Col. 1:10, so that God may be glorified when Christ returns, 1 Pet. 2:12.

FAMILY

God instituted marriage as a monogamous, lifelong relationship, Mark 10:2-12, to be established in a home separate from that of the parents, Eph. 5:31. Adultery is so serious as to be the subject of the seventh commandment, Ex. 20:14, where it stands between murder and stealing.

The husband is given the place of headship, but he is to love his wife enough to be willing to be crucified for her, Eph. 5:22-33. He bears the responsibility to provide for his family, 1 Tim. 5:8, and to rear the children in the nurture and admonition of the Lord, Eph. 6:4; Deut. 6:6, 7. He is warned not to provoke or discourage them, Col. 3:21.

The wife is given the place of subjection to her husband, Eph. 5:22-33; 1 Pet. 3:1-6, but she is to have the place of honor in the home, 1 Pet. 3:7. If either fails to give the other the place accorded by Scripture, their prayers are hindered.

Children occupy the place of obedience to both parents, Eph. 6:1-3; Prov. 22:15; 23:13, whom they must honor and requite, Eph. 6:2; 1 Tim. 5:4; John 19:26.

Servants in the household are to be given fair treatment by their employers, Col. 4:1. On their part, they are required to be obedient and honest, Tit. 2:9, 10, and faithful in their work, Col. 3:22-24.

FLESH

The expression "the flesh" often carries a special doctrinal meaning in the NT. In this usage it does not refer to the body, but to the old nature of the believer, with its tendency to sin even after the miracle of the new birth.

While believers should be spiritual, some are fleshly or carnal, 1 Cor. 3:1. These individuals are said to walk according to the flesh, 2 Cor. 10:2. They serve the law of sin, Rom. 7:25. Walking in the flesh is contrasted with walking in the Spirit, Rom. 8:4, 5.

Christians are admonished to make no provision for the flesh, Rom. 13:14, and its filthiness, 2 Cor. 7:1. A dreadful list of the works of the flesh appears in Gal. 5:19-21. They that are "in the flesh" cannot please God; their minds are at enmity with Him, Rom. 8:7, 8. The flesh is contrary to the Spirit, Gal. 5:17. No good thing dwells in the flesh, Rom. 7:18.

The notion that spiritual Christians may eradicate the old nature by a superior form of holiness is in error, 1 John 1:8-10. The teaching of Scripture is that in a believer the flesh is controlled by the Spirit, Gal. 5:16. The secret of this control is found in Rom. 6:6-13. It is based on knowing, v. 6; reckoning, v. 11; and yielding, v. 13. Gal. 5:24 states the result of this victory.

FORGIVENESS

An eternal unchanging law of the universe is revealed in Heb. 9:22. Without the shedding of blood there is no remission—that is, no forgiveness. Because human forgiveness simply remits a deserved penalty, men need the revelation that because of His holy character God can forgive men only on the basis of the full execution of the penalty. This is why the offering of a sacrifice for atonement was necessary in OT days, Lev. 4:35.

Christ shed His blood for the remission of sins, Matt. 26:28. All who trust in Him as the Lamb of God are forgiven all trespasses, past, present, and future, Col. 2:13; 1 John 2:12. They are forever delivered from all condemnation, John 3:18; 5:24. Forgiveness is sometimes thought of as the negative aspect of salvation, which also includes justification, Rom. 5:1, an inheritance, Acts 26:18, and much more.

When Christians fall into sin, fellowship with the Father is broken. The remedy is confession of the sin to God, 1 John 1:9. He freely forgives and restores. Failure to judge and forsake sin brings chastisement to a believer, 1 Cor. 11:31, 32. This family relationship is also in view in Mark 11:25, 26, where a forgiving spirit is required before the Father will forgive His children. A concise statement of this principle appears in Eph. 4:32. Believers are to forgive one another, even as God for Christ's sake has forgiven them.

GIFTS

The Spirit of God has given to every believer one or more gifts or divine enablements for serving Christ. These differ from one another, Rom. 12:6-8. Nine gifts are listed in 1 Cor. 12:4-11, but this is not exhaustive, because gifted men are mentioned elsewhere who possess totally different gifts: apostles, evangelists, pastors, teachers, and others, 1 Cor. 12:28; Eph. 4:8-11. Gifts are given to men, while gifted men are given by the Lord to the church.

The divine order regarding gifts puts apostles first, prophets second, teachers third. Others follow in order, with tongues mentioned last, 1 Cor. 12:28. During apostolic days gifts were sometimes imparted with the laying on of hands, 1 Tim. 4:14; 2 Tim. 1:6. Christians were instructed to desire gifts, especially that of prophecy, 1 Cor. 12:31; 14:1, which is defined in v. 3. It was revealed that some gifts would cease, 1 Cor. 13:8.

Instructions for the use of gifts are given in 1 Pet. 4:10, 11. The parable of the pounds establishes the principle that rewards will differ for differing degrees of diligence in their use, Luke 19:11-27. The parable of the talents establishes the principle that rewards will be equal for equal faithfulness on the part of believers, Matt. 25:14-30.

GLORY

The glory of Lebanon was its trees, Isa. 60:13; that of Solomon was his kingly splendor, Matt. 6:29. The word may be briefly defined as manifested excellence. Its most important use in Scripture is with reference to God and Christ in the visible bright effulgence of their deity.

The first mention of the glory of the Lord, at the giving of the manna, describes it as like devouring fire, Ex. 16:7, 10; 24:17. It is likened to a bright rainbow with a Man on a throne at its center in Ezek. 1:26-28.

The glory of the Lord seen in the tabernacle and temple was called by the Jews the *Shekinah,* from a root meaning to tabernacle or to dwell. Amazingly, the Hebrew word in Ex. 40:33, 34 and the Greek word in John 1:14; Rev. 21:3 are formed of the same consonants. God's glory was reluctantly withdrawn from the people of Israel because of their sin, Ezek. 9:3; 10:4, 18; 11:23, 24.

When the glory returns at the time of the inauguration of the kingdom it is seen to be a Person, Ezek. 43:2-6, identified as the Lord Jesus Christ in Jas. 2:1, AV marg. God's glory, an unseen treasure in the hearts of believers now, 2 Cor. 4:6, 7, will become visible to the universe when they appear with Christ in glory at His return to the earth, Col. 3:4; Rev. 21:9-11.

GOSPEL

The word means good news or glad tidings. Popularly applied to the four NT records of the first coming of Christ, in Scripture it is used only of good news concerning major aspects of divine revelation.

The gospel of the kingdom is the good news that God is going to establish a kingdom. It was preached by John the Baptist, Matt. 3:1, 2; by Christ before He was rejected, Matt. 4:23, and by the disciples during the period when their ministry was restricted to Israel, Matt. 10:5-7. Its message, "Repent: for the kingdom of heaven is at hand," Matt. 4:17, is not given during the present age, but it will again be proclaimed during the great tribulation, Matt. 24:14; Rev. 7:9, 14.

The gospel of salvation by grace through faith in Christ crucified and resurrected is mentioned under various descriptive terms some 85 times in the NT. It is described in 1 Cor. 15:1-5 as consisting of the death, burial and resurrection of Christ. A curse rests upon the preaching of "another gospel," Gal. 1:6-9; 2 Cor. 11:4, such as the teaching that men are saved by keeping the law.

The everlasting gospel of Rev. 14:6, 7 is not defined as are the others, but its theme, "Fear God, and give glory to him," is related to the final consummation of His purposes in the hour of final judgments.

GOVERNMENT

"The powers that be are ordained of God," Rom. 13:1. "The most High ruleth in the kingdom of men, and giveth it to whomsoever he will," Dan. 4:17. God permits both evil and good men to rule, Prov. 29:2. Satanic forces are often dominant, Luke 4:5, 6; Rev. 13:2; Dan. 10:13, 20. Pilate was given power from above, John 19:11. Capital punishment is a necessary part of government, Rom. 13:4; Gen. 9:5, 6.

God's people are not to meddle with changes sought by enemies of rulers, Prov. 24:21. Evil men seek rebellion, Prov. 17:11. Apostates, and not God fearing people, despise government and speak evil of authority, 2 Pet. 2:10; Jude 8. When the wicked seek to oppress the godly, the principle of obedience to God rather than man may be invoked, Acts 5:29.

Believers are required to be subject to the higher powers, Rom. 13:1. Nero was ruling when this precept was written. They are to obey magistrates, Tit. 3:1; to pay taxes, Rom. 13:7; Luke 20:25;

to submit to every ordinance of man for the Lord's sake, Rom. 13:2; 1 Pet. 2:13.

Christians are instructed to pray for all in authority, 1 Tim. 2:1, 2. The people of Israel were told even to pray for, and to seek the peace of the cities where they were held captive, Jer. 29:7.

GRACE

The dictionary defines grace as the unmerited favor of God toward men. This does not do justice to the richness of the biblical use of the term, which appears scores of times. Grace is the favor God is able to show to men because Christ died for them; "by grace are ye saved," Eph. 2:8. Because of His holy character, God could not save men simply because of His mercy and love. The claims of divine righteousness had to be satisfied before He could save sinful men, therefore Christ died in the place of the ungodly, Rom. 5:6.

Grace is distinguished from the law, John 1:17; from works, Rom. 11:6; and from debt, Rom. 4:4. Salvation cannot be earned by law keeping or by good deeds of any kind. Men are chosen by grace, Rom. 11:5; justified by grace, Rom. 3:24; continue in grace, Acts 13:43; approach God in prayer at the throne of grace, Heb. 4:16. They grow in grace as they grow in the knowledge of Christ, 1 Pet. 2:2; 2 Pet. 3:18. Men do not fall from grace by sinning, but by putting the law in the place of grace, Gal. 5:4.

A remarkable summary of the teaching of grace is found in Tit. 2:11-14. It includes the denial of wrong things, and the positive instruction that we must live soberly, righteously, and godly as we look for the blessed hope of the Lord's return.

GREAT COMMISSION

The challenge given by Christ to His followers just before His ascension has sparked missionary activity all over the world ever since the present age began.

He commanded the eleven to go, teach and baptize all nations, Matt. 28:18-20. The RV changes the word teach to "make disciples of." His words as they were given on another occasion, recorded in Mark 16:15, called for preaching the gospel to every creature. Preaching in His name among all nations is the theme of Luke 24:47.

Our Lord's last words are recorded in Acts 1:8. Perhaps the most famous missionary text in the Bible, they are a command to bear witness in the power of the Holy Spirit unto the uttermost part of the earth. The orderly progress of this testimony was to be in Jerusalem where the apostles were at the time, then in the surrounding area and the adjoining region, and finally to the far places.

The most comprehensive commission is found in Acts 26:16-18. Christ appeared to Paul for the purpose of making him a minister and a witness among the Gentiles. He was made responsible to open their eyes, 2 Cor. 4:3, 4; to turn them from darkness to light, Col. 1:13; and from the power of Satan to God, Heb. 2:14, 15, so that they could receive forgiveness, Eph. 1:7 and an inheritance, 1 Pet. 1:3, 4.

HEALING

God has healed in the past by prescription, 2 Ki. 20:7; 1 Tim. 5:23; through physicians, Luke 5:31; Col. 4:14; by direct intervention, Mark 3:1-5; in answer to the faith of friends, Mark 2:5; in response to prayer, Jas. 5:15, 16; and in spite of unbelief, Mark 6:5.

It did not please God to heal Daniel, Dan. 8:27; Elisha, 2 Ki. 13:14; Timothy, 1 Tim. 5:23; Epaphroditus, Phil. 2:26; Trophimus, 2 Tim. 4:20; or Paul, 2 Cor. 12:7-10. God is able to heal anyone at any time, but the Bible reveals that it is not normally His purpose to do so. Evangelicals therefore believe in divine healing, but not in divine healers.

Sickness and infirmity are permitted for a number of revealed reasons: so that God's works may be made manifest, John 9:3; for His own glory, John 11:4; for our profit, Psa. 119:67; Heb. 12:5-10; so that we may be able to comfort others, 2 Cor. 1:4; to make us more fruitful, John 15:2; Heb. 12:11; to prepare us for future glory, Rom. 8:17; 2 Cor. 4:17.

God always provides a way to escape, 1 Cor. 10:13. It comes through prayer, Matt. 6:13; Heb. 4:16. It may also come through self judgment, in the light of the Word, 1 Cor. 11:31; 2 Chr. 7:14. If God does not heal, His grace is sufficient, 2 Cor. 12:9.

HEAVEN

Heaven is a place. God the Father is there, Matt. 6:9. So are His throne, Psa. 11:4, and His angels, Mark 13:32. Christ came down from heaven, John 6:38. To it He ascended, Acts 1:9-11, to sit on the right hand of the Father, 1 Pet. 3:22. The Holy Spirit was sent down from heaven, 1 Pet. 1:12. That is where the believer's hope is found, Col. 1:5; his inheritance, 1 Pet. 1:4; his reward, Matt. 5:12; his treasure, Mark 10:21; and his name, Luke 10:20.

Heaven is thought to be a sphere, Job 22:14 marg. Its size is inconceivable, because from it the new Jerusalem descends, described as 1500 miles square, Rev. 21:10-16. It is "up," above the atmospheric and starry heavens, Gen. 7:23; 22:17, possibly in the north, Isa. 14:13; Psa. 75:6, 7. It is called the third heaven, 2 Cor. 12:2; Eph. 4:10.

Believers go to be with Christ in heaven at death, Phil. 1:23, far better than life on earth, being a place of joy and pleasure, Psa. 16:11. From heaven they will descend with Christ when He returns to the earth, 1 Thess. 3:13; 4:16. The calling of Christians is heavenly, Heb. 3:1, in contrast with the earthly calling of others, Rev. 21:24. Evidently because of the poverty of language, the eternal state is described in terms of the absence of sorrow, pain, death, and other "former things," Rev. 21:4.

HELL

The major OT Hebrew terms for the unseen world of the departed are Sheol and pit. The major NT Greek words are Hades, Gehenna, Tartarus, and the lake of fire.

Sheol and Hades are identical, Psa. 16:10; Acts 2:27. They refer to a place beneath the earth where Pharaoh and all other wicked men of ancient times are confined, Ezek. 31:16-18; 32:17-32; Luke 16:23-28. It has gates, Isa. 38:10; Matt. 16:18; and bars, Jon. 2:2-6. Christ has the keys to it, Rev. 1:18. It will some day give up its dead for judgment, Rev. 20:11-15.

Four words are translated pit in the OT. It is the place within Sheol into which the wicked descend at death, Num. 16:30-33; Ezek. 26:20. Infernal locusts are confined in the bottomless pit, Rev. 9:1-11. Satan will be cast into the pit of the abyss, Rev. 20:1-3, RV.

Tartarus is mentioned only in 2 Pet. 2:4, Gr. Sinning angels are bound and held there for future judgment in what are described as dark underground caverns, Gr.

The lake of fire is the final abode of Satan, his angels and all wicked persons, Matt. 25:41; Rev. 20:10, 15. It is identical with Gehenna, the "hell fire" of Matt. 5:22. It was named for the ancient valley of Hinnom where fires consumed refuse and worms fed on dead bodies, Josh. 15:8; Jer. 19:2-6.

HOPE

Believers are delivered from the great misery facing mankind of "having no hope," Eph. 2:12. At least seven revealed certitudes are eagerly expected by Christians. All of them are doubtless comprehended in "the hope of His calling," Eph. 1:18, "the hope which is laid up for you in heaven," Col. 1:5. The seven are:

1. The blessed hope of the personal return of Christ, Tit. 2:13.

2. The resurrection of the body in a glorious new form, never again subject to sickness, weakness or death, Acts 23:6.

3. The restoration of loved ones who have fallen asleep in Christ, 1 Thess. 4:13-18.

4. Fellowship with converts and other saints, 1 Thess. 2:19.

5. Being presented spotless, 2 Pet. 3:14 and faultless, Jude 24, in unutterable glory, Col. 1:27.

6. Entering into eternal life with all it means, such as reigning with Christ, Rev. 3:21; 22:5, and knowing God, John 17:3.

7. The receiving of an inheritance which is reserved in heaven until that moment, 1 Pet. 1:3, 4.

This exceedingly rich array of blessings is to believers a source of joy, Rom. 5:2; of comfort in sorrow, 1 Thess. 4:18; of confident assurance, Heb. 6:18, 19. It is an incentive to holy living, 1 John 3:3. Christians are said to be saved in hope, Rom. 8:24, RV, a hope based on the written Word of God, Psa. 119:49.

HOUSEHOLD SALVATION

An extensive revelation deals with the theme of God's plan for the salvation of families. The purpose of God to provide for entire households in His offer of salvation is seen in Gen. 7:1 and Acts 11:14; the words "thou and all thy house" are found in both the OT and the NT. This divine provision of deliverance for entire households extended even to children's children, Psa. 103:17, 18.

As the program of God unfolded, the families of Abraham and Joshua were saved as the patriarchs recognized their responsibility for them, Gen. 18:19; Josh. 24:15. Households were provided for on the night of the Passover, Ex. 12:3, 4. God's plan for ensuring as far as possible the salvation of children is revealed in Psa. 78:5-7. Rahab was given responsibility for her father, mother, brother, and others, Josh. 2:18, 19. Wives bear some responsibility for unsaved husbands, 1 Pet. 3:1, 2. The practical means whereby David sought to win his loved ones is seen in Psa. 101:2-7; that of Jacob, in Gen. 35:2-4.

Divine promises bearing on this theme are found in Prov. 22:6; Acts 2:39; and Acts 16:31. That which is implied in Deut. 5:29 is clearly stated in Acts 11:14. Such texts offer great encouragement to parents and others to pray for the salvation of members of their families, and to live with this in view.

IMMORTALITY

The word as used in the Bible means deathlessness, or exemption from the physical death of the body. It is not to be confused with the eternal life of the saved or the unending existence of the lost, though popular usage confuses these terms. The word is used only with reference to the body, Rom. 6:12; 8:11, and never in connection with the soul. Men are unable to kill the soul. Only God can destroy it, Matt. 10:28, where a word is used which does not mean to deprive the soul of life.

With the coming of Christ, light was cast upon the subject of immortality, which had been clothed in obscurity since OT days, 2 Tim. 1:10, Gr. Only Christ now possesses immortality, 1 Tim. 1:17; 6:16. All men, including saved persons, are now mortal, Job 4:17; 1 Cor. 15:22; Heb. 9:27. Men will continue to die until death is destroyed, 1 Cor. 15:26.

At the translation of the church, all believers will put on immortality. They will be clothed with deathlessness as with a garment, 1 Cor. 15:51-54. Mortality will then be "swallowed up of life," 2 Cor. 5:4, and believers will never again be able to die. In the same moment that their bodies become immortal, they also become incorruptible, or immune to change and decay.

INHERITANCE

Believers are "heirs of God, and joint heirs with Christ," Rom. 8:17. Not only do they receive forgiveness of sins, but an inheritance as well, Acts 26:18. This is in contrast with the inheritance of Israel, which the OT identifies some scores of times as the land of Palestine, Ex. 32:13; Isa. 60:21.

The Christian's inheritance is said to be in Christ, Eph. 1:11, and "in light," Col. 1:12. We are made fit for it by God the Father, Col. 1:12. The earnest or guarantee that we shall receive it is the Holy Spirit who, in the moment we are saved, seals us unto the day of redemption, Eph. 1:14.

Believers are given their inheritance by reason of the fact that they have been born again into the family of God. It is described in brief but astonishing terms in 1 Pet. 1:3, 4. It is incorruptible, or beyond the reach of decay and ruin. It is undefiled, or beyond the reach of sin. It does not fade away, which puts it beyond the reach of time and change. It is reserved for us in heaven, so that it is beyond the reach of loss.

Not only is our inheritance kept safely for us, but Scripture reveals that we who are to receive it are kept by the power of God until it becomes ours in the last time, 1 Pet. 1:5.

ISRAEL

Israel is the most prominent theme of the Bible, taking up four fifths of its pages. Only this people out of all the nations had its history written in advance, Deut. 28, 30. They are remarkable for their antiquity, their influence, and their preservation during centuries of persecution.

Descended from Abraham through Isaac and Jacob, Israel was chosen by God to reveal Him, to produce the Bible and to bring the Saviour to men. After being given Palestine by divine decree, Gen. 15:7, they occupied it for hundreds of years, then were taken captive, Jer. 25:11, and eventually were scattered over the face of the earth, Luke 21:24.

The present world dispersion will end when He who scattered them regathers them, Jer. 31:10. After large numbers of unbelieving Jews have returned to their land, Zech. 12:9-14, and suffered great tribulation, Jer. 30:1-7, they will be delivered by their Messiah as He returns to the earth, Zech. 14:1-3. He will then restore all Israel to the land, Deut. 30:1-3; Ezek. 39:28, bless and rule them from His throne in Jerusalem, Jer. 3:17.

During the present age when the nation Israel has been set aside for rejecting Christ, Rom. 11:15, individual Jews are being saved as God gathers out a people for His name from all mankind, Acts 15:14-17.

ISRAEL AND THE CHURCH

Many clearly stated distinctions between Israel and the church make it impossible to confuse the two. Israel's history began with Abraham, Isaac, and Jacob, Gen. 12:1-3, while that of the church began at Pentecost. It is made up of both Jews and Gentiles, Matt. 16:18; Acts 2; Gal. 3:26-28.

Israel's relationship to God was based on a covenant, Gen. 17:7, 8; that of the church, on a new birth into God's family, John 1:12;

1 Pet 1:23. Israel was promised earthly blessings, Deut. 28:1-14; the church is blessed with all spiritual blessings in heavenly places, Eph. 1:3; Heb. 3:1. On earth Christians are to be content with food and raiment, 1 Tim. 6:8.

Israel is the subject of OT prophecy; the church is not even mentioned in the OT, being the subject of an entirely new revelation, Rom. 16:25, 26; Eph. 3:1-6. Israel worshipped at Jerusalem, Psa. 122:1-4; the church worships wherever two or three are gatheied in the name of Christ, Matt. 18:20. Israel lived under the law, Ezek. 20:10-12; the church is not under law, but under grace, John 1:17; Rom. 6:14. The destiny of Israel is inseparably linked with the land of Palestine, Isa. 60:18-21; the church is to be taken away from the earth when it is complete and its destiny begins to unfold, 1 Thess. 4:13-18.

JEHOVAH

Whenever the words LORD or GOD (caps) appear in the AV, they represent *Jehovah* in the Hebrew original. It is a major OT name for Christ, used nearly 7,000 times, Isa. 6:1-12; John 12:37-41, revealing His redemptive character, grace and faithfulness.

The key to the meaning of this remarkable name is found in Ex. 3:14, where the Lord revealed Himself to Moses as the I AM, by using the root of the Hebrew *Jehovah*. In this apparently incomplete expression, He may be said to have given His people a blank check on which to write in their own needs as they prayed.

The Jews revered the word *Jehovah* so much that when Christ stood before them and identified Himself as the I AM of the OT, they sought to stone Him for blasphemy, John 8:24, 58, 59. When He took that same name on His lips in Gethsemane, some display of His glory caused His enemies to fall to the ground, John 18:5, 6.

Christ also filled in the blank seven times. He said, "I am the good shepherd," John 10:11, who meets the needs of all who want His care. The other examples are found in John 6:35; 8:12; 10:9; 11:25; 14:6; 15:1. These NT illustrations of the full meaning of *Jehovah* illuminate His promise, "Whatsoever ye shall ask the Father in my name, He will give it you," John 16:23.

JERUSALEM

Its history goes back 4000 years to Melchizedek, Gen. 14:17-20. It is mentioned well over 1000 times under its various names. Often destroyed, it has risen from its ashes to continue its astonishing world influence. There Christ was crucined and resurrected, and there the Holy Spirit descended to inaugurate the age of the church.

God made and fashioned the site long ago, Isa. 22:11, placed it "in the midst of the nations and countries that are round about," Ezek. 5:5, and chose it for His habitation, Psa. 132:13. There His glory dwelt, and will one day return, when the millennial temple is erected, Ezek. 11:23; 43:2.

The times of the Gentiles are said to be fulfilled when they no longer control the city, Luke 21:24. Gentile times will end when Christ reigns from Jerusalem, Zeph. 3:14-17. The holy city is to become a source of world wide trouble in the last days, Zech. 12:2, 3. All nations will gather against it to battle, Zech. 14:2. The Lord will return and deliver the city, Zech. 14:3, 4.

During the kingdom age, it is to be the world metropolis from which Christ will rule all nations, Jer. 3:17; Isa. 24:23. It will be elevated above the countryside; from it will flow a great river, Zech. 14:8-10. Rejoicing will fill the streets of the city, Jer. 33:1-16. It will be the joy of the whole earth, Psa. 48:2.

KINGDOM OF GOD

God is a King. His kingdom is glorious, majestic, everlasting, Psa. 145:1, 11-13; Dan. 4:3. It is universal, "His kingdom ruleth over all," from a throne in the heavens, Psa. 103:19. Mentioned some 70 times in the NT, the kingdom of God was the subject of Christ's post-resurrection ministry, Acts 1:3, and that of the apostles, Acts 8:12; 19:8. God's natural laws govern the world of nature; His written laws were given to govern and control men.

God's kingdom includes things that are seen: "all the earth," Psa. 47:7; material things as well as living creatures, Psa. 104; men and their rulers, Dan. 4:17. Its visible establishment on the earth was announced at Christ's first coming, Mark 1:15. It will be set up at His return, Rev. 12:10.

The kingdom also includes things invisible. Believers enter it at the new birth; the unsaved cannot see it, John 3:3, 5. Characterized by righteousness, peace, and joy, Rom. 14:17, it is not inherited by flesh and blood, 1 Cor. 15:50.

Angels are a part of God's kingdom, Psa. 103:20-22. Satan and demons are answerable to it, Isa. 24:21, 22; Rev. 20:1-3. Men are to seek it, Matt. 6:33. Believers are to be worthy of it, 2 Thess. 1:4, 5. It is never identified with the church in Scripture, nor are men anywhere told to build the kingdom.

KINGDOM OF HEAVEN

The expression is found only in Matthew, where it appears about 30 times. It is derived from Dan. 2:44; 4:25, 32. The kingdom of God is also mentioned in Matthew, five times out of 70 occurrences in the NT.

Some regard these two terms as identical because of similarities between them. Both are to be established on the earth, Matt. 3:2; Mark 1:15. Mysteries are associated with both, Matt. 13:11; Luke 8:10. Christ associated the parable of the leaven with both, Matt. 13:33; Luke 13:21.

However, differences between the two make it clear that the terms are not identical. The kingdom of God is entered only by the new birth, John 3:3, 5; not so the kingdom of heaven, Matt. 5:20; 7:21. The kingdom of God is eternal, Dan. 4:2, 3; Heb. 1:8, but not the kingdom which precedes it, 1 Cor. 15:24; Rev. 20:6. Only the saved are in the kingdom of God, John 3:3, 5, where they are safe, John 5:24; 10:28, 29, but unsaved persons are found in the kingdom of heaven, out of which they will be cast, Matt. 13:41-43, 47-51.

The kingdom of heaven therefore may be regarded as the rule of heaven over the earth by Christ when He establishes His kingdom on earth, while the kingdom of God is His sovereign rule in the universe and in the hearts of His people, Psa. 103:19.

LIFE AND DEATH

Only in the Bible can any satisfying light be found on the mysterious and baffling subjects of life and death, Deut. 30:19. In the beginning God breathed life into the nostrils of the man He had created, Gen. 2:7. That breath was the spirit of man. "The body without the spirit is dead," Jas. 2:26.

The normal life span is 70 years, Psa. 90:10. Those who keep God's precepts ordinarily live longer than those who do not, Prov. 3:1, 2. Life is likened to a shadow, Psa. 144:4, and a vapor, Jas. 4:14. "A sound heart is the life of the flesh," Prov. 14:30. "The life of the flesh is in the blood," Lev. 17:11.

By one man came death through disobedience, Gen. 2:17; Rom. 5:12. Under the permissive will of God, Satan has the power of death, Job 2:6. The fear of it brings men into bondage, Heb. 2:14, 15. Death is an enemy which will finally be destroyed, 1 Cor. 15:26. Christ has the keys to it, Rev. 1:18. It will be banished from God's new order, Rev. 21:4. For believers, "to die is gain,"

Phil. 1:21. For all others, after death there is judgment, Heb. 9:27.

Like Enoch and Elijah, believers who are living at the time of the translation of the church will never die, 1 Cor. 15:51, 52; 1 Thess. 4:14-18. All unbelievers will ultimately experience the second death, Rev. 20:14, 15.

LORD'S SUPPER

All who accept the invitation to the gospel supper, Luke 14:15-24 are sure to be present at the marriage supper of the Lamb, Rev. 19:7-9, and they have the privilege of enjoying the Lord's Supper in the meantime, 1 Cor. 11:23-29. At this communion service, they participate in a present activity which commemorates a past event and looks forward to a future consummation. It is a feast of love, a memorial of faith, a prophecy of hope. Believers meditate on a crucified Saviour's love, a living Saviour's intercession, and a coming Saviour's glory.

The Lord's Supper has its roots in Ex. 12:1-11, for it is Christ our passover who is sacrificed for us, 1 Cor. 5:7. On the night the blood of the passover lamb was shed, the people of Israel inaugurated a feast so they would afterward remember that they were saved by blood, as they enjoyed present fellowship and received strength for the wilderness journey ahead.

Believers take the cup of remission, Matt. 26:28, the cup of remembrance, Luke 22:19; the cup of the Lord's return, 1 Cor. 11:26. The table is prepared in the presence of their enemies, Psa. 23:5. Demons behold and tremble, Jas. 2:19. As Christians experience the Lord's presence, Matt. 18:20, their eyes affect their hearts, Lam. 3:51. As they are reassured of His love, they receive new strength.

MILLENNIUM

The thousand years during which Christ is to rule the world is popularly known as the millennium. As to where it belongs in the program of God, the discredited postmillennial view placed it before the physical return of Christ to the earth. The amillennial view rejects the literal meaning of the Bible text. The premillennial view accepts kingdom prophecies as literal, placing the return of Christ before the millennium is established.

This will be earth's golden age, when all of God's promises concerning His future kingdom will be fulfilled. It is described in the largest body of prophecy still unfulfilled. Creation will be liberated,

Rom. 8:18-23. The curse will be lifted, Isa. 11:6-9; 35:5, 6. The earth will be fruitful, Amos 9:13. Wars cease, Psa. 46:9, as the devil and his demons are imprisoned, Isa. 24:21, 22; Rev. 20:1-3. The Lord is king over all the earth, Zech. 14:9; Luke 1:32, 33, and believers reign with Him, 2 Tim. 2:12; Rev. 5:10.

The millennium is to endure for 1000 years, Rev. 20:4-6. As it begins, all wicked people will be cast out, Matt. 13:41-43; but as it ends, a final rebellion precedes the dawn of eternity, Rev. 20:7—21:5. Matt. 5-7 is widely regarded as the constitution of the coming kingdom, which is thought to be identical with the kingdom of heaven.

MISSIONS

The word missions does not appear in the Bible, but a vast revelation is given to the theme of missionary work. The words evangelist, Eph. 4:11, and witness, Acts 1:8, come closest in meaning to the subject.

OT references to the divine purpose of having God's Word proclaimed include Prov. 14:25-27; Isa. 6:8; cf. Acts 10:43; 14:17. OT missionary activity is seen in Josh. 2:18, 19; 2 Ki. 5:2-4; Jon. 1:2; 3:2. Psa. 96 is known as a missionary Psalm.

During the present age, God is seeking men, John 4:23. For this reason He calls His people to preach the gospel everywhere, Matt. 28:19, 20; Acts 1:8. Believers have an obligation to be ambassadors of Christ, Rom. 1:14-16; 2 Cor. 5:20. They are assured of the presence of Christ, Matt. 28:20; Heb. 13:5.

They are put in trust with the gospel, 1 Thess. 2:4, and sent forth, John 17:18, through open doors, 1 Cor. 16:9, into "the regions beyond," 2 Cor. 10:16. They are to preach the gospel, Acts 10:42, 43, which is defined in 1 Cor. 15:1-4. They work under divine compulsion and use every means possible, 1 Cor. 9:16, 22.

Missionary activity is of primary importance. It is the secret of blessing upon the local congregation. Missionaries are to be helped by prayer, 2 Cor. 1:11, and supported by the home churches, 1 Cor. 16:1, 2, as workers together with God, 2 Cor. 6:1.

MUSIC

The first sacred music on record is found in Job 38:7, where the morning stars sang together at the creation of the material universe.

The earliest recorded singing by men appears in Ex. 15:1, when the people of Israel rejoiced over their salvation from Egypt.

A number of remarkable facts are revealed concerning sacred music. It brings refreshment, and drives away evil spirits, 1 Sam. 16:23. It provides an atmosphere favorable to the ministry of the Word, 2 Ki. 3:15, 16. It helps to bring men to God, Psa. 40:1-3. It contributes to the defeat of the enemy, 2 Chr. 20:21, 22. It fills the house of God with glory, 2 Chr. 5:13, 14.

The people of Israel lost their song while in captivity because of sin, Psa. 137:1-4, but recovered it again after they were restored to the land, Ezra 3:2, 11. In the NT it is revealed that the secret of the song of the redeemed is found in the word of Christ dwelling in the heart, Col. 3:16. It is one of the results of the filling of the Holy Spirit, Eph. 5:18, 19.

The new song of heaven begins on the earth. It is praise to the Lamb for having redeemed men to God by His blood out of every kindred, tongue, people and nation, Rev. 5:9.

MYSTERIES

The popular concept that a mystery is something mysterious or secret tends to obscure the fact that it is not used in this way in Scripture. In the NT the word refers to divine truth which is now revealed after being hidden from men in OT days. It appears 27 times.

In Matt. 13:11 Christ began to reveal "the mysteries of the kingdom of heaven," a series of truths having to do with the previously undisclosed period between His first and second comings. The church age is a mystery "kept secret since the world began," Rom. 16:25, but made known to the apostles, Eph. 3:1-12. This revelation makes it clear that Israel cannot be identified with the church.

Other NT mysteries include the change in believers at the translation of the church at the end of the age, 1 Cor. 15:51, 52; 1 Thess. 4:13-17; the mystery of the church as the bride of Christ, despite the fact that He is also Israel's Messiah, Eph. 5:23-32; the mystery that Christ dwells within believers, Gal. 2:20; Col. 1:26, 27; the mystery of God in Christ, 1 Cor. 2:7; Col. 2:2, 9; the mystery of the gospel, Eph. 6:19; the mystery of godliness, 1 Tim. 3:16; the mystery of God's purposes in "the dispensation of the fulness of times," Eph. 1:9-12; the mystery of Israel's present blindness, Rom. 11:25; the mystery of iniquity, 2 Thess. 2:7; the mystery of the seven stars, Rev. 1:20; the mystery of Babylon, Rev. 17:5, 7.

NAMES OF GOD

A vast amount of truth is revealed in the various names for God used in the Bible. An understanding of the meanings of these names is necessary to the full understanding of hundreds of passages.

There are three primary names, indicated in the AV by the use of various type faces. When the text reads simply God, Gen. 1:1, it is *Elohim* or *El* in the Hebrew, meaning "the Strong One." Where the text reads Lord, Gen. 15:2, it stands for *Adonai* in the original, meaning "master." LORD or GOD in capitals stand for *Jehovah*, "the self-existent One," Gen. 2:4.

These three primary names also appear in seven different combinations with other names, in contexts of profound meaning. They are: Almighty God, or *El Shaddai*, "Giver of Strength," Gen. 17:1; most high, or most high God, or *El Elyon*, "God the highest," Gen. 14:18; everlasting God, or *El Olam*, "the eternally existent One," Gen. 21:33; mighty God, or *El Gibbor*, "the powerful One," Isa. 9:6; LORD God, or *Jehovah Elohim*, "the self-existent strong One," Gen. 2:4; Lord GOD, or *Adonai Jehovah*, "the Master who is self-existent," Gen. 15:2; and the LORD of hosts, or *Jehovah Sabaoth*, "the self-existent Supreme Commander of all the heavenly forces," 1 Sam. 1:3.

NATIONS OR GENTILES

The four words, Gentiles, heathen, nations, and people, found some 760 times in the AV, represent only one OT Hebrew word and one NT Greek word in the original. They are distinguished from the Jews and the church, 1 Cor. 10:32. A political era called "the times of the Gentiles" began when God gave them world rulership, Dan. 2:38; Jer. 27:6, 7. These times are to be fulfilled as their end draws near, Luke 21:24. Their end will come when Christ sets up His kingdom, Dan. 2:44; Rev. 11:15.

Five principles determine the destiny of the nations: their relationship to God, Psa. 33:12; to the law, Prov. 14:34; to Satan, Isa. 14:12, 16; to God's present program, Acts 15:14; to the people of Israel, Gen. 12:3.

Sixty passages speak of all nations in the time of the end. For example, iniquity, distress, and perplexity will come to them, Matt. 24:12; Luke 21:25. Multitudes of Gentiles will be saved during the great tribulation, Rev. 7:9, 14. War, famine, pestilence, and earthquakes will threaten the existence of the entire human race, Matt. 24:7, 22. A beast ruler will be given satanic power to rule all nations, Rev. 13:7. After all nations gather at Armageddon, Zech. 14:2; Rev. 16:13-16, Christ will return in judgment, Rev. 19:11-21. Righteous Gentiles will enter His kingdom, Matt. 25:31-34, and serve Him, Dan. 7:14. They will continue into eternity, Rev. 21:24-26.

OCCULT

Scripture condemns such occult practices as spiritism, divination, and astrology, Lev. 19:31; Deut. 18:9-12. The Bible warns against the occult, describing it as an unseen world of wicked spirits called "hairy ones," Lev. 17:7, Heb.; "destroyers," Deut. 32:17; Heb.; and demons throughout the NT, wrongly translated "devils."

An innumerable horde of these unclean bodiless spirits seek to possess or control men and animals, Mark 5:1-13. They are the evil seducing spirits of the last days who deceive men into holding doctrines of demons, 1 Tim. 4:1. They believe and tremble, Jas. 2:19, recognizing Christ as the Son of God who will eventually cast them into torment, Matt. 8:29. Possessing superhuman knowledge, they are able to speak the truth as well as lies, 2 Chr. 18:21; Acts 16:17, 18. They can be overcome only by the power of Christ, Matt. 10:8.

Satan rules the world of the occult, Matt. 12:24-28, through a hierarchy of principalities and powers, Dan. 10:12, 13, 20; Eph. 6:12. Sacrifices and gifts offered to idols are actually offered to demons, Deut. 32:17; 1 Cor. 10:19-21.

Just before the return of Christ, Satan will direct demons to gather all nations together for the battle of Armageddon, Rev. 16:13-16. The devil and his occult forces will be imprisoned by Christ after He returns, Isa. 24:21-23; Rev. 20:1-3.

PALESTINE

Called "the navel of the earth," Ezek. 38:12, Heb., the land of Israel is at the crossroads of three continents where most of the world's population is concentrated, and where the yellow, black, and white races meet. It is "Jehovah's land," Hos. 9:3, the only land ever given by God to any people, Gen. 13:14-17. It is Israel's inheritance, Psa. 105:9-12; Isa. 60:21, in contrast with the heavenly inheritance of the church, 1 Pet. 1:3-5.

Because of Israel's sin, the land became desolate after its people were removed, Jer. 9:11-16. It lay barren and sparsely inhabited until the twentieth century. Prophecy announces that it is to become fruitful again after the Jews return, Ezek. 36:8-12. The desert is to blossom as the rose, Isa. 35:1, 2.

When Christ returns with His saints, Zech. 14:5; 1 Thess. 3:13, an earthquake will level the hills of Palestine, Zech. 14:3, 4, 10, and make Jerusalem a mountain, Isa. 66:20. A deep wide river will flow from Jerusalem into the Dead Sea and the Mediterranean, making the city a fresh water port, Zech. 14:8; Ezek. 47:1-12. Cities will be rebuilt, Isa. 61:4, and the population will greatly increase, Ezek. 36:38. The land will become the center of world government under the Lord Jesus Christ, Psa. 22:27, 28; 72:8, 9.

PEACE

Three divisions of the doctrine are of special interest to believers. We have peace with God from the moment of our salvation; the peace of God is a Christian's normal experience afterward; eternal peace will be ours at the coming of the Lord.

"Being justified by faith, we have peace with God through our Lord Jesus Christ," Rom. 5:1. There is no peace to the wicked, Isa. 57:21, but Christ made peace for His people through His blood, reconciling us to God and abolishing the enmity contained in the law, Eph. 2:13-16; Col. 1:20.

The peace of God is the experience of believers as they engage in prayer, supplication, and thanksgiving, Phil. 4:6, 7; as they honor the Word, Psa. 119:165; Phil. 4:9; and as they trust in the Lord, Isa. 26:3.

Christ spoke both of peace with God and the peace of God in John 20:19-21. He referred to the peace of salvation when He said, "Peace be unto you," and showed them His hands and His side. Then He referred to the peace of service when He spoke the same words, but sent the disciples forth. Both are anticipated in John 14:27. Christians are to preach peace, Rom. 10:15, and to exhibit it in their lives, Gal. 5:22.

Abundance of peace as long as the moon endures will characterize the coming kingdom, Psa. 72:7, and it will continue into eternity, Isa. 9:7.

POWER

One reason why God saves men is "that he might make his mighty power to be known," Psa. 106:8. The heavens are the work of His fingers, Psa. 8:3, but our salvation required the baring of the right arm of His power, Isa. 52:10; 53:1.

Christ promised power to His followers in His last words before the ascension, Luke 24:49; Acts 1:8. The prayers of Paul exhibit a deep desire that believers might know this power, Eph. 3:16. It is seen not only in great works, but also in patience and long-suffering with joyfulness, Col. 1:11. God's power was manifested in the preaching of the apostles, Col. 1:27-29; 1 Thess. 1:5. Power belonged to God in OT days, Psa. 62:11, was given to Jesus Christ, Matt. 28:18, and He passed it on to believers, Acts 1:8.

Christians today receive power through feeding on the Word of God, Acts 6:4, 8, contr. Lev. 26:14, 37; and in answer to prayer and supplication, Gen. 32:28; Hos. 12:4; Phil. 3:10. God's strength is given to those who wait upon Him, Isa. 40:29-31, in recognition of their own weakness, 2 Cor. 12:9.

The remarkable revelation is given in Eph. 3:20 that God is able to do far more than we ask or think, according to the power that works in us. This is intended to be normal Christian experience, enabling believers to sing of it from day to day, Psa. 59:16.

PRAISE AND THANKSGIVING

Praise is an expression of approval or admiration; thanksgiving expresses gratitude. The two are linked in worship, 1 Chr. 23:30. When the trumpeters and singers united in praising and thanking the Lord at the dedication of Solomon's temple, the glory of the Lord filled the house of God, 2 Chr. 5:13, 14. Praise always glorifies Him, Psa. 50:23. When Paul and Silas prayed and sang in prison, God acted on their behalf, Acts 16:25. Their praise was literally hymn singing.

God delivered the people of Israel from their enemies when they began to sing and to praise, 2 Chr. 20:21, 22. This is an important element in the missionary enterprise, Psa. 96. Even though it may be only a joyful sound, Psa. 66:1, 2, it characterizes the homes of the godly, Psa. 118:15. Christ is said to praise God in the midst of the church, Heb. 2:12.

Thanksgiving can be expressed with vocal and instrumental music in worship, Psa. 147:7. As an indispensable element in prayer, the promise of peace is associated with it, Phil. 4:6, 7. The ungodly do not give God thanks, Rom. 1:21, but it is the revealed will of God that all Christians thank Him in everything, 1 Thess. 5:18. One mark of the filling of the Spirit is the giving of thanks to God always for all things, Eph. 5:18-20.

RACE

At least a dozen books in the Bible refer to the divine separation of mankind into races or nations, Gen. 10:25; Deut. 32:8. Within Israel it was forbidden to intermarry with other nations, Deut. 7:1-3. Such marriages were called a trespass which brought down the wrath of God, Ezra 10:2, 14. King Solomon's unions with women from other nations were referred to as a great evil, Neh. 13:23-27.

Abraham forbad Isaac to marry outside his own people, Gen. 28:1. Esau's marriage to Hittite girls brought grief to his parents, Gen. 26:35, and Moses' marriage to an Ethiopian woman resulted in family trouble, Num. 12:1. Later intermarriages broke up families and led to tragedy for children, Ezra 10:19, 44. Such records anticipate the social problems produced by miscegenation throughout history and in modern times.

Nations or races will continue on into the eternal state, Rev. 5:9; 21:24. It is a striking fact that the original threefold division of mankind into descendants of Shem, Ham, and Japheth, Gen. 9:18-27, reappears in the NT offer of salvation. An Ethiopian is saved in Acts 8:26-38, a Semite in Acts 9:1-16, and a Japhethite in Acts 10:1-48. Whatever may be the reason God has made a difference among the races of mankind, it does not extend to the universal offer of eternal life through Christ.

RAPTURE

The word popularly applied to the translation of the church at the end of the present age comes from a Latin verb *rapio,* to seize or to snatch away. The first clear revelation of the rapture of believers is found in John 14:3, where Christ promised to come again and receive His followers unto Himself. Some see this prefigured in the translation of Enoch prior to the destruction of the antediluvian world, Heb. 11:5.

The central passage dealing with the rapture is 1 Thess. 4:13-18. The Lord will descend from heaven, the dead in Christ will rise first, then all living believers will be caught up together with them to meet the Lord in the air, to be with Him forever after. This revelation expands the outline of events given by Christ in John 14:3 by adding a number of previously unrevealed details. The change which is to take place in Christians in the twinkling of an eye at the rapture is described in 1 Cor. 15:35-54. It will be accomplished by the power with which Christ will "subdue all things unto himself," Phil. 3:20, 21.

As believers await their translation to be with the Lord, they are to be waiting, 1 Thess. 1:10; watching, 1 Thess. 5:6; looking for Him, Tit. 2:13; loving His appearing, 2 Tim. 4:8; putting one another in remembrance, 1 Tim. 4:6; and exhorting one another as they see the day approaching, Heb. 10:25.

REDEMPTION

The comprehensive theme of redemption is dealt with in 150 texts of Scripture, where a dozen Hebrew and Greek words are used. The term means to deliver by paying a price, to sever from bondage.

In OT days a lost inheritance could be redeemed, Lev. 25:25, as could an Israelite who had sold himself into bondage, Lev. 25:47, 48. The plan called for a kinsman redeemer, a near relative who was willing, Lev. 25:48, 49; Ruth 3:12, 13 and able to redeem, Lev. 25:26; Ruth 4:3-6.

A series of 18 passages in the OT present God as Redeemer, Psa. 19:14; Isa. 41:14; 48:17. The most famous of these texts is Job 19:25, "I know that my redeemer liveth." Such passages speak of Christ our Brother, Isa. 8:18; Gal. 4:4, 5; Heb. 2:9-15. He was able and willing to redeem lost humanity, Heb. 10:4-10, "sold under sin," Rom. 7:14. He paid the price of His own blood, John 10:11, 18; Acts 20:28; 1 Pet. 1:18, 19.

Three important words are used of redemption in the Greek: (a) to buy in the market, 1 Cor. 6:20; Rev. 5:9; (b) to buy out of the market so that the person or thing cannot again be sold, Gal. 3:13; 4:5; (c) to set free, Tit. 2:14; 1 Pet. 1:18. A time of restitution of all things is coming, Matt. 19:28; Acts 3:21, when believers will experience the redemption of their bodies, Rom. 8:18-23.

RESURRECTION BODY

The central passage describing the resurrection body of believers is 1 Cor. 15:35-54. It is likened to the transforming change which a grain of wheat undergoes when it springs forth from the ground after it has been planted. No two bodies will be alike, but all will be celestial rather than terrestrial. They will no longer be dishonored, but glorious; incorruptible, that is, no longer subject to decay and ruin; powerful, not weak; heavenly, not earthly; immortal rather than mortal or subject to death. They will be spiritual, or suited to the life of the spirit in another realm, and no longer suited to the life of the soul as now.

At the sepulchre, Peter and John saw that the body of Jesus was gone, but the linens in which He had been wrapped were undisturbed, John 20:6-8. The original language makes it clear that He had passed through the grave clothes, as He later passed through closed doors and moved instantaneously from one place to another, John 20:19.

When we see Him, we shall be like Him, 1 John 3:2. He will change these present bodies of humiliation so they become like His own glorious resurrection body, Phil. 3:20, 21. This important revelation means that we will no longer be subject to natural law after He has come to receive us unto Himself, 1 Thess. 4:16, 17.

SABBATH, LORD'S DAY

The Sabbath was made known to Israel and made a commandment at the giving of the law, Ex. 20:9-11; Deut. 5:15; Neh. 9:13, 14. The word first appears in Scripture in Ex. 16:23. The Lord's day began to be observed by common consent in apostolic days, Acts 20:7.

The Sabbath was a sign between God and the Jews, Ezek. 20:10-12. It was never given to the Gentiles or to the church. The Lord's day commemorates the resurrection of Christ, Psa. 118:22-24; Luke 24:1-3, 33-36.

Rest and inactivity characterized the Sabbath, with the death penalty imposed for breaking its laws, Ex. 35:2; Num. 15:32-36. The nation went into captivity for disregarding it, Lev. 26:33-36; 2 Chr. 36:20, 21. For the church, the Lord's day is a time of Christian activity, rejoicing, and worship.

Each day belongs to a different age. The Sabbath was in force from Moses until the law was done away in Christ, Rom. 7:6; 10:4. Its cessation is predicted in Hos. 2:11, its restoration is mentioned in Ezek. 46:1; Matt. 24:20. The Lord's day began in apostolic times and will be observed until the Lord returns, 1 Cor. 11:26. The epistles mention the Sabbath only in Col. 2:16, 17. They do not list Sabbath-breaking as a sin. The expression "Christian sabbath" is not taken from the Bible.

SAINTS

The Bible does not support the popular idea of what constitutes a saint. The NT word does not mean a person who is pious or unusually good in the eyes of men. The Greek root means separate or set apart. It is used of all Christians, 1 Cor. 14:33; Phil. 1:1, including some who were by no means saintly, because they were guilty of various sins, 1 Cor. 1:2, 11; 5:1, 2. The holy men and women mentioned in 1 Pet. 3:5; 2 Pet. 1:21 were simply persons set apart to God. The NT condemns all who think themselves holier than others, Luke 18:9-14; cf. Isa. 65:5.

Saints may be poor, Rom. 12:13; 15:26, but they have an eternal inheritance, Col. 1:12. They are joint heirs with Christ, Rom. 8:17. Their prayers rise to heaven like incense, Eph. 6:18; Rev. 5:8; 8:4. The faith was delivered to them, and not to an ecclesiastical organization, Jude 3. Christ will be glorified in them when He returns, 1 Thess. 3:13; 2 Thess. 1:10. What He will have done for them will astonish the world. Their righteous deeds are said to form the white robe of His bride, Rev. 19:8.

The saints mentioned as living on the earth after the church has been translated, Rev. 13:7, and later during the kingdom age, Rev. 20:9, are people set apart by God to a destiny which is altogether different from that of church saints.

SALVATION AND REWARDS

A number of clear contrasts between the two appear in Scripture. Salvation is for the lost, Matt. 18:11, while rewards are for the saved, Prov. 13:13. The salvation offered to all who believe is the same for everyone, Acts 16:31; Heb. 10:39, while rewards will differ, Rev. 22:12. Salvation is a free gift, Isa. 55:1; Rom. 6:23, but rewards are earned, 1 Cor. 3:8. Salvation is received in the present, John 5:24; rewards are to be received in the future, Matt. 16:27.

When the day for rewards has come, fire will test every man's work. All that survives will be rewarded, and salvation will not be affected, 1 Cor. 3:11-15. Every man will have praise of God, 1 Cor. 4:5. Keeping the precepts of Scripture has always brought great reward, Psa. 19:11.

Christ spoke of rewards as being in heaven, Matt. 5:12. He will bring them with Him at His return, Rev. 22:12. A reward is to be given even for the offering of a cup of cold water, Matt. 10:42. God is a rewarder of them that diligently seek Him, Heb. 11:6. It is a worthy motive to serve Him with the promised rewards in view. Even Moses "had respect unto the recompense of the reward," Heb. 11:26. All believers are encouraged to have full confidence in the fulfillment of everything God has promised, Heb. 10: 35-37; Prov. 11:18.

SECURITY

"The security of the believer" is a theological expression based on Scriptural revelations underlying the doctrine of assurance. While this doctrine is rejected by some, others find it of great spiritual value to accept without question what the Bible teaches about the safekeeping of the people of God.

The believer's life in Christ is said to be everlasting or eternal—that is, it will never end, John 3:16; Rom. 6:23. Believers shall never perish, neither shall any man pluck them out of the Father's hand, John 10:28, 29. They are said to be "kept by the power of God," 1 Pet. 1:5; kept for Jesus Christ, Jude 1, RV. Christ declared that all who believe have everlasting life, and shall not come into condemnation, John 5:24. He is able "to save them to the uttermost that come unto God by him," Heb. 7:25.

The entire Trinity is involved in the safekeeping of Christians. The Father has given believers to the Son, John 17:9. The Son has asked that they be kept, John 17:11, 20. The Holy Spirit is to dwell within every believer forever, John 14:16; 1 Cor. 6:19. These revealed truths have nothing to do with human experience, but only with the divine purpose and promise. Passages which seem, to some, to contradict the doctrine of security are found to be related to rewards, chastisement, and the fact that an absence of good works reveals a lack of genuine faith, Phil. 2:12, 13; 2 Pet. 3:9-17.

SERVICE

What God expects of Christians is made clear throughout the NT. Nearly forty exhortations appear in Rom. 12 alone. The apostolic creed found in Tit. 2:11-14 outlines the Christian life as the denial of ungodliness and worldly lusts, accompanied by self restraint, righteousness, godliness and the expectation of the return of Christ. Another such outline in Heb. 10:19-25 calls for prayer, public testimony, a good example to others and assembly for worship.

It is reasonable, or spiritual, RV, to present one's body to God as a living sacrifice to serve Him, Rom. 12:1. This service must be exclusive, Luke 16:13; given with the spirit, Rom. 1:9; rendered with reverence and godly fear, Heb. 12:28; motivated by love,

Gal. 5:13. It calls for following Christ, John 12:26, whom all Christians serve, Col. 3:24, as they serve God, Acts 27:23.

Believers are described as persons who have turned to God from idols to serve the living and true God, 1 Thess. 1:9. This service may take the form of fasting and prayer, Luke 2:37, or ministering to the poor and needy, or giving oneself to prayer and the ministry of the Word as did the apostles, Acts 6:1-4.

When Christian service is rendered in righteousness, peace, and joy, the believer is acceptable to God and approved of men, Rom. 14:17, 18.

SPIRITUALITY

The biblical concept of a spiritual Christian is one who is governed by the Holy Spirit rather than by his lower nature. "He that is spiritual" is contrasted with "the natural man," that is, the soulish (lit.) or unregenerate individual, in 1 Cor. 2:14-16. The spiritual person is also set over against the carnal or fleshly believer who is still a babe in Christ, 1 Cor. 3:1-4.

Christians are exhorted to grow by feeding on the Word, 1 Pet. 2:2. The Holy Spirit teaches them by means of the Scriptures, John 16:13. They are led by the Spirit, Rom. 8:14; walk in the Spirit, Gal. 5:16; bear spiritual fruit, Gal. 5:22, 23; are strengthened by the Spirit, Eph. 3:16; and are filled with the Spirit, Eph. 5:18.

Spiritual Christians enjoy life and peace, Rom. 8:6. They acknowledge the epistles of Paul to be the commandments of the Lord, 1 Cor. 14:37. Far from thinking themselves to be on a higher spiritual plane than others, they seek to restore fallen believers in a spirit of meekness, lest they themselves face the same problem, Gal. 6:1-3.

Eph. 5:18-21 may be considered to be a description of a spiritual person, filled with joy and walking in humility, Jas. 4:6. Spiritual understanding, Col. 1:9, enables the believer to impart spiritual gifts to others, Rom. 1:11.

STANDING AND STATE

Standing refers to the believer's position in Christ. He is a child of God, John 1:12; justified by faith, Rom. 5:1; has access to God, Rom. 5:2; is an heir of God and a joint heir with Christ, Rom. 8:17; is the temple of the Holy Spirit, 1 Cor. 6:19; is baptized into the body of Christ, 1 Cor. 12:13. He is blessed with all spiritual blessings in Christ, Eph. 1:3; accepted in the beloved, Eph. 1:6; sealed with the Holy Spirit, Eph. 1:13; born unto an inheritance reserved for him in heaven, 1 Pet 1:3, 4. All of these things and many more are acts of God which accompany salvation, and are not changed by human frailty or sin.

State is a theological term which describes a believer's actual spiritual condition, which may fall short of what is enjoined in Scripture. Believers in Corinth were saints, as to their standing, being called unto the fellowship of Christ, 1 Cor. 1:1-9. Nevertheless, their state was characterized by divisions, carnality, and sin, 1 Cor. 1:11; 3:1; 5:1, 2.

The believer's standing in Christ is perfect and unchanging. His state may change for the better or the worse. The purpose of Christian growth is to bring the Christian's state into conformity with his standing, 2 Pet 3:18.

STEWARDSHIP

A faithful Christian's use of his possessions, time and talents is governed by New Testament principles. The central passage is 2 Cor. 8, 9, which sets forth Christ as the believer's example in giving. Extraordinary promises and revelations have to do with stewardship. "Give, and it shall be given unto you; good measure, pressed down, and shaken together, and running over," Luke 6:38. "It is more blessed to give than to receive," Acts 20:35. "He who soweth bountifully shall reap also bountifully," 2 Cor. 9:6. "God is not unrighteous to forget your work and labor of love," Heb. 6:10. "With such sacrifices God is well pleased," Heb. 13:16.

As Christians distribute to the necessities of saints, Rom. 12:13, they are to do it cheerfully, 2 Cor. 9:7, with simplicity, (liberally, RV), Rom. 12:8, to the glory of God, 1 Cor. 10:31. Money is to be set aside on the first day of the week as God has prospered us, 1 Cor. 16:2. It is to be used to bring people to God through missions, schools, churches, Luke 16:9-13. Faithfulness is required of stewards, whether or not their gifts are large, 1 Cor. 4:2; Luke 21:1-4.

The teaching of the NT is in keeping with such OT passages as Deut. 15:10; Psa. 112:9; Prov. 11:24, 25; 19:17; Eccl. 11:1; Hag. 2:15-19; Mal. 3:10.

SUFFERING

An important theme of 1 Peter is the sufferings of Christ and the glory to follow, 1:11. Alongside this is a revelation about the sufferings of believers and their own future glory. They may suffer wrongfully, 2:19; for doing well, 2:20; for righteousness' sake, 3:14; because they are Christians, 4:16; "according to the will of God," 4:19; being called to this very experience, 2:20, 21.

Christians should not think that fiery trials are a strange thing. They are partakers of Christ's sufferings in a world that hated Him, 1 Pet. 4:12, 13; John 15:18, 19. Reproach for His name means that the Spirit of glory already rests upon the believer, 1 Pet. 4:14. The remarkable connection between present sufferings and coming glory, mentioned in this passage, is found also in Rom. 8:17, 18. "If we suffer, we shall also reign with him," 2 Tim. 2:12.

Present trials are only temporary. They are "for a season, if need be," with praise, honor and glory to come when Christ appears, 1 Pet. 1:6, 7. In the meanwhile, blessings are promised in the present, 5:10. Christians who experience supernatural comfort during trials are enabled to comfort others because of it, 2 Cor. 1:3-6. One reason God has given us the Bible is so that we may find help and encouragement in the records of the suffering prophets, Jas. 5:10.

SUPPLICATION

Works on prayer seldom mention this word, which occurs 60 times in the AV. It is a form of intensified prayer by which God's help is fervently implored in a time of special need. It is to prayer what fire is to incense.

Supplication may be no more than a cry to God; the word is used in 1 Pet. 3:12, RV as a translation of the word cry in Psa. 34:15. The same word is used of the cry of the Jews during their Egyptian bondage, Ex. 3:7. Sometimes it is a wrestling with God like that of Jacob when he would not let the angel go until he blessed him, Gen. 32:24-29. The encounter was so intense that Jacob wept on that occasion, after which he was given power with men and with God, Hos. 12:3, 4.

The outstanding NT example is Christ in Gethsemane. His supplication was accompanied by "strong crying and tears," Heb. 5:7. Our Lord's mighty works were done with no sign of effort, but in this prayer He experienced travail and anguish of soul. Paul's deep concern for the salvation of Israel resulted in supplication, Rom. 10:1, RV.

The word is found in Phil. 4:6 between prayer and thanksgiving.

An outstanding revelation about supplication appears in Jas. 5:16. A new disclosure informs us that Elijah prayed, 1 Ki. 18:42, where the OT is silent. Associated with this fact is the statement that supplication (RV) avails much.

TEMPTATION

The Bible presents a threefold division of temptation. We read of "the lust of the flesh," or the desire to enjoy; "the lust of the eyes," or the desire to obtain; "the pride of life," or the desire to accomplish, 1 John 2:16. Each refers to an area of normal, God-given desire, which can become sin when it goes beyond the limits established in Scripture. It is not a sin to be tempted, because Christ was, but yielding becomes "the transgression of the law," 1 John 3:4.

Satan used all three of these avenues to the human heart when he tempted Eve, Gen. 3:1-6. Eating the forbidden fruit appealed to the lust of the flesh. The words "your eyes shall be opened," appealed to the lust of the eyes. The promise, "ye shall be as gods," appealed to the pride of life. Eve capitulated in all three areas, v. 6.

The devil used the same three approaches in tempting Christ, Luke 4:1-13. He still tempts people today to sin through appetite, avarice, or ambition. Christ has given us the means of deliverance. Like Him, we are to be filled with the Spirit, Eph. 5:18; led by the Spirit, Rom. 8:14; empowered by the Spirit, Rom. 15:13; Luke 4:1, 14.

The Lord triumphed by using the Word of God, quoting the particular verse which suited the occasion. So may we, Eph. 6:17; Jas. 4:7.

TONGUES

The first time tongues are mentioned in the NT they refer to known languages, Acts 2:4, 6, as they do when last mentioned, Rev. 17:15. Many believe tongues were sometimes ecstatic utterances, unintelligible until interpreted, the least of several gifts of the Spirit, 1 Cor. 12:28, 31; 14:5. Several principles for their proper control are given in 1 Cor. 14, which spiritual believers must acknowledge to be the commandments of the Lord, v. 37.

1. Five words which can be understood are better than 10,000 in a tongue, v. 19.

2. Two or three persons at the most are to speak at any one meeting, v. 27

3. These are to speak one at a time, v. 27.

4. No one is to speak in tongues unless an interpreter is present, v. 28.

5. Each speaker is to exercise control over himself to avoid confusion, v. 32, 33.

6. Women are to keep silent in the church, vv. 34, 35. The word "unknown" found in the AV is not in the original text.

It is implied in 1 Cor. 13:11; 14:20 that prophecy is more suited to mature Christians than are tongues. Prophecy is defined as speaking to men to edify, exhort, and comfort them, 14:3. Inasmuch as tongues are associated by some with the baptism or outpouring of the Holy Spirit, it is a notable fact that when the Spirit is poured out after the Lord's return it leads to prophecy, not tongues, Joel 2:28, 29.

TRIBULATION

Prophecy describes a time of great world tribulation unlike anything in history, Dan. 12:1; Matt. 24:21. More space is devoted to it in the OT than to the coming of Christ. Every NT writer refers to it. The Revelation is largely a description of its leading events. This hour of tribulation, Rev. 3:10 is not to be confused with tribulations of the hour, John 16:33; Acts 14:22.

All nature is drawn upon to emphasize the terrors of those years. We read of smoke, fire, great heat, lightning, darkness, beasts, falling stars, earthquakes. There are voices from heaven, trumpets, thrones, great armies, battles, blood, plagues, scenes of judgment. The supernatural bursts in upon the earth. Angels and demons are active. The bottomless pit is opened. Terrifying signs become visible; fearful announcements are made from the sky.

Heaven and earth are terribly shaken, Isa. 2:19. The entire race is involved as God punishes the world for its iniquity, Isa. 13:11; Rev. 3:10. The devil and his angels are cast into the earth, Rev. 12:9. Unclean spirits gather men to Armageddon, Rev. 16:13-16. People hide in dens and rocks to escape the wrath of the Lamb, Rev. 6:15-17. God shortens the days to preserve the race, Matt. 24:22. The tribulation ends with the return of Christ, Matt. 24:29, 30.

WAR

The wars of the Lord are prominent in the OT, Num. 21:14, when God helped His ancient people against their enemies, 1 Sam.

17:47; 1 Chr. 5:22. "The captain of the Lord's host," Josh. 5:15; 23:10, led the armies of Israel. Even the stars in their courses fought for them, Judg. 5:20. Some wars were fought to destroy nations of unspeakable wickedness, Deut. 7:1-10; Lev. 18:24, 25.

World war is predicted for the last days. After war in heaven, Satan is cast into the earth, Rev. 12:7-12, which becomes engulfed in warfare, Matt. 24:6; Rev. 6:4. The climax is reached at Armageddon, "the battle of that great day of God Almighty," Rev. 16:14-16. It ends when the Lord descends from heaven, defeats the armies of earth, and binds Satan, Zech. 14:1-3; Rev. 19:11-14; 20:1-4. During the ensuing kingdom age, wars will cease unto the ends of the earth, Psa. 46:9; Isa. 2:4. One final conflict precedes eternity, Rev. 20:7-10.

Behind man's wars, which rise from his wicked heart, Jas. 4:1 is a continuing invisible spiritual warfare. Believers are struggling against unseen hosts of wickedness, Eph. 6:12-17. The weapons of their warfare are mighty through God, 2 Cor. 10:4. They are called upon to war a good warfare, 1 Tim. 1:18; 2 Tim. 4:7, as good soldiers of Jesus Christ, 2 Tim. 2:3, 4.

WILL OF GOD

God knows that men are incapable of planning their own lives, Jer. 10:23; Isa. 53:6. Only He knows the future, Isa. 46:9, 10. Therefore He promises to direct the paths of believers whose trust in Him is sincere, exclusive and complete, Prov. 3:5, 6. Christians may "prove" His good will by presenting their bodies to the Lord, letting Him transform them until they are no longer conformed to the world, Rom. 12:1, 2.

God wants us to know His will, Col. 1:9. He commands .hat we obey it, Eph. 5:17; 6:6. A number of clear and specific statements describe His will for everyone. These include our sanctification, 1 Thess. 4:3; prayer and thanksgiving, 1 Thess. 5:17, 18; good works, 1 Pet. 2:15; and suffering, 1 Pet. 4:19.

Practical rules for discovering the will of God call for the surrender of our own wills, Luke 22:42; placing the written Word above all personal impressions, Jer. 10:23; seeking the mind of the Lord through prayer, Psa. 143:8, and the use of the Bible, Psa. 40:7, 8. Providential circumstances sometimes become a factor, Prov. 4:14, 15; Acts 17:10.

We are instructed to stay where we are, 1 Cor. 7:20, and to be content, Phil. 4:11, until He leads us elsewhere. "He that doeth the will of God abideth forever," 1 John 2:17.

WORLD

A strange mistranslation in the AV has confused many in their desire to understand the prophetic Scriptures. The expression, "the end of the world," found in Matt. 13:39, 40, 49; 24:3; 28:20; Heb. 9:26 does not refer to the world at all in the original text. It is rather, "the end of the age," the original word being *aion*, meaning age, and properly translated in Eph. 2:7; Col. 1:26. It is also wrongly translated in other passages like Luke 1:70; Acts 3:21.

Two other Greek words are translated world. One is *oikumene*, meaning the inhabited earth. This was taxed, Luke 2:1; experienced famine, Acts 11:28; is to pass through the great tribulation, Rev. 3:10; will hear the preaching of the gospel of the kingdom, Matt. 24:14; will be involved in world war, Rev. 16:14.

The most widely used word translated world is *cosmos*, meaning the created earth, Acts 17:24, which Christ made, John 1:10. Its foundation is spoken of in Eph. 1:4. The final end of the world (a different word) is mentioned in 2 Pet. 3:7, 10, when it will be burned up. The word *cosmos* carries other meanings also, such as the world of men, John 3:16. It is used of the evil world system, Eph. 2:2; 1 John 2:15-17, which is at enmity with God, Jas. 4:4. It lieth in the wicked one, 1 John 5:19, RV, who is its prince, John 12:31. It is overcome by the faith of believers, 1 John 5:4, 5.

Moody Press, a ministry of the Moody Bible Institute, is designed for education, evangelization, and edification. If we may assist you in knowing more about Christ and the Christian life, please write us without obligation: Moody Press, c/o MLM, Chicago, Illinois 60610.

INDEX